SCROLL SAW
HANDBOOK

SCROLL SAW
HANDBOOK

■ ■ ■ ■ ■

Patrick Spielman

 Sterling Publishing Co., Inc.   New York

Library of Congress Cataloging-in-Publication Data

Spielman, Patrick E.
  Scroll saw handbook.

  Includes index.
  1. Jig saws. 2. Woodwork. I. Title.
TT186.S67 1986   684'.083   86-14352
ISBN 0-8069-4770-5 (pbk.)

Copyright © 1986 by Patrick Spielman
Published by Sterling Publishing Company, Inc.
387 Park Avenue South, New York, N.Y. 10016
Distributed in Canada by Sterling Publishing
% Canadian Manda Group, P.O. Box 920, Station U
Toronto, Ontario, Canada M8Z 5P9
Distributed in Great Britain and Europe by Cassell PLC
Villiers House, 41/47 Strand, London WC2N 5JE, England
Distributed in Australia by Capricorn Ltd.
P.O. Box 665, Lane Cove, NSW 2066
Manufactured in the United States of America
All rights reserved

Table of Contents

ACKNOWLEDGMENTS   7

INTRODUCTION   9

Scroll Saw Fundamentals   19

    1.   History of Scroll Saws   20

    2.   Scroll Saw Basics   31

    3.   Blades, Speeds, and Feeds   42

Commercially Available Scroll Saws   57

    4.   Rigid-Arm Scroll Saws   58

    5.   Light-Duty Scroll Saws   72

    6.   Kit and Reproduction Pedal Scroll Saws   79

    7.   Hegner Saws   86

    8.   Excalibur Saws   101

    9.   RBI Scroll Saws   111

    10.   Woodmaster and Strong Scroll Saws   128

    11.   AMT and Jet Scroll Saws   134

    12.   Delta C-Arm Scroll Saw   138

    13.   Sears "Walking Beam" Scroll Saw   145

Sawing Techniques   155

    14.   Safety   156

    15.   Sawing Basics   161

16. Patterns and Projects   173

17. Sawing Inside Openings   188

18. Sawing Small Pieces and Thin Stock   196

19. Sawing Joints   201

20. Compound Sawing   210

21. Bevel Sawing   214

22. Inlays, Reliefs, and Recessing   223

23. Marquetry Basics   238

24. Sawing Nonwood Materials   247

CURRENT BOOKS BY PATRICK SPIELMAN   254

ABOUT THE AUTHOR   255

METRIC EQUIVALENCY CHART   255

INDEX   256

ACKNOWLEDGMENTS

It was a genuine pleasure to communicate by phone, mail, and visit personally with a number of experts who specialize in certain scroll saw areas. One who was especially generous with his expertise and provided many prompt and generous contributions is Hanns Derke of Advanced Machinery Imports. His one-on-one seminar with me and follow-up consultations have made this a much better book. Ray Seymore of Seyco Sales Co. is another individual who knows his business and shares this knowledge. Many thanks to him for his visit and valuable demonstrations with the Excalibur saws. Thanks also to Kris Rice, Sam Keener, and Don Kennedy for giving me the "inside story" on the RBI scroll saws. Chuck Olson of The Olson Saw Company was a great source of information about blades, and provided valuable material for Chapter 3. The tips and "leads" from Glenn Davidson are also appreciated.

Thanks to my son, Bob Spielman, for his support and interest in this work, and for his innovative ideas. Thanks, also, to my wife, Patricia, for her generous help with this book and for all of her immeasurable talents in project designs and drawings for our companion book, the *Scroll Saw Pattern Book*. And with much gratitude, Mrs. Pat and I express our special appreciation to Julie Kiehnau, who quickly mastered the scroll saw, created and produced some excellent projects, and did all of the typing—all of this while under the pressure of helping customers.

Thanks to Carmen Lucke, curator of the Jens Jacobsen Museum, Washington Island, Wisconsin for her terrific cooperation as I photographed in the museum one cold fall day. Thanks to my friend and colleague, Bill Dehos, for his help on the "Island Journey," and to Walter Schutz, who allowed me to photograph and use his collection of delightful scroll-sawn silhouette designs.

Thanks also to J. Philip Humfrey for his generous support, contributions, and overall interest in this work. Willard Bondhus provided some great ideas and photos for do-it-yourself scroll-saw construction in Chapter 6. The photos provided by Silas Kopf of his outstanding examples of marquetry are a real treat and inspiration for everyone.

I would also like to extend my appreciation to the following individuals and organizations who have in one way or another helped in this work:

Dan Bechtel, American Machine & Tool Co.
Jay Beck
Russell Bott, Sawdust Trail Woodshop
Mrs. Val Box, American Intertool, Inc.
Mike Brainerd, Dremel Power Tools
Dwight Check, The Tool Company
Jessica Collignon
Delta International Machinery Corp.
Jay Dykstra, Oliver Machinery Co.
James and Roland Ehlers
Vic Kluesner, Emerson Electric Co.
Mindy Kolof of Sears
Jim and Cheri Langsather
John Miller, Woodmaster Tools, Inc.
John Oberg, The Puzzler
Old Sturbridge Village
Dick Powel, The Corn Crib Workshop

Powermatic-Houdaille, Inc.
Dean Ruffner, Jet Equipment and Tools
Kim and Rob Russell, The Russell Works
Mortimer V. Schwartz, The Fine Tool Shops
Shopsmith, Inc.
Gene Sliga, Delta International Machinery Corp.

Tom Stratton, Foley-Belsaw Co.
Donald Strong, Strong Tool Design
Vega Enterprises, Inc.
Don Zinngrabe

Patrick Spielman
Spielmans Wood Works

INTRODUCTION

For the purposes of this book, the terms "scroll saw" and "jigsaw" have essentially the same meanings. The majority of manufacturers today call their machines scroll saws, and *Webster's New International Dictionary* (second edition) defines a scroll saw as "a ribbonlike saw stretched in a frame, adapted for sawing curved outlines . . ." Some of the new manufacturers of scroll saws do refer to the design of older-style, rigid-arm machines as jigsaws. Regardless of their preferences, for consistency all sawing machines discussed will be called scroll saws.

The scroll saws that have become available in recent years are simply fantastic machines. They should probably carry warning labels like: "Use of this machine could become addictive." The more you use a scroll saw, the more you want to use it, and the more you find to do with it. This is because scroll-sawing today is exciting, relaxing, and often very therapeutic. The scroll saw user's confidence and skills grow quickly with each new project. The intoxicating aroma of freshly cut wood, the quickness and high quality of cut, and the pure joy and satisfaction of working with scroll saws has captured the fancy of amateur, veteran, and professional woodcrafters alike. (See Illus. 1 and 2.) Men, women, and children from ages 10 to 100 can become very skilled in a short time. (See Illus. 3 and 4.) One manufacturer estimates that 25 to 35 percent of all total sales is to women. Scroll-sawing has even become a "family experience" in many households.

Illus. 1. Eleven-year-old Jessica Collignon—a beginner —gets some experience on one of the new constant-tension scroll saws.

Illus. 2. The scroll-saw marquetry on the typewriter and the book design on the tambour of the roll front desk are by professional woodworker Silas Kopf.

Illus. 3. Julie Kiehnau's first scroll-sawn, bevel-cut inlays fit perfectly.

Illus. 4. Some plywood ornaments by Julie Kiehnau.

The scroll saw is an exceptionally safe machine to use. Most woodworking accidents happen when woodworkers try to cut small pieces of wood on a machine. In the case of the scroll saw, however, the design is such that you can cut small pieces of wood very safely. Furthermore, there is no danger of pieces flying or kicking back, which can happen with other woodworking machines. With a scroll saw, you'll be able to make something from every piece of scrap safely, regardless of how small it is. (See Illus. 5 and 6.)

With new scroll saws, you can saw very intricate designs into softwood or hardwood two inches and more in thickness. Sawing is done with a variety of very narrow blades, some so small they are hairlike in size. (See Illus. 7.)

The scroll saws that were available as recently as ten years ago required wide blades for cutting thick stock. (See Illus. 8.) Today, the new constant-tension machines permit swift changes in cutting directions without relief cuts. You can make sharp right-angle turns or complete 360° on-the-spot turnarounds without blade breakage. The cut surface is so smooth it does not have to be sanded, and it is perfectly square to the face without being "bellied" or angled.

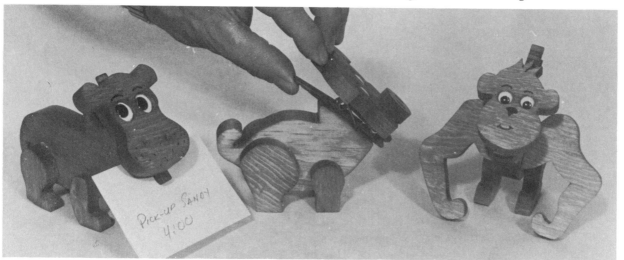

Illus. 5. These note holders are designed to incorporate spring-loaded clothespins. They are produced by Russell Bott in his "Sawdust Trail Woodshop."

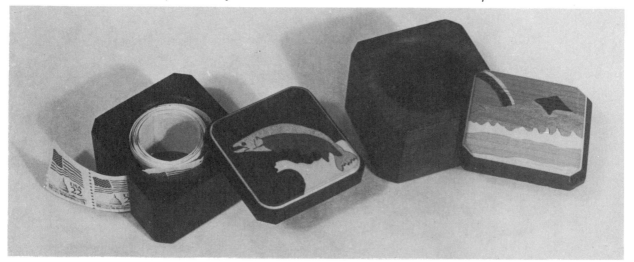

Illus. 6. These small boxes with marquetry inlaid tops—made by Jim and Cheri Langsather—are good examples of how to turn small scraps into useful projects.

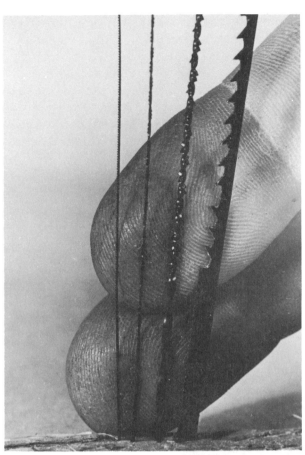

Illus. 7. With recent improvements in scroll-saw design have come new blade configurations in a wide range of sizes.

Illus. 8 (below). As recently as ten years ago, scroll sawing required wide blades and relief cuts for sawing curves in thick stock.

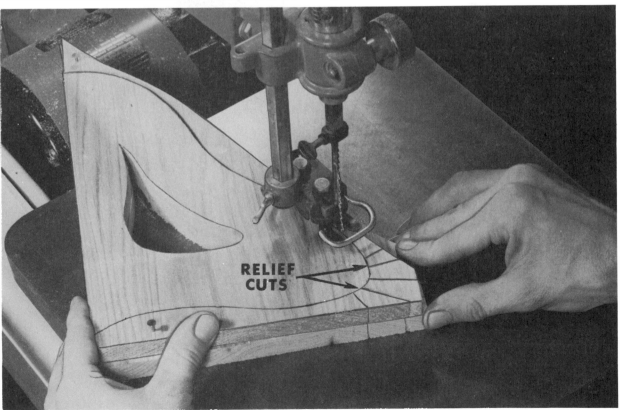

RELIEF CUTS

A wide variety of projects can be made with just the scroll saw. However, a hand drill is helpful in some cases. You can keep your entire scroll saw shop or business stored in the space of a small closet. Then, after hours you can, if you wish, turn your kitchen, apartment, or basement into a family-run minifactory.

Scroll saw woodcrafting is a lot different from cabinetmaking or furniture making. It is suited for both those woodworkers short on patience and those who can work away countless hours cutting out fancy scrolling, fretwork, making models (Illus. 9 and 10), or working at advanced marquetry (Illus. 2). There are literally thousands of easy-to-make designs that can be cut out in a matter of minutes that make great gifts or saleable items. (See Illus. 11 and 12.)

Many woodworkers utilize the scroll saw in their woodcraft business. Some even depend entirely upon the scroll saw for their income. Scroll saws are generally portable and they will draw crowds and onlookers at craft shows and art fairs.

The scroll saw is a natural for toy makers (Illus. 13) and for those who make wood signs and other wood items commercially. (See Illus. 14.) All kinds of wood objects, from large lawn ornaments (Illus. 15) to small and delicate tree ornaments (Illus. 16) to works of art (Illus. 17), can be made and sold.

Illus. 9. This model of an old-time harvest wagon, 24 inches long, was completely cut out in less than three hours.

Illus. 10. This model steam engine, 16 inches long, is made of wood scraps, steel, brass, copper, aluminum, and acrylic plastic—all cut with a scroll saw.

Illus. 11. A simple cutout makes an interesting wall decoration.

Illus. 12. Country cutouts are popular. See the companion book, the Scroll Saw Pattern Book, *for over 450 designs of these and other patterns.*

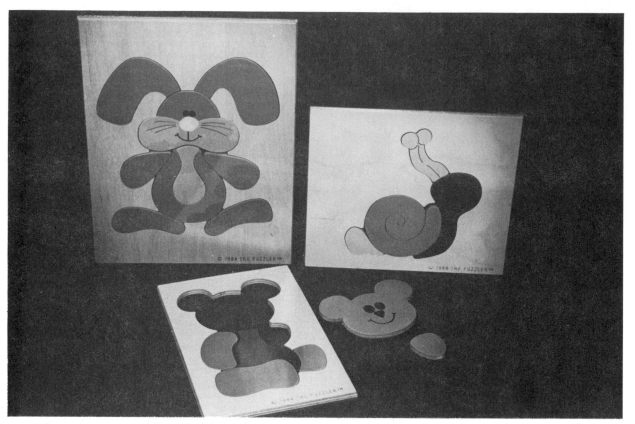

Illus. 13. Shown here are the works of "The Puzzler," John Oberg, whose copyrighted designs are marketed nationally.

Illus. 14. Julie Kiehnau at work.

Illus. 15. James and Roland Ehlers specialize in lawn ornaments, which are sold locally from this front yard display.

Illus. 16. These thin cutout ornaments are marketed as "Kim's Kritters" and sold at craft fairs and directly to stores. The designs are copyrighted and produced by Kim and Rob Russell of the Russell Works.

Illus. 17. This one-of-a-kind work of art by Jay B. Beck consists of individual cutout pieces with contoured edges, and selective staining mounted to a framed backing.

If you are thinking about buying a scroll saw, check the "field" carefully. All scroll saws are not alike in style, size, cutting capabilities, or price. To provide some assistance in making a decision, I have included in Chapter 2 scroll saw features to look for and those to avoid when shopping. Chapters 4 through 13 describe and review the general types of scroll saws available today and the specific brands.

Scroll-sawing today with one of the new machines is considerably different from scroll-sawing years ago. In this book, I will compare and describe the capabilities of the old machines with those of the new ones. Also, jobs and projects you can make with a good scroll saw are described and illustrated. You will find information about how to make patterns, bevel-saw, make inlays, do incise work, make duplicate cuts, cut thick, thin, and small parts, make compound cuts, cut a variety of materials other than wood, and make woodworking joints. You'll even find ideas on how to use your scroll saw to prepare stock for wood turnings and how to make things from simple scroll saw puzzles to easy-to-make elegant, dovetail joints. As you'll find out in the following pages, the scroll saw is incredibly versatile!

Patrick Spielman
Spielmans Wood Works

SCROLL SAW FUNDAMENTALS

1
HISTORY OF SCROLL SAWS

Man's effort to substitute energy other than his own muscle power for sawing wood dates back before the discovery of America. Early saw mills were powered by animals, wind, and water.

Between 1600 and 1620, the first American saw mills appeared in Maine and Virginia. Some of the saws that cut logs into lumber had long blades rigged in a frame; these blades were spaced to cut boards of equal width. The saws moved up and down in a reciprocating action, and the cut was made only on the downward stroke of the saw. This reciprocating blade movement is the same basic cutting action incorporated in all scroll saws today.

The first scroll saws were handmade wood parts, except for a crude metal blade. The blade was strained or tensioned by attaching one end to a flexible wooden rod (used as a spring) that was attached to the shop ceiling. The blade extended downwards through the table, with the lower end connected to a foot treadle near the floor. (See Illus. 18.) The operator depressed the treadle to pull the blade downwards for the cutting stroke. The wooden spring rod raised the blade again when the foot pressure was released.

It is believed that the first fine scroll saw blades were invented by a German clockmaker in the late 1500s. Until the advent of the machine age, narrow-cutting blades were held in frames similar to the coping or fret saw frames still available today that are used for hand-sawing.

Illus. 18. The earliest forms of scroll saws employed a reciprocating cutting action produced by a foot treadle. The blade was tensioned by a wooden spring rod attached to the ceiling.

Scroll-sawing machines made with metal parts first appeared in the mid-1800s. They were moved up and down by a foot-powered treadle or pedal mechanism. The use of cast iron in the manufacture of scroll saws and other woodworking machines provided the necessary weight and rigidity. (See Illus. 19–21.)

No. 1 Amateur Saw.

Complete with Borer,	-	$10.00
Without Borer,	- - -	8.00

This machine will cut pine of any thickness up to 1½ inches, and harder woods of proportionate thicknesses. It admits a swing of 18 inches around the blade, and accomplishes every branch of sawing within the range of general amateur work.

The table does not tilt, but sawing for inlay work can be done by placing a beveled strip under the stuff being sawed.

The price of the machine complete is **$10.00.**

The price of the machine without Boring Attachment is **$8.00.**

It weighs 40 pounds.

Boxed ready for shipment it weighs 63 pounds.

Illus. 19. This reprint from the 1907 W.F. & John Barnes Catalog shows an early scroll saw probably designed for the home workshop.

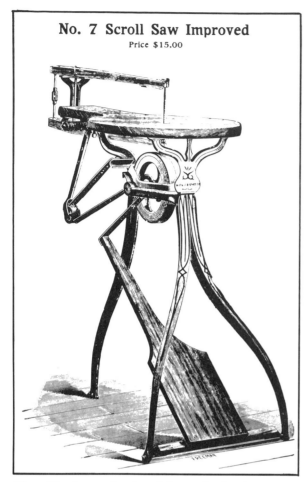

No. 7 Scroll Saw Improved
Price $15.00

Illus. 20. A saw developed for professional, non-factory use featured larger cutting capacities.

Scroll Saw No. 7
Price $15.00

This machine is designed for practical service in the workshops of carpenters and builders, cabinet makers and other wood workers.

WARRANTY

We warrant it to be well made, of good material and workmanship, and with reasonable practice to saw at the following rates: Pine, 2 inches thick, 1 foot per minute; 1 inch thick, 4 feet per minute; walnut, 3 inches thick, ½ foot per minute; 1 inch thick, 2 feet per minute, and other woods and thicknesses at proportionate rates.

The ordinary rate of speed when sawing is from 800 to 1200 strokes per minute. The saw leaves the work as smooth as is possible for any saw to do, and can be taken out and replaced in an instant for inside work.

The swing around the blade under the arm is 24 inches.
The length of the blade is 7 inches.
The table and arms are made of hard maple.
The frame is made of cast iron, strong, yet light.
The balance wheel runs on a steel arbor.
The machine weighs 60 pounds.
Boxed for shipment, 95 pounds.
We include one dozen blades with each machine.

The above cut shows our No. 7 Scroll Saw arranged with a countershaft. The price of countershaft, including the connecting band wheel on the machine, is $10.00. The price of No. 7 Scroll Saw, arranged with countershaft only (no foot power), is $20.00.
Speed of countershaft 500 R. P. M.
Tight and loose pulleys 4 in. diameter x 2 in. face.

Illus. 21. This factory scroll saw was belt-driven from the line shaft.

Early factories powered their machines from water wheels through long line shafts. The line shaft usually extended throughout the total length of the plant along the ceiling or floor. Each individual machine in the factory was belt-driven from that one line shaft. (See Illus. 21.) This system continued until electric power was introduced. However, many factories continued to employ the line shaft until the mid-1930s, even though small electric motors became available in the early 1900s.

Although cast iron was used for many parts on the earlier scroll saws, the flexing quality of wood remained essential to the design and function of the early constant-tension-saw frame arms. Almost all early manufacturers of scroll saws used hardwood for the arms and worktables.

One company that probably was the largest manufacturer of scroll saws in the 1800s was the W. F. and John Barnes Company located in Rockford, Illinois, which manufactured a complete line of "Patent Foot and Hand Power Wood Working Machinery." Their line included many different scroll saws, and even circular saws and wood turning lathes that were efficiently foot-powered.

Some selected pages from the 1907 Barnes Company Catalog (No. 67) are shown in Illus. 19–22. Note their prices and their designs, which are in some cases similar to the constant-tension saws that are so popular now.

The most famous of the Barnes scroll saws was the Velocipede Scroll Saw No. 2. (See Illus. 22.) This machine had an optional boring device that was attached to the machine for convenient drilling of holes necessary for making inside cuts and fretwork. The table and arms were made of hard maple. The original Velocipede and some of the other Barnes saws carried blades seven inches in length, whereas almost all of the modern saws carry five-inch blades. The worktable did not tilt. The Velocipede had a 24-inch throat capacity, a weight of 90 pounds and essentially the same cutting capabilities as the Barnes No. 7 saw shown in Illus. 21.

The Barnes Velocipede No. 2 Saw is available again today. It is being brought back by a new manufacturer, and is being marketed as an authentic reproduction—which apparently it is, except that the new version has cast-aluminum rather than cast-iron parts. (See page 84 for more information concerning this reproduction saw.)

The Jens Jacobsen Museum on Washington

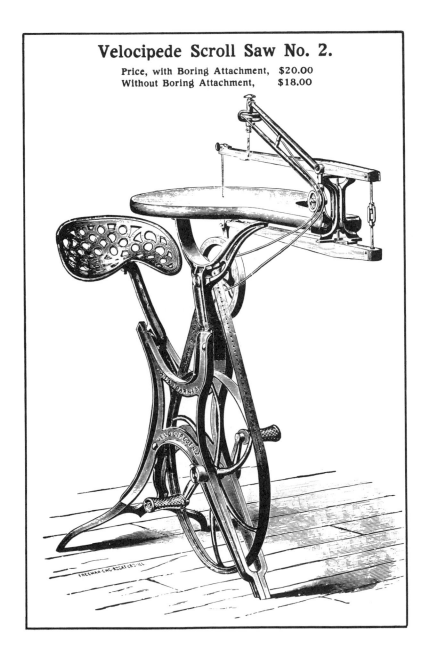

Velocipede Scroll Saw No. 2.

Price, with Boring Attachment, $20.00
Without Boring Attachment, $18.00

Illus. 22. The original Velocipede Scroll Saw No. 2 is available today (without the boring attachment) as a functional reproduction. The original was cast iron, and the reproduction is cast aluminum.

Island in Wisconsin exhibits an antique scroll saw made by New Rogers manufacturer, along with a variety of fretwork pieces made by Jacobsen with this saw. New Rogers scroll saws were manufactured around the same time as the Barnes saws. Illus. 23–27 show the construction features of this early saw. Note again that the design configurations are similar to the modern constant-tension saws. Jacobsen's fretwork projects attest to the cutting capabilities of those crude saws of more than a century ago. Some of Jacobsen's work is shown in Illus. 28–33.

In the early 1900s, small electric motors were used in individual woodworking machines. During this period, scroll-sawing became extremely popular. Scroll saws were used by furniture makers, cabinet shops, mill-work factories, and custom-home builders. They were used to cut all of the ornate scroll or fretwork popular during the Victorian period and at the turn of the century. Today, scroll saws are used in the repair, restoration, and recreation of those intricate and elegant designs found on the grills, delicate brackets, and other decorative pieces from these time periods.

Illus. 34 is a page reprint of a January 1932 *Deltagram* publication introducing their "new" 24-inch Delta scroll saw. This machine incorporated a revolutionary design concept—a rigid arm with an upper-coil spring to help pull the blade as it was pushed upwards by the lower chuck linkage. This machine is the forerunner of the present Delta 24-inch scroll saw that has remained virtually unchanged in appearance for the past 50 or so years. (See page 62 for more information about today's Delta 24-inch rigid-arm saw.)

Illus. 23 (left) and 24 (above). Overall views of Jen Jacobsen's New Rogers treadle saw. The original blade is broken and the drive belt is missing.

Illus. 25. A slot in the wooden arm cradles a pin on the eccentric. This converts a rotary motion to an up-and-down movement of the lower arm. This saw has a steel table that can be tilted.

Illus. 26. The eccentric shaft and pulley for a round-belt drive.

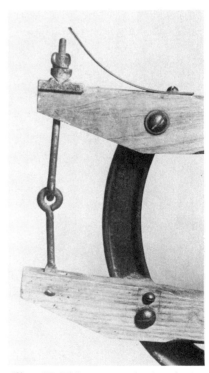

Illus. 27. This rear tensioning device looks similar to rear tensioning devices on modern constant-tension saws.

Illus. 28–32. Examples of fretwork made by Jens Jacobsen of Washington Island, Wisconsin, in the early 1900s.

Illus. 29.

Illus. 30.

Illus. 31.

Illus. 32.

Illus. 33. Cut-through lettering made by Jens Jacobsen.

Illus. 34. The forerunner of today's rigid-arm Delta scroll saw appeared in the early 1930s. This machine was followed shortly afterwards with an improved version, the "Deluxe" Delta scroll saw, whose design has remained virtually unchanged to this day.

Many proponents of the currently popular constant-tension scroll saws claim that the development of the rigid-arm scroll saw was a step backwards. Other veteran craftsmen who perfected their scroll-sawing skills on these saws are not eager to give them up. They have learned to work around the saw's obvious inefficiencies and the restrictions of sawing thick stock with fine blades. (See Illus. 35–37). Some of those woodworkers who practice marquetry prefer the rigid-arm machines, provided they are equipped to cut at the proper speed and are fitted with the proper chucks and blade guides. Apparently others agree because very recently a few new rigid-arm machines by other manufacturers have entered the scroll saw market.

In the late 1940s and mid-fifties, Sears,

Illus. 35–37. Some delicate silhouettes cut out of ¼-inch plywood with the older Delta scroll saws. These silhouettes were made around 1935 by an unknown New York artist, and are part of a collection owned by Walter Schutz.

Illus. 37.

Illus. 36.

Roebuck and Company carried several scroll saws in different price ranges. One was called a "spring-loaded" type. This had a rigid, cast arm with a spring that produced the upstroke of the blade as it was loaded or stretched on the power (or downwards) stroke. Another type of scroll saw sold by Sears in the post-World War II era was its first "walking beam" saw. (See Illus. 38.) Rather than a spring to effect the upwards stroke, power and tension were applied to both ends of the blade on both the upwards and downwards strokes by means of a walking beam mechanism. As stated in an old manual: "Since the drive system is not subjected to sudden loading on the successive downstrokes, this type of jigsaw assures smooth, uniform-cutting action which eliminates, to a considerable extent, blade breakage and vibration." (Chapter 13 discusses the current "walking beam" saw sold by Sears.)

A portable, handheld electric scroll saw was manufactured by Dremel for a number of years. Apparently the woodworking consumer didn't buy it, as Dremel stopped manufacturing it in 1972. (See Illus. 39.)

No other dramatic design changes in scroll saws really occurred until the Hegner saws, from West Germany, appeared in 1975. They signaled the return of the walking beam, constant-tension, parallel-arm machines, but with many significant technical refinements. A growing number of other manufacturers have since followed Hegner's lead.

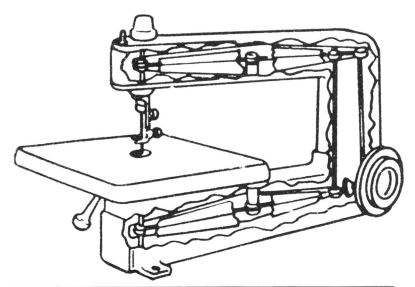

Illus. 38. A sketch showing the workings of an old Sears "Walking Beam" scroll saw sold in the 1940s and 50s. This constant-tension saw evenly distributed power (tension) to both ends of the blade with all of the moving parts safely enclosed.

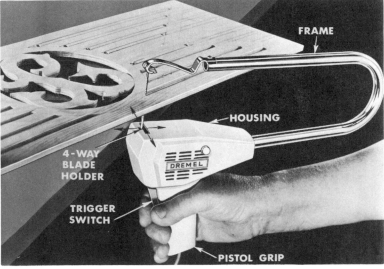

Illus. 39. Here is an interesting concept that didn't make it. This handheld power scroll saw was discontinued by Dremel in 1972.

2
SCROLL SAW BASICS

HOW SCROLL SAWS WORK

All scroll saws must have some way of converting the rotary motion of the motor to an up-and-down reciprocating action. (See Illus. 40.) Scroll saws are designed so the blade cuts on the downwards movement, so the teeth of the blade should always point downwards. How fast the blade goes up and down is specified as the strokes per minute (spm) or the cutting strokes per minute. The speed can vary from machine to machine. It depends upon the speed of the motor, which is specified as revolutions per minute (rpm). If a scroll saw is direct-drive type, which many are (it's the most basic), then the cutting strokes per minute will equal the revolutions per minute or speed of the motor. Sometimes it is better to change or slow down the cutting speed, particularly when sawing metal, plastic, or very thin material such as veneer.

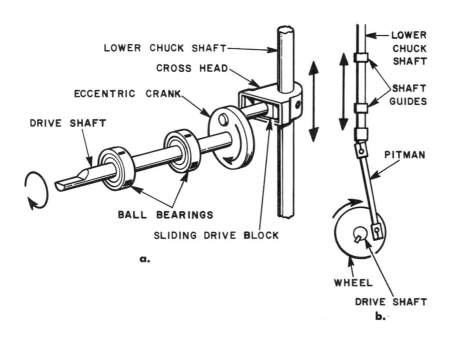

LOWER CHUCK SHAFT
CROSS HEAD
ECCENTRIC CRANK
DRIVE SHAFT
BALL BEARINGS
SLIDING DRIVE BLOCK
a.

LOWER CHUCK SHAFT
SHAFT GUIDES
PITMAN
WHEEL
DRIVE SHAFT
b.

Illus. 40. Conventional methods of converting rotary motion into reciprocating motion: (a) Eccentric crank on the left, and (b) the wheel and pitman drive.

Saws having speeds different from the speed of their drive motors are either belted-drive systems or variable-speed controlled saws. A belted-drive saw makes use of a combination of different size pulleys that are fitted on to the drive shaft and/or to the motor shaft. A belted-drive system is simple in design. It is easy to maintain and provides precise control of specific speeds. (See Illus. 49 on page 38.)

A mechanical means of actually changing the pulley sizes (diameters) with a single control crank while the saw is running is one form of a variable-speed saw. The motor speed does not change, but the spm does. This type of variable speed is found on the older, heavier, rigid-arm machines, such as the Delta and Powermatic. The other variable-speed system is activated electronically inside the motor, and actually slows or speeds up the rotation (rpm) of the motor shaft simply by the turn of a hand dial. Generally, the higher speeds are preferred for almost all wood-cutting jobs except sawing thin veneers.

The length of the cutting stroke equals the vertical distance travelled by the blade in one complete stroke. Stroke lengths vary from approximately ⅜ to 1⅛ inches, with a range of ¾ to 1 inch being the most common. Short-cutting strokes reduce saw efficiency and cutting speed when sawing medium to thick stock. Consequently, the longer strokes are usually preferred, but only if the mechanics of the saw provide proper vertical travel of the blade or proper tension throughout the stroke. Few saws available today have a provision for changing to a shorter stroke length. A shorter stroke length provides a higher degree of accuracy; this is beneficial when production-cutting thin materials such as metals, veneer, etc.

The throat of a scroll saw is that horizontal distance from the blade to the rear or vertical part of the saw frame. Throat capacities range from 12 to 26 inches, and again the middle range of 14 to 18 inches appears to be the most popular.

The depth of cut is the thickest piece of wood that can be "potentially" cut on a saw. Remember, hardwoods and softwoods cut a lot differently. You may be able to cut 2-inch oak, but how long will it take to complete the cut and what will be the quality of the cut? Will it be rough, smooth, or burned? Will it be straight with the cut edges flat and true, or will the cut surfaces bulge or slant and be out of square? (See Illus. 41.)

Illus. 41. The quality and trueness of cut are important, especially in thick stock. This 1½-inch pine should have a square edge. What will happen when thick hardwood is cut on the same saw?

BASIC SCROLL SAW DESIGNS

The styles or designs of scroll saws today fall into two distinct groups: *rigid arm* and *constant tension*. The constant-tension saws can be further divided into *C-arm* and *parallel-arm* saws.

Rigid-arm Saws

Rigid-arm saws (Illus. 42) have cast or tubular overarms that are stationary. The only visible movement is the blade going up and down. A spring-loaded plunger is located on the upper arm. With rigid-arm saws, the downstroke is the power stroke; the upstroke is produced by the spring action, located in the upper tube of the plunger assembly. In operation, the spring is loaded (or stretched out) on the downstroke (cutting stroke).

The drive system of the rigid-arm machine, by virtue of its design, is subjected to

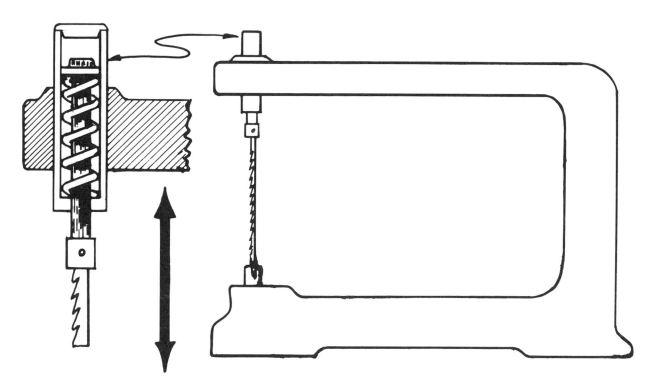

Illus. 42. How rigid-arm scroll saws work.

sudden loading and unloading of the blade tension during each stroke. In other words, the tension is not consistently the same throughout the entire stroke. If, because of feeding pressure or sawdust clogging, the upper spring does not pull the blade up, after the downstroke, the blade is too flexible as it is pushed upward by the drive system of the machine. This situation, combined with feeding pressure, places strain on the blade; the result is premature breakage. To prevent this from happening, reduce stock thickness or use stiffer and wider blades; these blades, however, will progressively limit the sharpness of the turn that can be made and the capability of making intricate cuts in thicker material.

In short, the disadvantages of rigid-arm saws well outweigh their advantages. I would seriously question why one would purchase this type of machine for home or professional use.

Constant-Tension Saws

Constant-tension saws include the C-frame and parallel-arm types. (See Illus. 43 and 44.) Throughout the stroke, the blade always maintains exactly the same tension on the upstroke as it does on the downstroke. The advantages of constant-tension saws include minimal blade breakage and the capability to cut with much thinner and narrower blades. This allows the operator to make incredibly sharp turns and saw accurate, highly detailed, intricate designs in thick as well as thin stock. As the blade reciprocates it enters slightly into the work on the downstroke and then backs away slightly on the upwards movement. (See Illus. 43 and 44.) The cutting action of constant-tension saws is much different from that of the rigid-arm saws. On a rigid-arm saw, the saw blade stays perfectly vertical in just one spot, moving up and down only within its own space. With constant-tension saws, the blade generally moves slightly forward into the wood on the downwards stroke and slightly back on the upstroke, or vice versa. The blade can also have a "mixed action" movement.

The blade motion of constant-tension saws does several important things: (1) It generally provides for better sawdust removal when fine blades are used, which means cooler cutting, less friction, and no burning of the cut; since less heat is generated, blades will stay sharp longer and don't break as often. (2) Some of the blade works against the walls or sides of the saw kerf; the results are extremely smoothly cut surfaces that need no or very little sanding. The blade "rasps" away ridges on the previously cut surfaces as it moves into and out of new wood during the reciprocating movement. (3) Less pressure is required to hold down the workpiece if the blade backs off on the upstroke, which is when the work normally tends to lift on the rigid-arm saws.

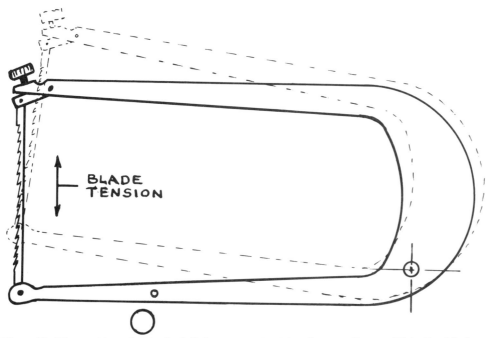

Illus. 43. The motion of a typical C-frame constant-tension scroll saw. Note the blade positions.

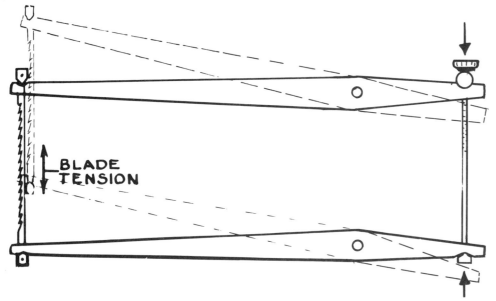

Illus. 44. The action of a true parallelogram constant-tension saw. Note the blade positions.

34

C-Arm Constant-Tension Saws. These saws are tensioned "up front." (See Illus. 43.) This is an advantage because it eliminates the reach to the back of the machine, where almost all parallel-arm saws are tensioned. (See Illus. 44.) The primary disadvantage of the C-arm saw design is the way the blade travels. As you can see in Illus. 43, the blade tips backwards on the upstroke. On some C-arm saws (the RBI Eagle, for example [see page 111]), the pivot point is even more centrally located, vertically; this means that when cutting, the blade tips slightly more forward beyond vertical, at the completion of the downstroke. (The blades of the Delta C-arm and Hegner Multimax I C-arm, however, are in a vertical position at the completion of the downstroke.) The tipping of the blade in and out of a vertical plane creates some problems when sawing along sharp irregular curves in thicker stock. It's likely that the curved cuts will not be as square, as sharp, and as true as when making straight line cuts in the same material with the same saw.

Parallel-Arm Constant-Tension Saws. These saws (Illus. 44) are regarded by most authorities as the best overall—at least in design theory, and that is with all other considerations being equal. A cheaply made parallel-arm saw, for example, is no better a buy than a cheap version of any other tool. The major advantage of true parallelogram saws is that the blade remains vertical throughout the total stroke. (See Illus. 44.) Although the blade moves slightly into the cut on the downwards stroke and moves slightly back on the upstroke, this design seems to produce the smoothest and truest cuts with the least blade breakage.

SCROLL SAW FEATURES

Blade suspension is one feature you will read about frequently in the chapters ahead. The term pertains to the way the blade is mounted to the forward ends of the C-arm or the parallel arms. It cannot be a "stiff" connection. The blade must hinge or pivot freely, even on the C-arm-type saws. Feeding pressure will cause the blade to bend, which is normal in fast cutting. When the feed is slowed to make a turn, the blade "catches up" and the cut made along the curve edge is vertical, as it should be.

There is a greater emphasis on the blade clamp's ability to pivot on parallel-arm-type saws than there is on the C-frame designs. Illus. 44 shows how the angle of the blade to the arm becomes more acute as the saw approaches the highest upward position of its stroke. Therefore, it is imperative that the blade is allowed to pivot freely. (See Illus. 45.) If the blade suspension system does not provide a good, free pivot action, the blade will be forced to bend at the point where it comes out of clamps. (See Illus. 46.) This causes strain and metal fatigue at this point; premature blade breakage is the certain result.

Illus. 45. A blade clamp pivots on a knife-like edge. The space above the clamp is intentional—it allows the blade clamp to pivot freely.

The bending of blades, shown in Illus. 46, can also be caused by careless installation. If the blade is not pointing in the right direction as it is clamped in the first blade holder or chuck, the blade must be bent to get the other end clamped. That's why some saws have locking pins. (See Illus. 47.) These pins hold the blade clamp steady while it is installed and tightened with a wrench.

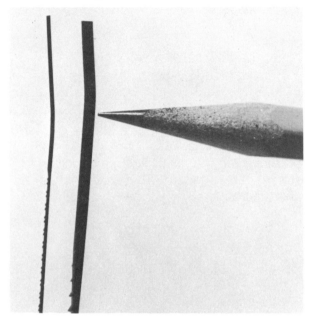

Illus. 46. Saw blades bent near the ends indicate a poorly designed blade suspension system or careless blade installation. Bending, as shown, results in premature and more frequent blade breakage.

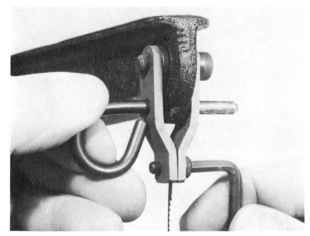

Illus. 47. A pivotal gimbal-type blade clamp has parallel jaws and a "locking pin" that's used to keep the clamp from "swinging around" when the blade is installed.

There are a lot of different types of saw tables available on the market today. When buying, pay attention to the following features: their shapes (round, rectangular, etc.), sizes, center openings, blade slots (for ease of blade installation), and their abilities to tilt right, left, or in either direction. Other important considerations include the accuracy of the tilting scale, the smoothness or ease of adjustment, and the clamp quality.

I sometimes find a large table a disadvantage because, since I seldom use the back of it, I just store unneeded pieces on it, which get in the way when I do need to swing a big piece of stock.

Pay attention to the design engineering (or lack of design engineering) on many of the new constant-tension saw tables. Some manufacturers advertise full 45° tilts either left or right, but some of these tables will not tilt to 45°. Others that do tilt to 45° do not permit cutting! On one machine, the lower arm strikes the saw table on the upstroke when it is set at just 34°, so you can't cut at 45° at all. On another machine, if you tilt the table a full 45° left (the only way the table tilts), you have less than ¼-inch clearance under the hold-down arm. On yet another machine, the hold-down arm must be removed to permit tilting the table to 45°.

One machine has a slot in the table that is either in the wrong location for a tilting operation or is just not big enough, because with the table tilted the blade cuts up the table and makes a very jagged blade opening. On another machine that must be bolted to the manufacturer's stand, the saw table strikes the stand just as it reaches the 45° tilt. In this case, your workpiece cannot be larger than the saw table, because if it extends over the edge of the table, the workpiece will strike the saw stand.

All these problems associated with poor table-tilt design can leave the potential customer shocked over the sloppy engineering that's evident in some machines and fairly well hidden by other manufacturers. For example, though full 45° cuts are not made that often on a scroll saw, the table should be designed to make that cut if that is what the manufacturer claims it can do. Why have a 45° mark on the scale if you can't even adjust the table to that setting?

A lot of design inefficiencies are the result of the manufacturer's intent to get a machine into the marketplace quickly without complete evaluation or testing. Several manufacturers make design changes and improvements as they go along. This is why it is essential for the buyer to be wary.

Make the following inspections when looking at a scroll saw: Check the side play of the arms. Look at the saw in operation to see if the travel of the saw blade is a blur or a crisp vertical line. Pay attention to saw vibration: Some saws are very loud and must be bolted down to a heavy workbench or special steel stand; otherwise, they bounce all over. Other saws run very quietly and so smoothly that you can actually balance a coin on its edge. (See Illus. 48.) The noise level can affect your health and comfort during extended periods of saw use.

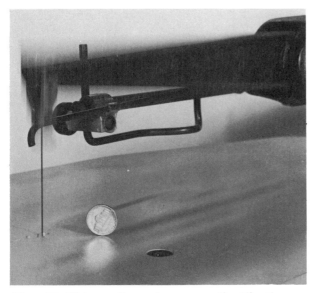

Illus. 48. This scroll saw has a smooth, vibration-free operation, as shown by the coin that is steadily balanced on edge while the scroll saw is on.

One machine I am familiar with practically requires a major overhaul just to change speeds. The guard must be removed, which is okay, but then the pulleys must be re-moved from the pitman shaft, reversed, aligned, and then secured again with two screws before the belt and guard are replaced. Another machine has one double pulley for speed changes, but no provision to adjust or move the motor.

A big throat capacity can be a disadvantage, especially if you have a saw with rear tensioning, because the adjustment control is difficult to reach on 19-, 24-, and 26-inch saws. On the other hand, if you cut a lot of large pieces, a big throat capacity is important. Also, remember that a tabletop machine that has a rear motor mount might require as much as three feet of space (front to back) for just a 19-inch throat capacity.

Check where the *switch* is; it should be easy to reach so the saw can be quickly shut down if necessary. An auxiliary foot switch is very useful for some kinds of sawing jobs, and it's a very good safety feature (See page 157.)

There are machines that require the use of a manufacturer's stand. Some stands take up considerably more floor space than is necessary. A stand should be solid, stand level, and not occupy excessive floor area.

Some machines have dust blowers. Some blowers work effectively; others either barely work at all or they can't be adjusted easily to the cutting area.

Foreign manufacturers are likely to require metric wrenches and metric replacement nuts and bolts. Believe it or not, one machine required one size allen wrench for the lower blade clamp, and a different size allen wrench to tighten the upper blade clamp. This is a problem the manufacturer should have corrected.

Weight and portability is an important feature for many woodcrafters. More weight does not necessarily mean a better value. Extra weight is one way for manufacturers to counteract machine vibration. If your saw must be stored away after every time it's used, or you use your saw at craft shows, portability is an essential consideration. However, remember that lightness may be that saw's only desirable feature.

The kind of motor, the machine base, and the kind and quality of bearings should also be investigated before you purchase a scroll saw. Motor size and quality can vary a great deal. Horsepower alone is not the best measure of a good motor. Amps are the best indicator of power, but most constant-tension saws have ample power for light, intermittent use. Continuous cutting and sawing of thick hardwoods and metals requires a durable and much more powerful motor. The range of sizes available is from 0.9 amps to a hefty 3.6 amps. Most machines specify ⅛ hp, which is probably adequate for average home-craft saw use.

Induction-type motors are more reliable and consistent, but also more expensive. Good-quality variable-speed motors are expensive. The less expensive variable-speed units have electronics like dimmer switches, and they lose power as the rpm is decreased.

The base of the machine (Illus. 49) is important in the same way that a good foundation is important to a house. Some machine bases are heavy castings or welded steel plate. Others are simply stamped sheet metal. The kind and quality of bearings, if any, at wear points and on moving parts (including motors) will determine the life of the machine. The various kinds of bearings include the sealed ball-bearing type, bronze, and/or nylon sleeves. Pivot points, rather than areas of full rotation, are available with either the sleeve or ball-type bearings. Most authorities agree that bronze-alloy sleeve bearings are the best choice at arm pivots and similar areas that wear.

The quality of work hold-downs vary considerably from manufacturer to manufacturer. This is not a major concern if you're a professional woodworker because eventually you'll probably not use hold-downs anyway. However, for schools and for other institutional use it is extremely important that hold-downs and guards be in place, ready, and easy to use. The hold-down is very helpful when a beginner or youngster starts on the saw; in fact, make sure they use hold-downs in your own shop.

The quality of the overall workmanship and engineering that has gone into the manufacture of a scroll saw can indeed be observed. You can answer the following questions by inspecting the machine: Are the edges left sharp or deburred? What's the quality of the paint job and the finish of polished metal surfaces? Do the welded joints have good penetration and smooth, clean beads? Are the appropriate materials used? (See Illus. 49.) Are the component parts—such as standard bolts, nuts, clamps, thumbscrews, bumpers, electrical cords and plugs—of minimal size, or standard and top quality? Has the machine been designed for not only convenience of the operator but to be used for a long time? The manufacturer's warranty also varies considerably in duration and substance from manufacturer to manufacturer. Does the manufacturer have easy accessibility to replacement parts and service? Be certain to verify this, especially if considering an imported saw.

One of the most important considerations of all is the time and convenience involved to make blade changes. There isn't anything more disheartening than fumbling around and wasting precious time changing blades. Even though constant-tension saws have a much lower frequency of blade breakage

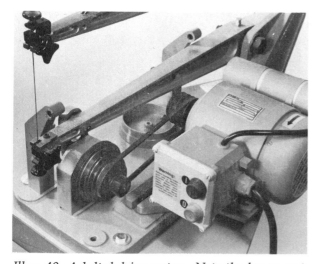

Illus. 49. A belted-drive system. Note the heavy cast base, machined steel pulleys, push-button switch, and totally enclosed induction motor.

than rigid-arm saws, blades will still have to be changed more often than you think, in part because of the sharp turn cuts and faster, highly detailed cuts in thick woods that can be made with thin blades (Illus. 50), and also because all blades eventually break or become dull. Also, making the many cut-outs of inside openings in fretwork requires very frequent blade threading and reclamping. (See Illus. 51 and 52.) With practice and repetition, you can shorten the time it takes to change blades with any system, but some saws are far easier and quicker to use than are others.

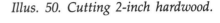

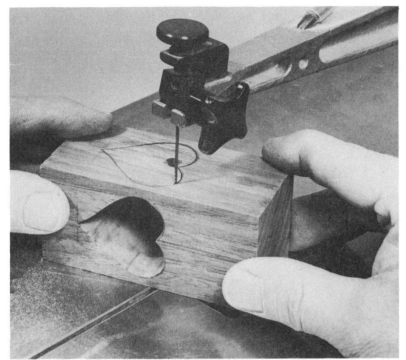

Illus. 50. Cutting 2-inch hardwood.

Illus. 51. These parts for a corner shelf require a lot of blade threading, reclamping, and retensioning.

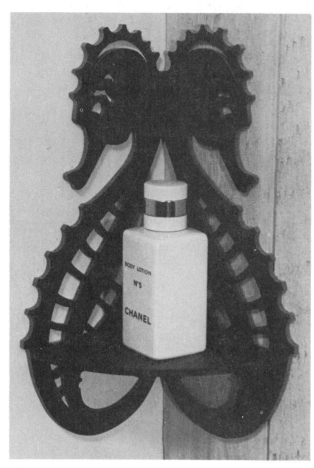

Illus. 52. The completed shelf.

For most saws, you have to bend over to see what's going on under the table when you install the lower blade end or work the lower blade clamp. There are some machines where this can be done simply by "feel," without looking.

Also, weigh the alternatives of loose-blade clamp pieces against those that are permanently attached to the machine. Are other auxiliary devices and tools such as stiffeners or clamp holders required when changing or reinstalling blades? Can these parts become lost or misplaced? Is it easy to thread the blade through large and thick pieces? Are there slots in the table to simplify such jobs?

In addition, consider what will happen if a blade breaks on the saw you are thinking of buying. Will a broken blade damage your workpiece? (See Illus. 53.) When a blade breaks, will it pierce your hand or finger be-fore you shut the power down? Or does the upper arm immediately lift up, stopping the reciprocating action safely?

Illus. 53. Ask the manufacturer about what will happen when a blade breaks. Will it damage the work, as shown, and could it pierce the operator's hand or fingers before the power can be shut down?

Finally, consider these additional questions: Is cleanup easy or are there areas that collect dust, cuttings, etc., that can only be cleaned by vacuum or compressed air? Are machine stands and machine bases provided with protective bumpers or glides so tables and floors do not become gouged or scratched?

This discussion of scroll saws features should be helpful when you purchase a scroll saw. However, consider some additional factors: What type of work do you expect to do with a scroll saw? How reliable must the machine be? (See Illus. 54.) How long do you want it to last? What kinds and range of materials will you cut? Is a large throat and a thick-material cutting capability important or is a smaller, more compact machine more practical? Will one speed serve your needs or will you be cutting plastics, metals, and veneer that are best handled at lower, variable speeds. Do you want portability, a bench-top unit, or one on a stand set up as a permanent ready-to-use workshop tool? Will the machine be used continuously as a production tool or just on an occasional weekend?

The bottom line is price. Scroll saws range in price from a little over $100 to nearly $2,000. Everyone has his own needs, expectations, and financial limitations. Scroll saws are like cars—some run well, some are "junkers" (new or used), and others fall in between. If the tool is to be part of your work—used in your business or used to make some extra money—then the machine that will provide the best quality for your needs is your best choice regardless of price. You'll have speed, convenience, and will spend very little time making repairs or waiting for parts. Otherwise, the medium-priced machines are good values if you can afford them. The most inexpensive machines are, in my opinion, poor saws that will either break down or present a problem to the saw operator eventually. And this often occurs just after the warranty period expires, or after the manufacturer has discontinued production and exited from the scroll saw business.

Chapters 4–13 explore the majority of scroll saws available today. As noted previously, manufacturers are continually making changes and improvements. Get up-to-date descriptions and prices from them. It's always best to actually operate the saw and examine it firsthand. This should be done leisurely, with plenty of time allotted for making all adjustments, changing blades, and cutting a variety of materials thick and thin, hard and soft. Talk to those who own or used the machine you are thinking about buying. Don't buy a saw sight unseen from a catalogue photo or description in an advertisement.

3
BLADES, SPEEDS, AND FEEDS

When the right *blade* (Illus. 55) is used on the material being cut, at the correct saw *speed* (cutting strokes per minute), and the operator feeds the material into the saw at the proper *rate*, the results will be an efficient cutting operation. (See Illus. 56.) That is, the wood (or material) will be cut with the smoothest finish, in the quickest time; also, there will be the least amount of wear and tear possible on the machine and minimal blade breakage if the blades were installed properly and used at the correct tension. With each new scroll-sawing experience, it becomes easier to coordinate these three basic factors. (If your machine is of a single-speed type, then you only have to concentrate on the blade selection and feed rate.)

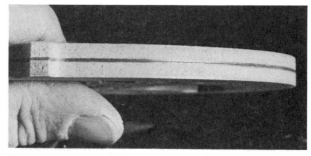

Illus. 56. Two thicknesses of ¼-inch hardwood plywood. The cut surface is so smooth it shines, and there is no splintering on the lower edge.

TYPES OF BLADES

Scroll saw blades are reasonably inexpensive, at least when compared to other cutting tools and to the price of a piece of good sandpaper. Blades range from around 14¢ to 50¢ each and more, depending upon the size, style, quality and quantity purchase at one time.

Traditionally, saw blades used in reciprocating sawing machines are of four basic types. These are: the plain-end blade (Illus. 57), the pin-type blade (Illus. 58), the sabre saw blade (Illus. 59), which is the widest and stiffest, and spiral blades (Illus. 60 and 61).

Today, however, the most widely used blades are the 5-inch plain-end blades, because these types of blades are used in almost all scroll saws. The narrower-sized blades are emphasized because with them

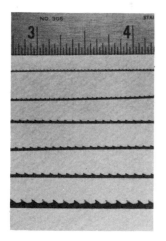

Illus. 55. Common fretsaw blades used in constant-tension saws. Above, a 2/0 fine blade with 28 teeth per inch. Below, a coarse blade with 9 teeth per inch.

the popular constant-tension saws will cut very sharp turns in thick and thin stock. In recent years, more attention has been given to the finer fret saw blades because they have proven reliable when used in the constant-tension saws. (See Illus. 62.) At one time, Delta illustrated over 30 different sizes and types of blades in their catalogue for their rigid-arm saws. Today, they illustrate only 17 blades, and only three of these blades are ³⁄₁₆ inch or more in width.

Illus. 58. Three-inch pin-end blades used in Dremel and Delta hobby scroll saws.

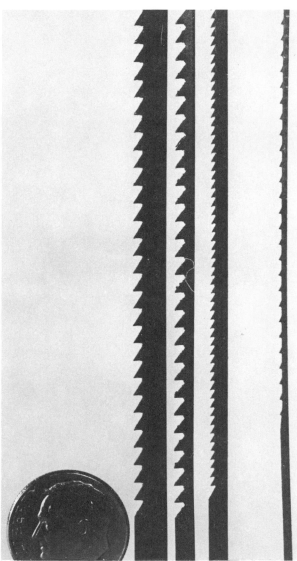

Illus. 57. Standard 5-inch, plain-end blades; the dime is for size comparison. From left to right: 10-tooth Delta scroll-saw blade, 10-tooth Trojan scroll-saw blade, 20-tooth Olson scroll-saw blade, and a No. 7 skip-tooth fret blade with 14 teeth per inch.

Illus. 59. Sabre-saw blades have 9 teeth per inch, are ³⁄₁₆ or ¼ inch in width, and chucked at one end, as shown. These blades are only used on rigid-arm scroll saws.

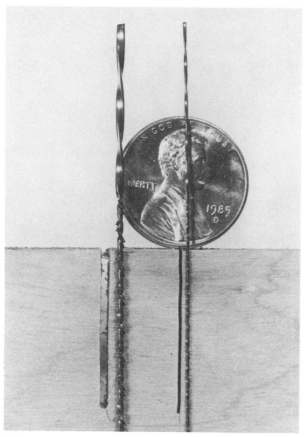

Illus. 60. These five-inch spiral blades, supplied by the Olson Saw Co., cut in all directions. They range from a 2/0 size (.025-inch kerf) at the right up to a No. 6 (.049) at the left. These are toothed blades that are twisted.

Illus. 61. At left: the Olson No. 6 spiral blade with 30 teeth per inch. At right: a length of Remington's rod saw that has particles of tungsten carbide bonded to a steel rod. This rod saw is recommended only for very hard materials like marble, glass, and ceramics.

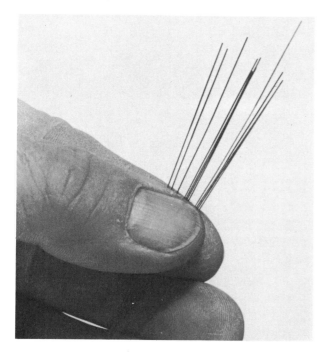

Illus. 62. Shown are a dozen incredibly fine blades that are used for the special cutting of veneers. They are about the size of "fat" hairs.

The blades available for use in scroll saws today range in size from 8/0 (.012-inch width, .006-inch thickness) up to ¼-inch in width (.028 inch in thickness). There are few manufacturers of scroll saw blades worldwide. Some are: The Olson Saw Company, Bethel, Connecticut 06801; The J.N. Eberle Co. of West Germany, with American Intertool, Inc. (1600 Jarvis Ave., Elk Grove Village, Illinois 60007) its exclusive United States distributor; and Hegner, which carries Pebeco, Gottfried, and Goldsnail (also a West German blade manufacturer), and which is sold through its exclusive United States distributor, AMI Limited, P.O. Box 312, New Castle, Delaware 19720.

The easiest method of categorizing the plain-end blades for scroll-sawing is the system that the Olson Saw Company uses. They have been in the saw blade business since 1918. Olson lists their blades under these four major headings: (1) "Scroll saw blades," (2) "Scroll/Fret saw blades," (3) "Metal piercing" or "Jewellers' blades," and (4) "Spiral blades." Saw blades are specified according to width, thickness, teeth per inch (Illus. 63), length, and style. Generally, for reasons of simplicity, blades are given "universal, generic numbers," starting from 8/0 (the narrowest and thinnest) upward to 2/0, 0, and continuing from No. 1 consecutively up to No. 12.

Amazingly enough, the blades specified as scroll saw blades are not really used as much for scroll-sawing as are the scroll/fret saw blades. Fret saw blades are much smaller in width and thickness. They range from a 2/0 (.010 inch thick, .022 inch wide) up to a No. 12 (.020 inch thick, .067 or about ¹⁄₁₆ inch wide). Illus. 64 compares the smallest scroll saw blade (.022 inch thick, .110 inch wide) to a No. 9, a medium-to-big fret saw blade (.018 inch thick, .053 inch wide). Scroll saw blades have regular-style teeth.

All fret saw blades have a "skip-tooth" design, which means that every other tooth is eliminated. (See Illus. 64.) Skip teeth provide faster, cooler cutting with greater chip clearance. Eberle manufactures a skip, double-tooth blade that is sold in sizes from 2/0 up to No. 11. Many marquetry experts prefer the Eberle blade design in the 2/0 size for veneer-sawing. Illus. 65 compares the Eberle 2/0 skip, double-tooth blade to their standard, wide-space, No. 9 skip-tooth fret saw blade of conventional design.

Illus. 64. The smallest blade in the scroll category, shown at the left, is being compared to a No. 9 blade, one of the larger sizes in the fret-saw group. Fret blades are much smaller than scroll-saw blades. The scroll-saw blade on the left has 20 standard teeth per inch. The fret blade has a skip-tooth configuration.

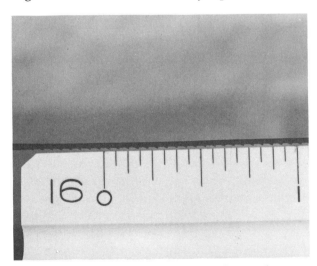

Illus. 63. Teeth sizes are specified as the number per inch. Here we have a skip-tooth configuration fret blade with 20 teeth per inch.

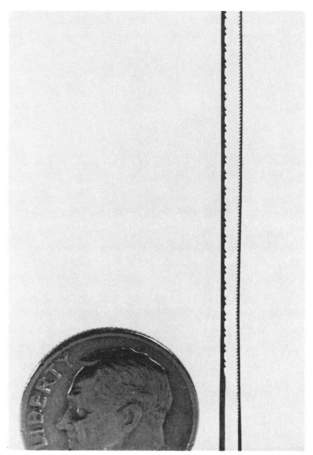

Illus. 65. Fret-saw blades by Eberle, (a German manufacturer). On the left, a 2/0 blade. On the right, a No. 9 blade.

Illus. 66. The No. 5 skip-tooth fret blade on the left is being compared to a No. 5 jewellers' metal-cutting blade on the right. Respectively, they have 14 and 36 teeth per inch.

Jewellers' or metal-piercing blades have regular saw teeth. They are made of hardened, tempered steel for cutting mild steel and other hard materials. They range in size from 8/0 to No. 12. Only those sizes from a No. 1 (.012 inch thick, .024 inch wide) up to the No. 12 (.023 inch thick, .070 inch wide) are recommended for motor-driven scroll saws. Jewellers' blades are not recommended for normal wood-cutting jobs, although some saw users do attempt to cut veneer with fine jewellers' blades. Silas Kopf, a marquetry expert, says "Jeweller's blades have the teeth too close together, and they can clog." Kopf recommends skip double-tooth blades for cutting wood veneer because they clear the dust away. Illus. 60 compares a 5/0 jewellers' blade to a 5/0 fret blade.

Spiral blades are unique because they saw in all directions without turning the workpiece. They are ideal for cutting small curves and openings in detailed fretwork, for 0° radius work, etc. Some 30 to 40 years ago, a wirelike blade with helical teeth was used in light crafts. At that time the blades were called drill saws. These blades also cut in any direction, but the shallow teeth limited their usefulness to just thin, soft materials. The spiral blades shown in Illus. 60 are a recent development by the Olson Saw Company. These are actually high-carbon steel, 5-inch blades with standard tooth forms that are twisted. They cut all kinds and thicknesses of material.

In addition to wood, spiral blades will cut nonferrous metals, plaster, bone, etc. Olson manufactures blades in 8 different sizes, from the smallest 2/0 with 51 teeth per inch, up to a No. 6 with 30 teeth per inch. The No. 6 cuts a big .049-inch kerf, which you might not want. It also kicks up a lot of sawdust. However, for some jobs, the No. 6 saw blade may be just what one needs.

Though the taut, highly tensioned fret saw blades permit on-the-spot turns, which might be considered a zero-radius turning capability, spiral blades can cut in all directions. However, although I have used spiral blades, I would not consider them a substitute or a cure-all for the standard fret blades. It is much easier to follow lines of larger radius curves and make straight line cuts with a fret blade than with a spiral blade. The spiral blade goes in all directions, often following the grain of the wood rather than the layout line. This makes it difficult to cut smooth, flowing curves without bumps or dips. Also, they do not cut surfaces nearly as smoothly as regular fret blades.

I did find one class of work for spiral blades that no other blade can handle— bevel-sawing letters for signs that all have to slant in the same direction. (See Illus. 67.) Illus. 68 shows the actual bevel-cutting with a spiral blade.

Illus. 67. A spiral blade is the only type of blade that can be used on a bevel-cut project such as this.

Illus. 68. When bevel-cutting with a spiral blade, you can cut in all directions without turning the workpiece.

Guidelines for Selecting Blades

It is difficult to make very specific recommendations in blade selection because of the following reasons: (1) The industry is not completely standardized. A number of variations among manufacturers do exist when scroll saw blades made by foreign manufacturers are included. (2) The performance of blades can vary from "batch to batch." For example, you may be able to put one blade to a lot of tension and get extensive use from it; however, though the next blade is identical to the first one, the second one will dull or snap in less than half the time, even though all of the other conditions appear the same. (3) The human element plays a part in determining which blade to use, because individual judgments are different. What is considered a moderate feed rate to one person can be interpreted as something entirely different by another individual.

There is no one blade that is the absolute best for a given job. Each blade will handle a range of jobs with various materials and different thicknesses. However, keep in mind these general guidelines for blade selection: The finer the blade, the less the thickness that can be cut without problems. With thick stock and thin blades, the feed must be slower; the results will be a smoother cut and less frequent blade breakage.

The first time I got my hands on a new constant-tension saw, I installed the finest blade on hand (a 2/0) and tried to cut ¾-inch hardwood—an unrealistic expectation. Remember, the thinnest blades are for the thinner materials. However, also remember that medium-size fret blades such as those in the 5 to 9 range are still very narrow when compared to the blades widely used for conventional cutting jobs with rigid-arm scroll saws.

One more general guideline should be noted: As the thickness of material increases, use blades with proportional fewer teeth. In short, use a coarse blade for thick material. Illus. 69 illustrates the importance of having at least two, preferably three, teeth in contact with the workpiece. Because of the unique

capabilities of the constant-tension saws, blades that are finer than usual can sometimes be used to cut thicker materials. However, don't feed the material too quickly. More tension is required; slow the feed rate at curves to avoid bellied or unsquare cuts. (See Illus. 70.) The amount of detail of your particular project is very specifically related to blade selection. Always use the widest blade possible, but one that will still allow you to make the desired curves with ease.

Tables 1–4 are taken from the Olson Saw Company's catalogue. They should provide guidelines for selecting the proper blade to use for a particular range of cutting jobs. The blade you choose should be based upon the following factors: operating and cutting speeds, quality of cut, and blade durability (wear and breakage) desired.

Illus. 69. At least two, preferably three, teeth should be in contact with the material at all times. Here, for example, a No. 9 blade with 12 teeth per inch is a good choice for sawing this ¼-inch material.

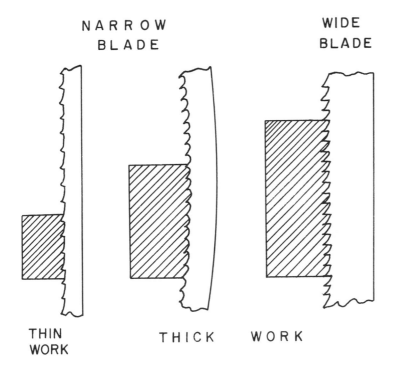

NARROW BLADE   WIDE BLADE

THIN WORK   THICK WORK

Illus. 70. The effect of blade width, feeding pressure, and material thickness.

Olson	Cross Reference Numbers		Material Cut	Width	Thickness	TPI
	Parker/ Trojan	Delta/ Rockwell				
403	520	40–164	wood	.110″	.022″	20
411	515	40–191	wall board, pressed wood, wood, felt, paper, bone, lead	.110″	.022″	15
412	510	40–192	hard/softwood, plastic	.110″	.022″	10
406	425	40–165	asbestos, mica, iron, steel, lead, copper, brass, aluminum, pewter	.250″	.028″	20
413	310	40–193	hard/softwood, plastic	.187″	.028″	10
414	407	40–194	hard/softwood, plastic	.250″	.028″	7

Table 1. Popular sizes of conventional scroll-saw blades with regular saw teeth.

Table 2. Spiral saw blades supplied by the Olson Saw Co.

Universal Generic No.	Kerf Size Thickness	TPI
2/0	.025	51
0	.026	46
1	.030	46
2	.032	41
3	.035	41
4	.038	36
5	.044	36
6	.049	30

Universal Generic No.	Material Cut/Usage	Width	Thickness	TPI
2/0	For extremely intricate sawing. Very thin cuts in ¹⁄₁₆″ to ³⁄₃₂″ materials. Excellent for cutting wood veneer, plastics, hard rubber, pearl, etc.	.022″	.010″	28
0		.024″	.011″	25
1		.025″	.011″	23
2	For tight radius work in thin materials, ³⁄₃₂″ to ¹⁄₈″ wood veneer, wood, bone, fibre, ivory, plastic, etc.	.029″	.012″	20
3		.032″	.013″	18
4		.033″	.014″	15
5	For close radius cutting in materials ¹⁄₈″ or thicker. Great for sawing hard/softwood, bone, horn, plastics, etc.	.037″	.015″	14
6		.040″	.016″	13
7	Popular sizes for cutting hard and soft woods ³⁄₁₆″ up to 2″. Also cut plastic, paper, felt, bone, etc.	.043″	.016″	12
8		.047″	.017″	11.5
9		.053″	.018″	11.5
10		.059″	.019″	11
11		.063″	.019″	9.5
12		.067″	.020″	9.5
Reverse tooth	For smooth, splinter-free finish on top and bottom sides. Excellent for hard/softwood, plywood, etc., with thickness of ¼″ or more.	.100″	.022″	9 with 3 reverse teeth

Table 3. The popular scroll/fret-saw blades widely used in constant-tension scroll saws. All are of a skip-tooth design.

Universal/ Generic No.	Width	Thickness	TPI
8/0	.012″	.006″	84
7/0	.013″	.006″	81
6/0	.014″	.007″	79
5/0	.016″	.008″	74
4/0	.017″	.009″	66
3/0	.019″	.0095″	61
2/0	.020″	.010″	56
0	.022″	.011″	51
1	.024″	.012″	48
2	.028″	.013″	43
3	.030″	.014″	41
4	.031″	.015″	38
5	.033″	.016″	36
6	.038″	.017″	33
7	.041″	.019″	30
9	.049″	.022″	25
11	.057″	.024″	20
12	.070″	.023″	17

Table 4. A list of the metal-piercing or jewellers' saw blades used for metals and other hard materials. All have regular saw teeth 8/0 to 2/0 and are not, as a rule, recommended for power sawing.

ACCESSORIES AND CUTTING TECHNIQUES

With some constant-tension saws you can perform jobs in addition to sawing. Some blade holders or clamps allow the installation of files (Illus. 71 and 72) and other cutting or abrasive tools that function with a reciprocating action. Small jewellers' files, the tungsten-carbide rod saws (Illus. 61), and one or more hack saw blades installed together can do filing and abrasive cutting jobs on a variety of materials.

Sometimes a wide kerf can be the specific cutting job. A uniformly wide kerf is desired for work requiring certain inserts. On some machines, two or three blades can be mounted side by side, and tensioned together, if they will all fit into the upper and lower blade clamps. If not, similar results can be obtained to some extent by installing one blade and then wiring another blade or blades (that have been cut shorter) to it. (See Illus. 73 and 74.) The effectiveness of the latter technique is limited to short-term cutting in soft, thin, and easily cut material. With the outside blades not being tensioned, they have a tendency to follow the grain or move in a new direction.

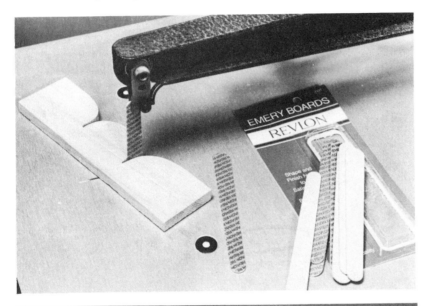

Illus. 71. Using fingernail files in this scroll saw converts it into a light-duty, reciprocating sanding machine.

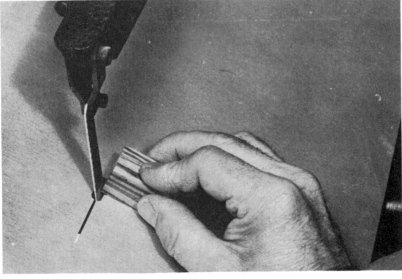

Illus. 72. With a tilted table, a power-driven fingernail file can chamfer an edge.

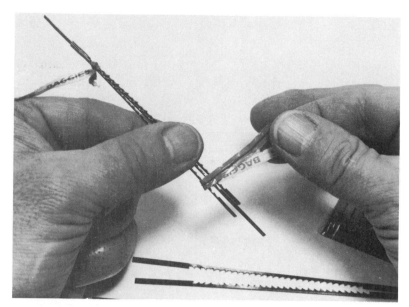

Illus. 73. Using plastic bag "ties" to wire three blades together for cutting a wide kerf. The center blade is chucked as usual, and the two outside blades are only "wired" to it.

Illus. 74. Making a wide kerf. The technique shown, with the blades wired together, should be limited to cuts in thin wood.

The 90° blade-twist trick (Illus. 75) is another technique that may be practical in some situations. To change the cutting direction of a blade, simply twist it on the ends. When it is twisted to 90°, you can feed the work from the side of the machine like a band saw. Most blades are not tempered at the ends so they can bend without breaking. Remember, however, that when the 90° blade-twist trick is done with C-arm and parallel-arm constant-tension saws, the result will be a less-than-ideal cutting stroke. In both cases, the arm action is such that the blade moves slightly from the back to the front of the machine with every stroke.

Most blade manufacturers package the blades in little bundles of a dozen wrapped with very fine wire. Getting a blade out of a bundle can at times be frustrating and time-consuming. If all the wire wrappings are removed, the blades can become mixed with other sizes; this makes it difficult for you to pick out the correct size. Lengths of ½-inch PVC (polyvinylchloride) plastic pipe with end caps or a cork make good storage vessels. (See Illus. 76.) PVC components are available at most hardware stores and plumbing supply centers. One final tip: Attach a length of adhesive-backed magnetic tape to an appropriate spot on the saw base or stand. This will hold a selection of blades conveniently. (See Illus. 77.)

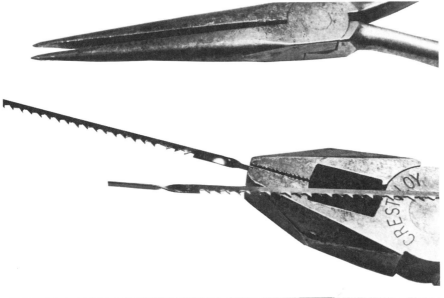

Illus. 75. When the ends of a blade are twisted, longer cuts can be made in a "band-saw fashion," which is feeding from the side, rather than the front of the machine.

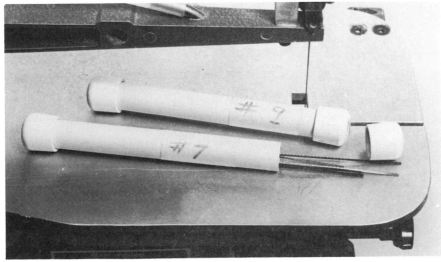

Illus. 76. One-half-inch-diameter PVC pipe and end caps make good blade storage containers.

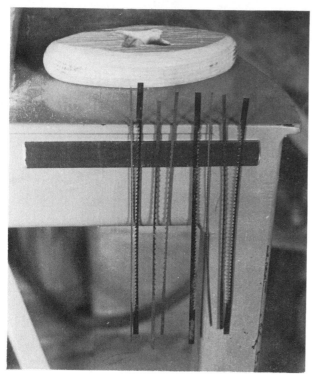

Illus. 77. A selection of blades can be kept conveniently ready with a length of adhesive-backed magnetic tape.

SPEEDS

Machine speed (strokes per minute) is not as important as the rate or speed at which the operator advances the material into the reciprocating new blade. Different feed rates mean different quality cuts. Commonsense regarding feed rates can prevent problems that might arise when using a single-speed machine. For almost all wood-sawing, the highest machine speed is best anyway—especially when the constant-tension saws are used. The only times slower speeds are important are when cutting unusually hard materials like hard metals and plastics. And slower speeds are normally best for sawing thin veneers, soft metals, bone, ivory, rubber, and laminated plastics.

Most one-speed or two-speed machines have around 1,200 to 1,800 cutting strokes per minute at the maximum. Hardwoods, softwoods, hardboard, plywood, and paper products over 1/16 inch thick can generally all be cut at the higher speeds. This covers about 95 percent of general wood-cutting

jobs. Medium machine speeds may be an advantage for cutting 1/16- to 1/4-inch-thick softwoods, for making puzzles and some inlay work. Cutting marquetry work and jewellery making are often best done at slower speeds, from less than 100 to 600 or 800 csm. Remember, for efficient cutting, as your material thickness increases, select wider blades with fewer teeth per inch.

FEEDS

If you occasionally cut materials such as soft metals or thin veneer-like wood and slow cutting speeds are recommended, you can often get by just by slowing the feed rate. As a general rule, slower feed rates result in a smoother finish on the cut surface. However, the best blade for the material being cut is one that not only produces smoothly cut surfaces but also is the most efficient as far as time is concerned.

Since feed rate is related to time and quality or smoothness of cut, let's look at a few examples. Illus. 78 shows a cut surface across the grain on 3/4-inch-thick white pine. A No. 9 fret blade with 11½ teeth per inch was used. The first inch at the left in the photo was cut at a rate of 10 seconds per inch of feed. The remainder of the cut was made at more than double that speed, cutting at the rate of 4 seconds per inch. Notice the obvious difference in surface quality. (Incidentally, pine is not one of the smoothest cutting woods. Walnut can burn at high cutting speeds, and poplar, a softwood, cuts smoothly and doesn't burn at high speeds.)

Illus. 79 shows three different finish qualities on hard maple. The first inch at the left in the photo was cut with a No. 9 fret blade with 11½ teeth per inch at a feed rate of 12 seconds per inch. The next inch was cut with the same blade but at three times the feed rate (4 seconds per inch). The final inch at the right was cut slowly, but on a band saw using a 1/4-inch skip-tooth blade.

Illus. 80 shows 3/4-inch red oak that was cut at two dramatically different rates. There was not a great deal of difference in the appearance of the surface qualities. However, tear-out on the bottom was greater at the faster feed rate. Slowing to a feed rate of about 6 or 7 seconds per inch increased surface quality considerably.

A reverse tooth blade manufactured by the Olson Saw Company is a production blade designed to minimize splintering on the bottom side as the blade exits through the wood. (See Illus. 81 and 82.) This blade has 9 teeth per inch and is designed to cut both hard and soft woods, plywood, etc., at ¼ inch or more in thickness. This blade may

not work effectively in your saw unless the lower reverse teeth match up at the proper height with the worktable. (See Illus. 82.) Regardless of how this blade is installed on some machines, the reversed teeth do not travel above the table surface, thus negating its intended purpose. However, I have been advised by the Olson Saw Company that they are now making a 5 reverse-tooth blade in addition to their standard 3 reverse-tooth blade. One of these blades will allow the opposed teeth to travel above the table surface.

Illus. 78. Three-quarter-inch pine cut at different feed rates. The inch at left was cut in 10 seconds; the remainder of the cut was made at a rate of 4 seconds per inch of cut surface. Note the bottom tear-out.

Illus. 79. Differently cut surfaces of hard maple. The one at left was cut at a feed rate ⅓ the speed of the center cut. The cut on the right was made on a band saw.

Illus. 80. Three-quarter-inch red oak: the cut at the left was made at 10 seconds per inch, and the rest of the cut was made at a feed rate of 4 seconds per inch.

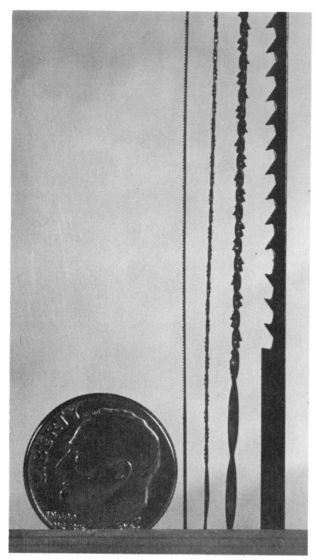

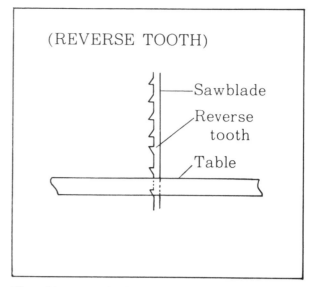

Sawblade

Reverse tooth

Table

Illus. 82. To work effectively, the blade must be installed with the lower tooth or teeth on the downstroke, as shown.

Illus. 81. A comparison of some unusual blades. From left to right: 6/0 jewellers' blade, 2/0 and No. 6 spiral blades, and a reverse-tooth fret blade designed to minimize bottom splintering that has 9 teeth per inch, and is .022 inch thick and .100 inch wide.

COMMERCIALLY AVAILABLE SCROLL SAWS

4
RIGID-ARM SCROLL SAWS

Scroll saws in the rigid-arm category include those older, larger, and heavier machines that have a straining device for the upper end of the blade. This blade-tensioning device usually consists of a coil spring inside a tube with a plunger that has a chuck with adjustable flat jaw(s) to grip the blade. Rigid-arm scroll saws have been around for more than a half century. Companies such as Delta International Machinery Corp. of Pittsburgh, Pennsylvania (Illus. 83 and 84), Powermatic Houdaille, Inc. of McMinnville, Tennessee (Illus. 85), and Oliver Machinery Co. of Grand Rapids, Michigan (Illus. 86 and 87), have been manufacturing these machines for years. Oliver's equipment is exclusively industrial. They incorporate some very interesting design features.

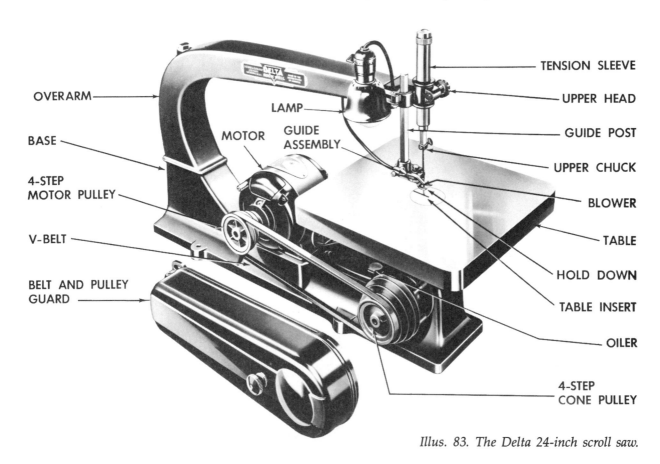

Illus. 83. The Delta 24-inch scroll saw.

Illus. 84. The Delta 24-inch variable-speed scroll saw being used to make an internal cut.

Illus. 85. The Powermatic 24-inch scroll saw with an optional variable speed controlled by the front hand wheel.

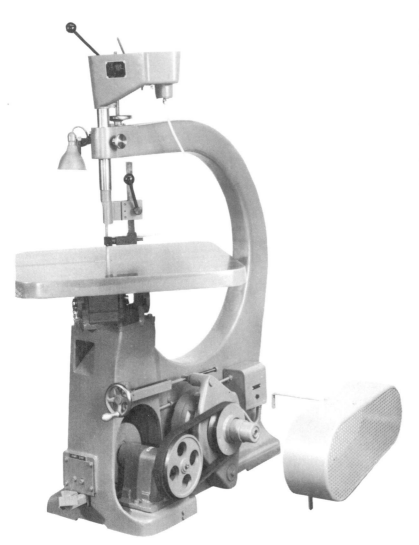

Illus. 86. The Oliver industrial heavy-duty variable-speed drive scroll saw weights 1,600 pounds. It can carry blades 10 to 18 inches in length; it cuts stock up to 10 inches thick, has a 2½-inch cutting stroke, a tilt table, and a 36½-inch throat capacity, with an overall height of 6 feet.

Illus. 87. An adaptation of the same Oliver machine with the overarm neck omitted. This ceiling-supported scroll saw can cut stock of any width or length. Note the casters on the worktable to facilitate the moving of heavy workpieces in this factory.

In addition to Delta and Powermatic, which have pretty well dominated school and professional markets for several decades, there are other scroll saw manufacturers that have, over the years, come and gone. Some of the current scroll saw manufacturers include: Boice Crane Industries, P.O. Box 249, Gothenburg, Nebraska; Vega Enterprises, Inc., P.O. Box 93, Decatur, Illinois 62526; and the Foley-Belsaw Company, 6301 Equitable Road, Kansas City, Missouri 64120. The Foley-Belsaw scroll saw is an adaptation of the old Sprunger machines that were produced by Sprunger Bros. of South Bend, Indiana, since World War II. Shopsmith, Inc., 6640 Poe Avenue, Dayton, Ohio 45414, has a rigid-arm scroll-saw attachment for their multiple five-in-one machine, as does Master Woodcraft & Machine Co., 800 Spruce Lake Drive, P.O. Box 669, Harbor City, California 90710, for their "5-in-1" multipurpose machine.

A few foreign manufacturers have just entered the United States market. "Jet" is a saw that is manufactured in Taiwan, and sold by various dealers. Asahi Koki Co., Ltd. of Japan, manufactures two new saws. Fine Tool Shops of Danbury, Connecticut is this manufacturer's exclusive United States distributor.

On the Delta and Powermatic scroll saws, and some other saws, the overarm can be removed to convert the machine to a sabre saw setup, as shown in Illus. 88. With this setup, you can make inside or outside cuts on stock of any length or width. The sabre saw setup requires special accessories, including an additional lower-blade guide (Illus. 89) and special sabre saw blades, which are much stiffer and wider than scroll saw blades. Sabre saw blades are only clamped at the lower end, and they are too wide to permit intricate cutouts or sharp turns.

Pages 62–71 discuss several brands of rigid-arm scroll saws available on the market today.

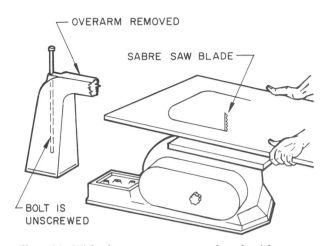

Illus. 88. With the overarm removed and with a sabre saw blade that's clamped only in the lower chuck, work on any size material can be cut.

Illus. 89. The Delta sabre saw setup. Note the lower support guide directly behind the blade.

DELTA 24-INCH SCROLL SAW

This saw is available in a four-speed belted-drive version or a variable-speed model. (See Illus. 83, 84 and 89–91.) The belted-drive model delivers a choice of 610, 910, 1,255, and 1,725 cutting strokes per minute. Motor sizes recommended are ⅓ hp. The variable-speed model has a range of 650 to 1,700 csm. Delta rigid-arm saws have a blade chuck (Illus. 92) that will clamp objects other than just saw blades—such as sanders and files; hold-downs, dust blowers, rollers, and blade guides (Illus. 93), are other features of this saw. The blade guide is necessary on all "non-constant-tension" machines to minimize "weaving" cuts. The Delta 24-inch scroll saw will convert to a sabre saw, as shown in Illus. 88 and 89. Files and/or a sanding attachment (Illus. 94) can be fitted to the lower chuck.

Special chucks and blade guides for using very fine fret blades are essential when doing marquetry or similar precision work. (See Illus. 95 and 96.)

Although the Delta 24-inch machine has a specified 1¾-inch-thickness cutting capacity (Illus. 97), as do other rigid-arm machines, it does not cut stock this thick as easily as the new constant-tension saws. In order to cut thick material on almost all rigid-arm saws, it is necessary to use a heavy, wider blade in order to minimize blade breakage. However, a wide blade severely limits the turning capabilities of the saw and the amount of intricate cutting or detailing that can be done in thick stock. A ¼-inch blade with seven teeth per inch will cut 2-inch-thick softwood slowly. The entire upper-blade support as-

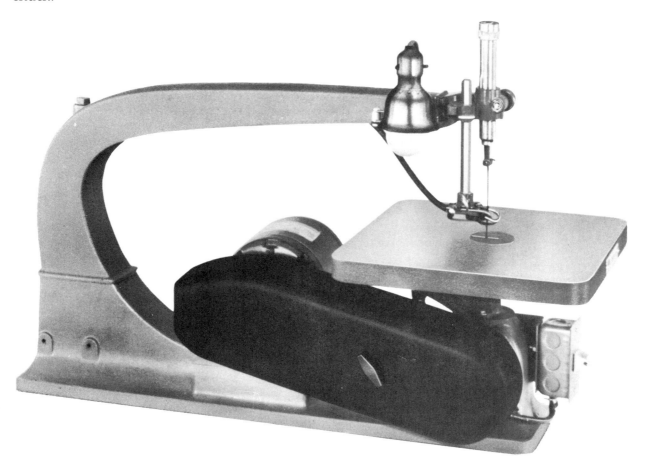

Illus. 90. The Delta bench mount, a four-speed model. All models have 14-inch square tables that tilt 45° right, 15° left, and 45° to the front.

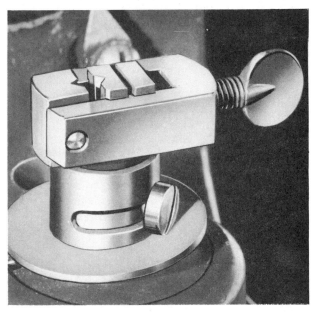

Illus. 92. The Delta blade chuck will hold not only flat blades, but round-shank sanders and machine files. The chuck also can be rotated 90° so an unlimited length of cut is permitted.

Illus. 91. The Delta variable-speed model, with retractable casters and lamp attachment, on stand.

Illus. 93. The Delta spring hold-down adjusted for a bevel cut. Note the blade guide, roller support, and the air blower directed to the cutting area.

Illus. 94–96. At far left, a sanding-attachment that has a combination flat and curved work surface. This fits into the lower chuck. At center, a self-centering lower chuck accessory. Fine blades are automatically centered and locked with the thumbscrew. At right, individual blade guides, valuable for accurate cutting, are matched to fit specific blade thicknesses.

Illus. 97. Wide blades are required for thick cutting. Here 1½-inch stock is being cut, but because of the wide blade size required, the sharpness of turns and/or the cutting of highly detailed designs in thick stock are severely limited.

sembly must be removed. In addition, the blade will wander and sometimes make non-vertical cuts. Also, only turns of minimal radii can be cut without prebored "turning holes."

One final note about the Delta 24-inch scroll saw concerns the calibrated exterior of the upper plunger casing (Illus. 98), which contains the coil spring for blade-tensioning. The entire assembly of spring, plunger, blade chuck, etc., is adjustable vertically to coincide with the optimum amount of tension selected for various types and sizes of blades. The numbers etched on the outside are merely for the operator's reference, and are not specific values for specific blades.

POWERMATIC SCROLL SAW

The Powermatic scroll saw (Illus. 85 and 99–101) is very similar to the Delta saw in overall specifications, design, and appearance. The Powermatic might be slightly heavier in gross weight. Both saws have a 1-inch stroke length, and their speed ranges are very close when the four-speed belted-drive and variable-speed models (Illus. 99) are compared. The Powermatic has a slightly larger table, 14 inches × 15 inches, with the same tilting options. The upper-blade chuck and plunger assembly with the other features are almost identical to the same units on the Delta saw. (See Illus. 100.) The lower chuck is also similar to the lower chuck on the Delta machine. (See Illus. 101.)

Illus. 98. This close-up look at a Delta saw shows the exterior of an upper plunger casing containing the coil spring for blade tension. This entire assembly is adjustable vertically to coincide with the optimum tension for various blades. Note the blade chuck at the bottom of the square plunger tube.

Illus. 99. A view showing the drive mechanism of the Powermatic variable-speed 24-inch scroll saw. Note the table-tilting trunnions and the heavy cast construction.

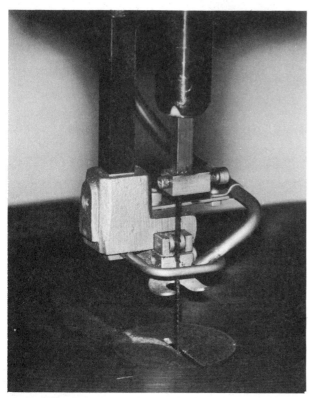

Illus. 100. Powermatic's upper blade-guide assembly. Note the front blade guard, the blade guide, dust blower tube, work hold-down, and the blade chuck with an allen-type cap screw.

Illus. 101. The lower chuck on the Powermatic saw.

JET SCROLL SAW

The Jet scroll saw (Illus. 102), manufactured in Taiwan, has the same cutting capacities as the Delta and Powermatic scroll saws; i.e., a 24-inch throat, and 1¾-inch-maximum stock thickness. The catalogue specifies a 6-inch blade length, whereas both Delta and Powermatic require a 5-inch blade. The motor is listed at ½ hp. The Jet comes only in a four-speed belted-drive model, with a choice of 790, 990, 1,250, and 1,600 cutting strokes per minute. The table size is 15½ inches × 15½ inches, with 45° right and 15° left tilts only. The saw has an upper-blade guide, dust blower, and hold-down. For more information on this machine, write to: Jet Equipment & Tools, 1901 Jefferson Ave., P.O. Box 1477, Tacoma, Washington 98402.

Illus. 102 (right). The Jet 24-inch rigid-arm scroll saw.

VEGA SCROLL SAW

The Vega scroll saw, Model No. 126 (Illus. 103), has some features that are different from other rigid-arm-type scroll saws. The upper-blade guides can be adjusted by thumbscrew. The upper-blade guides are actually rollers. A roller is located on each side of the blade, and on the back of the blade; this setup is similar to the blade-guide systems found on the more expensive band saws. This machine has plenty of room for access to the lower-blade chuck for changing blades because the table-support trunnions are spaced farther out towards the table's front and rear edges. The motor is bolted on an elastomer mounting material to isolate it from the base and to reduce noise and vibration.

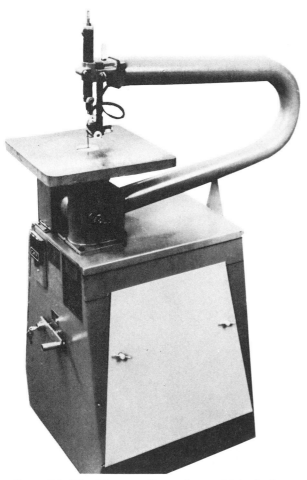

Illus. 103. The Vega scroll saw has a 26-inch throat clearance, and can cut stock up to 2½-inches thick with a variable-speed drive.

The Vega saw will carry either 5- or 6-inch blades. A 1½-inch thickness is the cutting capacity with the 5-inch blade, and a 2½-inch thickness can be cut with blades 6 inches in length. When blade lengths are changed, a simple tension change is made on the upper assembly. The variable-speed motor is ⅓ hp, with speeds variable from 430 to 1,725 rpm. A speed-changer crank control is lockable (with a removable key) so that very low speeds can be assured when beginners are using the machine. Finally, sabre-sawing can be performed on this machine with the removal of the structural steel-tubing overarm, and the use of an accessory sabre blade support.

FOLEY-BELSAW SCROLL SAW

The Foley-Belsaw scroll saw (Illus. 104), as mentioned earlier, is a remake of the old Sprunger scroll saws that were first manufactured in the 1940s. The entire line of woodworking machinery was taken over in 1985 by the Foley-Belsaw Co., which added some new features. This saw, like the others discussed in this chapter, is of the plunger type with a typical upper-blade tension system. The throat capacity is 20 inches, and the maximum thickness that can be cut is 2 inches. A 12-inch × 12-inch table tilts a full 45° left and right. A ¹⁄₁₅-hp enclosed variable-speed motor provides a range of 600 to 2,000 strokes per minute.

The Foley-Belsaw scroll saw carries all standard 5-inch blades in chucks that have stop pins for proper positioning of the blade. An allen wrench is necessary for tightening the blade chucks. This saw has both upper and lower rotating chucks. When set screws are loosened, the chucks can be rotated a full 360°. This is convenient when cutting a pattern that requires a full 360° rotation of the workpiece, and where the location of the pattern and the length of the piece will result in interference with the overarm frame. When the workpiece comes in contact (or strikes) the arm, the saw is stopped, the chucks rotated, and the cut is completed.

Illus. 104. The Foley-Belsaw scroll saw has a 20-inch throat capacity and $\frac{1}{15}$-hp variable-speed motor with a cast-iron overarm frame and 12-inch × 12-inch tilting table. An adjustable flexible shaft with a small pin light is mounted on the overarm, and a dust blower is directed to the cutting area. The machine can be purchased alone for workbench mounting or on the accessory stand, as shown.

ASAHI KOKI SCROLL SAW

The Asahi Koki scroll saw (Illus. 105–107) consists of two models, both with a 20-inch throat capacity. One is considered a "beginner's" saw (Illus. 105) and the other is called the "professional" model. The professional model is heavier and has a 1-inch cutting stroke; the beginner's model has a ¾-inch stroke. The table on the professional model is 12 inches × 16 inches; it is only 10 inches square on the beginner's model. Both tilt 20° right and left. The blade holders on the professional model can be adjusted so that the blade will cut in any direction, and the upper guide has a roller to keep the blade straight. Otherwise, the specifications are very similar. Both machines have 1,100 cutting strokes per minute, and are advertised as having the capabilities to cut wood 2 inches thick, as well as brass and ferrous materials in thinner thicknesses.

SHOPSMITH SCROLL SAW ATTACHMENT

The Shopsmith scroll saw attachment (Illus. 108 and 109), is another rigid-arm machine. The tubular arm construction has an 18-inch throat and 90° "indexing chucks" that give the operator a choice of four different blade-cutting directions. The overarm can be removed for conversion to do sabre saw type of cutting, and with a machine file installed you can do power-filing jobs. This power-tool attachment also features a tilting table and a dust blower system.

Illus. 105. The Asahi Koki "beginner's" scroll saw features a hinged arm and 20-inch throat capacity.

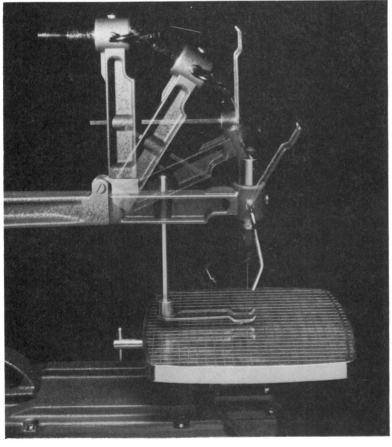

Illus. 106. Stop-action photography illustrates the hinging feature of the arm, which facilitates the threading of a blade through a hole for interior cutouts.

Illus. 107. The Asahi Koki "professional" model also has a 20-inch throat capacity and will cut 2-inch stock, as will the beginner's saw.

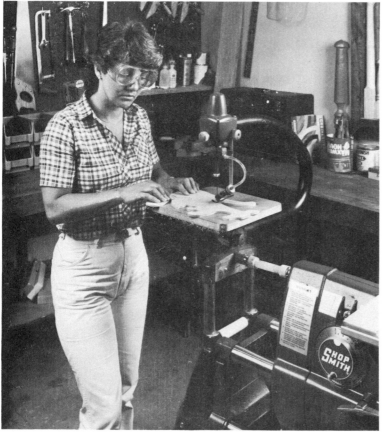

Illus. 108. The Shopsmith 18-inch scroll saw in use; it is attached to the Mark-V multiple machine, which is its power source.

Illus. 109. A close-up look at the Shopsmith unit shows the table tilt, hold-down, air supply, upper chuck, and enclosed tensioning system.

5
LIGHT-DUTY SCROLL SAWS

Illus. 110 and 111 show two bench top saws that are very similar to each other in design and function. They can be used for light-duty sawing and—with the use of their accessory attachments—can perform many other light woodworking jobs.

The Dremel saw (Illus. 110) is called the "Basic Scroll Saw/Sander"; with a flexible shaft and its accessories added it's called the "Moto-Shop." (See Illus. 112.) It has been around for many years. (The scroll saw/ sander is available in many hardware stores and is sold by Sears, as are extra blades, sanding discs, and the 30-inch flexible shaft

kit.) The overarm, table, and base are made of pressed sheet steel. The table measures 8 inches × 9½ inches and tilts 45° left and right. (See Illus. 113). You can mount a 4-inch disc sander (Illus. 114 and 115) and a 30-inch flexible hose with a collet chuck to the side-mounted power takeoff drive. This is a "kitchen-table" workshop that's ideal for light craft work, making models, etc. It has suction cups on the base, and it does not have to be attached to a workbench unless desired. The saw alone has a total shipping weight of only 16 pounds, which makes it easy to carry around.

Illus. 110. The Dremel scroll-saw sander has a 15-inch throat capacity and can cut stock 1¾ inch thick.

Illus. 111. Delta's new 15-inch hobby scroll saw comes with a disc sander and has features very similar to those on the Dremel saw. The table tilts 45° right and left; the saw has a variable-speed motor (1,100 to 2,000 cutting strokes per minute), and it can also be fitted with a flexible shaft attachment.

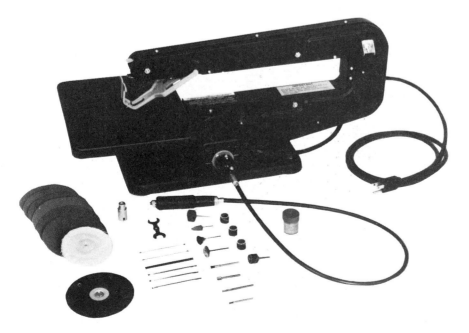

Illus. 112. The Dremel saw with the flexible shaft and all accessories is called the "Moto-Shop."

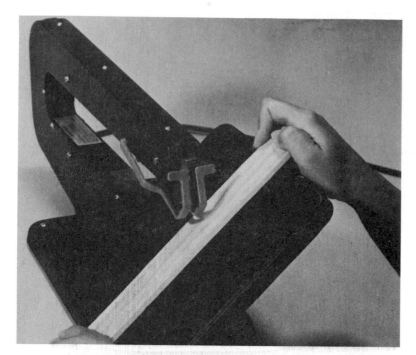

Illus. 113. Making a 45° cut with the Dremel saw.

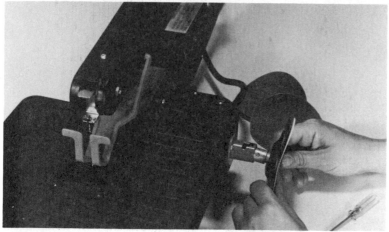

Illus. 114. Mounting the disc sander to the power takeoff.

Illus. 115. The disc sander smooths and shapes edges. Work must be held on the left or forward and downward side of the disc.

Whenever the power takeoff is used with an accessory the scroll-saw blade must be in position on the saw. The Dremel saw carries a 3-inch pin-type blade. Illus. 116–118 show blade installation. A plastic blade guard is easy to remove or install without tools. It simply snaps into position with two pins that fit into matching holes on the arm. (See Illus. 119.)

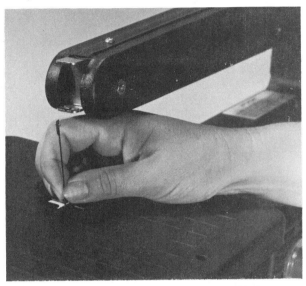

Illus. 116. Installing a blade. A pin-type blade "hooks" into upper and lower blade holders.

Illus. 118. A close-up look at the upper blade holder. The pins set into the small "v's." The blade can be installed to cut in any of four directions.

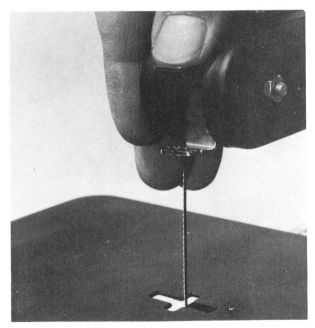

Illus. 117. The upper-blade lever holder is a spring that is depressed for blade installation. No tools are needed to change blades.

Illus. 119. The plastic blade guard. It does not function as a hold-down.

This saw will cut softwoods up to 1¾ inch thick, but it is better suited to cutting thinner materials. The saw has a direct-drive motor that delivers 3,450 strokes per minute. The length of the stroke is not specified, but it is short. With continuous cutting of thin materials, the wear on the blade can be shifted by raising the table. This brings a new, unused segment of the blade to the cutting area.

The flexible shaft can be fitted with a drill; it can also be fitted with carving burrs, a sander, grinders, etc. (See Illus. 120.) The drill is used to make entry holes for threading the blade through the workpiece when making interior cuts. (See Illus. 121–123.)

The Delta 15-inch hobby saw (Illus. 111), like the Dremel, has suction cups that firmly secure it to any tabletop or bench top. The

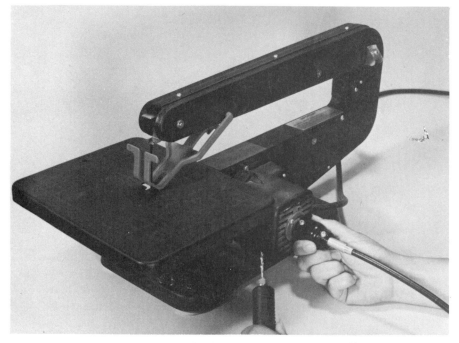

Illus. 120. Attaching the flexible shaft to the power takeoff.

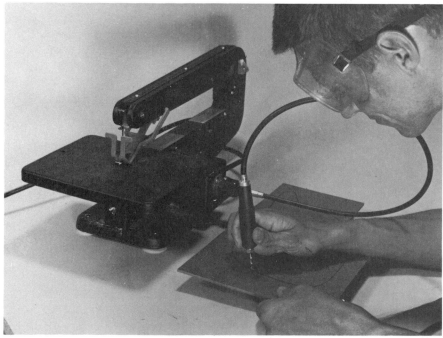

Illus. 121. A drill in the hand piece is used to make an entry hole for the blade so an inside cut can be made.

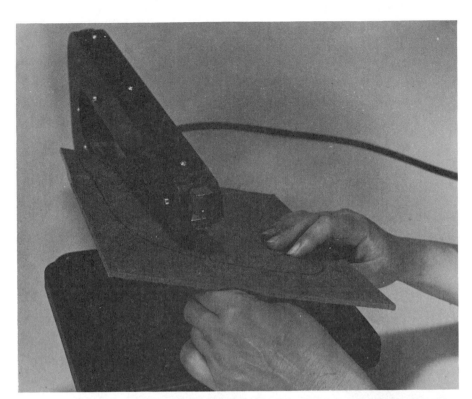

Illus. 123. Making the inside cut.

table is 8 inches × 9½ inches and tilts right and left. The motor is a universal, variable-speed type that locks in anywhere between 1,100 to 2,000 strokes per minute. The vari-able-speed feature is important if you intend to cut materials other than wood—such as metal and plastics.

The Delta hobby saw comes with a 4-inch-diameter disc sander; it can also drum-sand, buff, and polish when the variety of accessory attachments available for the power takeoff are used. The blade holder is a three-position type, so the blade cutting direction can be from the front or either side. Delta literature states that the saw can cut wood 1½ inches thick but it does not specify if that's hardwood or softwood. The pin-type blade used is 3 inches long. The blade guard looks and functions the same as the blade guard on the Dremel saw. The shipping weight is only 15 pounds, which makes it easy to carry around and use for light wood crafting.

6

KIT AND REPRODUCTION PEDAL SCROLL SAWS

KIT SAWS

Constant-tension scroll saws can indeed be homemade, especially when castings and other parts that are commercially available are used. Two parallel arms are cut out of hard maple, and a simple turnbuckle device is employed to provide the tension. Essentially, these parts are made just like the parts on the old treadle-powered saws of the 1800s.

Illus. 124. A kit saw is made with wooden arms, wooden stand, a table with castings, and an electric motor.

However, unlike those saws, you can power your homemade or kit machine with an electric motor. (See Illus. 124.)

The Tool Company, 5271 Raintree Parkway, Lee's Summit, MO 64082, sells kit scroll saws. The kit scroll saw is complete except for the stand and motor. Motors are available.

The kit saw has a 1⅛-inch stroke length. The standard throat clearance is 24 inches, but a much greater distance would be a definite possibility for special applications. Likewise, the table surface can be made almost any size, with a table 19½ inches × 31½ inches being the size recommended. It's suggested that the table work surface be covered with plastic laminate.

The kit is designed to be of the floor-standing type similar to the one shown in Illus. 124. It does not have table-tilting options. The scroll-saw kit package with all parts, including the arms, castings, blade holders, and pulley, plus plans weighs only nine pounds. (The stand and motor are not included.)

A modified version of a scroll saw made from a basic, standard kit was designed by Willard Bondhus, a woodworking colleague from Minnesota, and is shown in Illus. 125–133. This has several design innovations made by Mr. Bondhus to satisfy certain performance requirements when the saw is used for marquetry cutting. The same general principles and techniques employed in building the Bondhus saw can be applied to make a customized scroll saw or one for a more general class of work.

Other than the purchased castings, all of the work parts were fabricated from typical scraps found in the Bondhus workshop. Basically, the major parts consist of a flat base with a couple of strips nailed under it to provide clearance for the fly wheel that was let into the base. (See Illus. 125 and 126.) Illus. 127 shows how the flywheel and pitman are connected to drive the lower arm. Although the pitman is made of wood, it has nylon bearings to lessen the wear. The motor is ac-

tually from a used Xerox machine and is only $\frac{1}{15}$ hp. However, for marquetry, other small motors, such as one from a sewing machine, would work as well. A small-motor pulley, a round sewing machine belt, and the foot switch from a used sewing machine can also be used. The Bondhus saw has approximately 60 cutting strokes per minute. The actual cutting speed will depend upon your motor rpm and the size of the motor pulley.

A "rear box" at the back of the base pro-

Illus. 125. This bench-model scroll saw was made from a basic parts kit. It was designed and built by Willard Bondhus.

Illus. 126. A view under the saw table shows the fly wheel let into the base, the motor drive, the pillow blocks, and the drive shaft.

Illus. 127. A close-up shows how the fly wheel and pitman arm are connected to the lower arm. Note the blade chuck with fine blade at the end of the arm.

vides the mounting for the arm pivot-plate hardware. Towards the front is a table pivot pin. (See Illus. 128 and 129.) The lower arm extends through openings in the vertical panels comprising the rear box. (See Illus. 128.)

One of the requirements for professional marquetry cutting with a scroll saw is a table that tilts both ways. (See Illus. 129 and 130.) A simple strap hinge and pin set into the front of the upper piece of the "rear box" facilitates the tilting feature. (See Illus. 128.)

The arm pivots are provided by the pivot-plate hardware. The pivot-plate hardware and the turnbuckle are shown in Illus. 131. The turnbuckle provides the necessary blade tension. A very innovative idea is the insertion of a large clear Plexiglas™ disc set into an opening cut into the table. (See Illus. 132.) Since the saw operator can see through the table, it is easier to install a blade into the lower-blade clamp. A small slot approximately ¾ inch in total length runs sideways, partly on each side of the blade. This is carefully cut into the Plexiglas™ disc. The exact location is determined with a paper pattern. There is a narrow slot rather than just a small hole for the blade; this slot is necessary for when the table is tilted. (See Illus. 132 and 133.)

Illus. 128. A view with the table removed. Note the simple strap hinge on the angled upright. The hinge, blade, and a pivot pin in the "back box" are all in alignment.

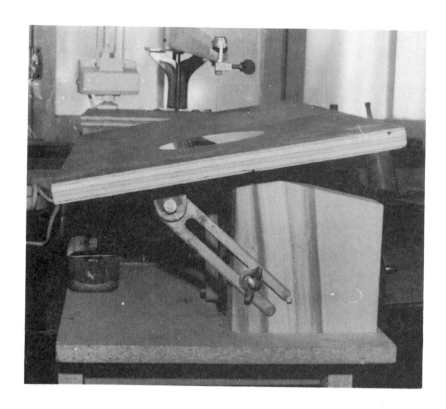

Illus. 129. One of the requirements was a table that tilted 12° in both directions. (Also see below.)

Illus. 129A.

Illus. 130. The table is set at 90° to the blade.

Illus. 131. This view from the rear shows the upper and lower arms, the turnbuckle for blade tensioning, and the pivot-plate hardware.

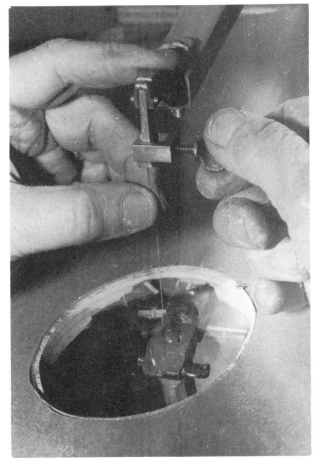

Illus. 132. Installing a fine blade in the upper chuck. A clear Plexiglas® disc covers the large opening for through-the-table visibility. Only a very small blade slot is cut into the plastic.

Illus. 133. Willard Bondhus with his custom scroll saw. Note the use of yet another feature—a hand wheel attached to the end of the drive shaft. This provides the option of manual operation when a very slow speed and "gentle touch" is desired. Here the table is tilted to the right. A commercial lamp/magnifying glass is attached to the rear.

REPRODUCTION SAW

If you like exercise, a pedal-powered reproduction of the Barnes Velocipede scroll saw is available, knocked-down, by mail order from The Tool Company. (See Illus. 134.)

The Barnes Velocipede scroll saw is an authentic reproduction of a saw that is visually appealing and one of the most efficient woodworking machines ever made. This is an exact copy of a machine patented in 1871 and manufactured by the John Barnes Company of Rockford, Illinois. The original was cast iron and weighed approximately 90 pounds, which was still light enough in the early days to be functionally portable. (See page 23.) The current reproduction, manufactured by The Tool Company, in Lee's Summit, Missouri, weighs only 50 pounds complete.

This muscle-powered machine provides surprisingly precise cuts easily in thinner material. Cutting thicker and heavier hardwoods requires proportionally more physical energy. Although more expensive than modern scroll saws of good quality, these machines are being purchased as nostalgic or museum pieces, and by wood-instrument makers and those who do marquetry. (This saw really attracts crowds at arts and crafts fairs.) The blade clamps are brass and accept all types of scroll saw and fret blades. The upper-blade clamp has a quick-release thumbscrew that's ideal when doing lots of internal cuts, as in fretwork. The work table is 20 inches wide at the widest point and more than 30 inches in overall length. The seat is adjustable vertically to permit optimum pedaling comfort for people of different sizes. The manufacturer even has a red pinstripe option for part of the machine, which lends a decorative touch.

Illus. 134. The pedal scroll saw is available today as a cast-aluminum reproduction of the Velocipede No. 2 Saw. It has a 24-inch throat capacity, a 1⅛-inch stroke length and, of course, the blade speed is variable, depending upon your energy level.

7
HEGNER SAWS

The Hegner machines are without question responsible for the resurgence of scroll-sawing in the last decade. (See Illus. 135–138.) Hegner saws were the first to combine innovative engineering and modern technology with the basic design elements of the old wooden-arm, walking beam saws that were around in the late 1800s.

Hegner describes its machines as "parallel-arm, patented blade suspension, constant-tension, high-performance, and universal precision scroll saws." Illus. 139 and 140 show the type of work that can be done with Hegner saws.

The design on the Hegner saws available today began in West Germany in 1974 when Helmut Abel was granted an international patent for a new scroll-saw blade suspension system. This became one of the major features exclusive to the Hegner saws that were first produced in 1975 for the world-famous woodworkers of Germany's Black Forest.

In 1978, Advanced Machinery Imports, Ltd. of New Castle, Delaware, introduced Hegner saws to the United States market. (Advanced Machinery Imports (AMI), Ltd. is currently the exclusive United States distributor.) They and their dealers pretty well controlled the United States market, paving the way with the only available "constant-tension" scroll saw. In 1982, the first competitor arrived: the American-made RBI, C-arm Eagle saw. Since then, about a dozen or so other saws have been introduced across the United States that are of American as well as foreign manufacture.

Today, Hegner and AMI offer four different models. Illus. 135–138 show these models, including their top-of-the-line machine, the Polymax-3 (Illus. 135). The Polymax-3 and the Multimax machines are parallel-arm saws. They are suitable for production work, and even capable of cutting steel up to ⅜ inches thick. The smaller Hobbymax (formally Multimax-1) is a light-duty saw with a C-arm design, which is best suited to cutting stock less than ¾ inch in thickness.

Illus. 135. Hegner's top-of-the-line machine, the Polymax-3, has a 19¾-inch throat capacity, optional stroke lengths of ⁹⁄₁₆ or ³¹⁄₃₂ inch, a belted drive that gives a choice of 700, 1,100, 1,270, or 1,600 cutting strokes per minute; it can cut stock up to 2 inches thick.

Illus. 136. The Multimax-3, on a typical Hegner stand, has a 25-inch throat capacity, stroke length of ⅜ or ⅞ inch, and a single speed of 1,660 cutting strokes per minute (variable speed is optional). This will cut stock as thick as 2⅜ inches.

Illus. 137. The Multimax-2 has a 14¼-inch throat capacity, cuts stock 2 inches thick with a ⅞-inch stroke, and has a single speed of 1,660 rpm (cutting strokes per minute), with a variable-speed motor as an option.

Illus. 138. Hegner's C-arm machine, the "Hobbymax," is designed to cut softwoods up to 1⁹⁄₁₆ inch thick and other material of 1 inch or less. It has a 14-inch throat capacity and runs at 1,560 cutting strokes per minute, each stroke ⁵⁄₁₆ inch in length.

Illus. 139. This butterfly design was cut out of a ¼-inch steel plate with a Hegner saw. If it can cut intricate designs in steel, imagine what it can do with wood.

Illus. 140. All of the pieces that comprise this coach project were cut on the Hegner Hobbymax.

ESSENTIAL FEATURES

Because the Hegner saws were the first in many areas of design innovation and are the most imitated saws today, we will take a close look at their major structural features.

Blade Suspension System

The most important feature of all is the famous Hegner blade suspension system, which plays an important part in the machine's precise cutting abilities and low blade breakage. The blade suspension system revolves around the triangular (prismatic) blade clamps. (See Illus. 141 and 142.) The blade clamps are set into the V-shaped openings on the ends of the arms. (See Illus. 143 and 144.) A hex-cap screw (Illus. 142) or optional plastic thumbscrew (Illus. 143) holds the blade in the slot of the blade clamp. A top thumbscrew is turned inwards towards the upper blade clamp, but not tightly against it, to hold the clamp when a blade breaks. The gap is shown in Illus. 143. On the Multimax models, a retaining spring, shown in Illus. 144, keeps the lower blade clamp from flying out in the event of blade breakage. Illus. 145 and 146 show the components of the upper blade suspension system of the Polymax-3.

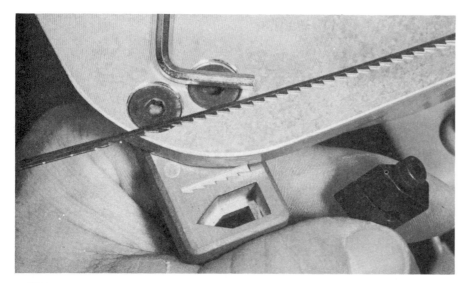

Illus. 141. A close-up look at the patented blade clamp with a knife-like pivoting edge. Note the blade-mounting device attached to the front corner of the saw table.

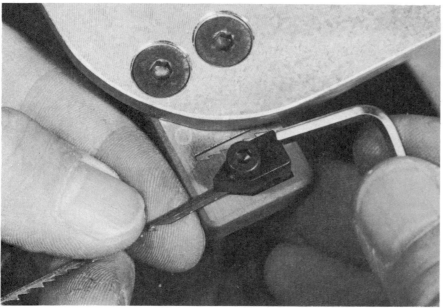

Illus. 142. A blade clamp is secured to each end of the blade. In practice, it's best to secure the bottom clamp first. As shown here, the teeth of the blade point towards the bottom clamp.

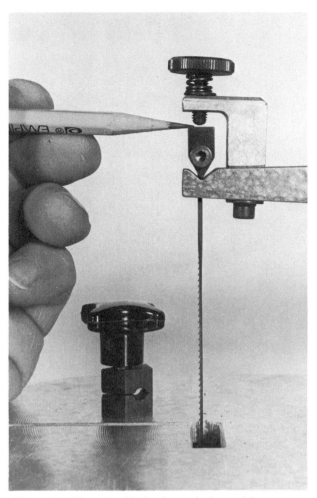

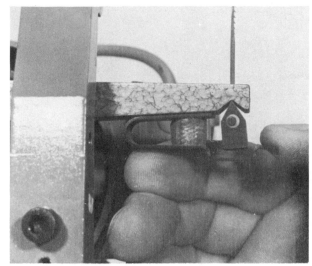

Illus. 144. The lower retaining spring.

Illus. 143. Here the blade clamp is in position on the upper arm of the Multimax-2. An intentional gap is left above the blade clamp when the thumbscrew is turned downwards. This allows the clamp to pivot freely on its "knife" edge during operation. Also, note that the blade clamp is used with a thumbscrew rather than with a hexcap lock screw.

Illus. 145. Here the blade clamp (with the plastic thumbscrew) is being placed into the "v" on the Polymax-3 arm. Note the blade opening and the slot in the table for easy blade installation.

Illus. 146. Here is an overall view showing the components of the Polymax-3 blade suspension system with the table removed.

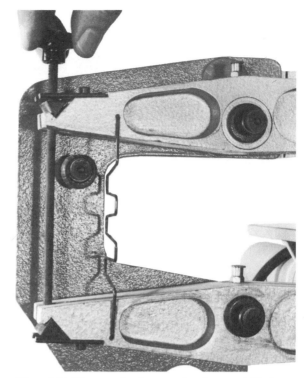

Illus. 147. The tensioning mechanism and blade retention system on the Polymax-3.

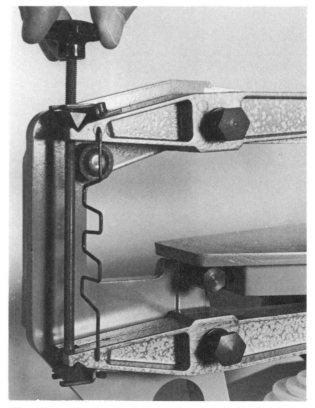

Illus. 148. The tensioning mechanism and retention system on the Multimax-2.

A distinct safety system is built into the tensioning mechanism at the rear of the arms. Illus. 147 and 148 show the tensioning knob on the threaded rod and the heavy-duty "harmonica" spring on both the Polymax-3 and the Multimax-2, respectively. The spring stops the motion of the upper arm immediately if the blade breaks during operation. It prevents a broken blade from piercing the operator's hand or damaging the surface of the workpiece.

Skilled and experienced operators know just how much tension is required for various types of blades. Before the power is turned on, the tensioning is done, as shown in Illus. 149. In Illus. 149 the operator is "plucking" the blade while turning the tension knob to check and feel for the correct tension. Some claim that the final adjustment in tension can be made with the machine running. This option is up to the operator. If the machine is noisy, it may indicate the need for more tension.

Illus. 150 and 151 show what happens when excessive pressure is applied to the blade. The blade clamps pivot when pressure is applied to the blade; they also pivot with or without blade pressure when the arms are in operating motion. The blade clamps are the front pivot points of a four-point parallelogram where the included angle is changed with every repeating stroke. If the ends of

the blade "leg" of the parallelogram did not pivot on the blade clamp's knife edges, or if a pivot with a high-friction design (such as a pin, ball bearing, or other rolling element) were used, the blade would have to bend sharply at the clamp area. This would strain the metal of the blade and increase the frequency of blade breakage. AMI states that this amount of blade breakage is what prevented constant-tension saws from being accepted in the past. The other two pivot points of the parallel arm or perfect parallelogram system are towards the rear of the arms. (See Illus. 152.)

Though the Hobbymax is of a modified C-arm design, it still uses the Hegner blade suspension system with tilting table and direct drive through an eccentric cam. The Hobbymax does not have a convenient blade-clamp holder attached to the table; rather, it is cast into the table itself.

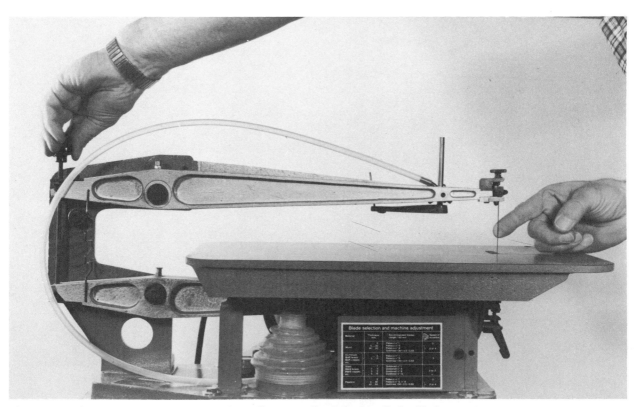

Illus. 149. The operator can check tension adjustment by "plucking" the blade.

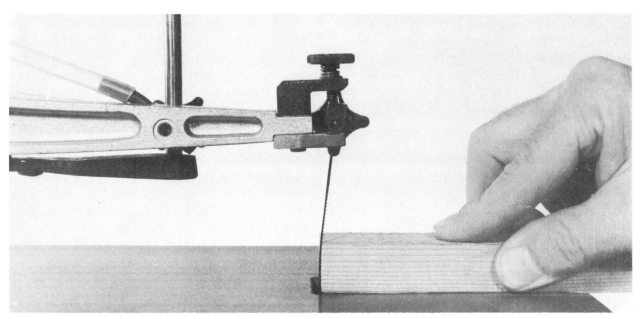

Illus. 150. This simple demonstration of force used against a blade shows the essential mechanical principles of the Hegner saws. Since the blade can't stretch, it has to bend, as do the I-beam arms, which have a spring-like quality, under this excessive force. Even with this kind of abusive treatment, the blade is difficult to break.

Illus. 151. In addition to the spring-like bending of the arms, the blade clamp pivots on its "knife edge."

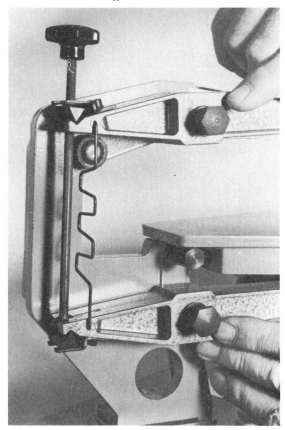

Illus. 152. The two rear pivots of the Multi-max-2 machine are heavy-duty sleeve bearings, the same as those in the Polymax-3.

Blade-Cutting Action

The three heavy-duty Hegner saws are perfect parallelograms, and the blades are always in a perfectly vertical plane throughout the complete up-and-down movement of the cutting stroke, during which they move slightly back-to-front. On these saws, the blade's movement is into the work on the downwards motion and then slightly back on the upwards part of the reciprocation. Illus. 153 depicts the cutting action of the Hegner saws. It shows an exaggerated positioning of the saw blades, representing the end of the upstroke at the left, and then moving to the right as it progresses forward into the work. The completion of the downstroke is represented by the blade on the right.

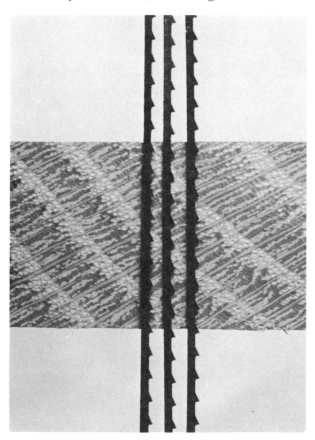

Illus. 153. These blades simulate the position of a single blade during a cutting stroke. The blade is always vertical, moving into the wood on the downward stroke. This slight back-to-front movement of the blade "works" over the previous saw cuts, creating a rasp or file-like action that results in a very smoothly cut surface.

The purpose, of course, to maintaining the saw blade in a perpendicular position is to ensure its ability to produce a consistently vertical edge on the workpiece; this characteristic is what clearly distinguishes Hegner saws from most others, including the old "walking beam" saws. Square edges are perhaps the most difficult and yet most important aspect of scroll-sawing; the inability to produce them is an important reason many scroll saws and band saws are generally ineffective for quality scroll work in 1 inch or thicker stock.

One further point should be noted: Even a parallelogram is incapable of producing square edges if the blade is not also held in a straight line. To accomplish this, one must consider both the tension required and how much can be applied. According to AMI, Hegner saws actually require less tension for proper operation than other machines, since the support points of the blade assembly are closer together. When this distance is decreased, less tension is needed to provide the necessary blade stability. Yet Hegner saws also possess a unique ability to generate high tension without the significant blade stress and resultant breakage that usually accompanies it, due to the ultra-low friction pivot of the patented blade clamps described previously. The result is maximum blade stability with minimal blade stress.

The cutting action on Hegner saws ultimately produces five key reactions:

1) Cuts are consistently vertical, perfectly perpendicular, and square to the working line without a bowed or bulging edge.

2) The front-to-back movement increases the cutting efficiency dramatically over straight up-and-down action, like the orbital sabre-saw movement which revolutionized that industry not so long ago.

3) By moving cleanly away from the workpiece on the upstroke, the blade has less tendency to lift up the workpiece.

4) The front-to-back motion prevents most of the chatter marks characteristic of band saws and up-and-down scroll saws, virtually eliminating sanding in most cases.

5) The rearward movement also reduces friction and heat buildup that is so destructive to saw blades; as a result, saw blades will last longer.

Drive Systems and Stroke Lengths

Hegner saws have several types of drive systems. The direct, single-speed drive of the Hobbymax and Multimax machines has a connector from the motor linked directly to the lower arm. (See Illus. 154 and 155.) A four-speed belted-drive powers the Polymax-3 (Illus. 156). Shifting the belt for speed changes requires only a slight movement of the motor base by loosening a single allen screw. Illus. 157 shows the eccentric side of the drive system on the Polymax-3. Illus. 158 and 159 show the eccentric positions in the full downstroke and upstroke, respectively. The vertical distance moved in one revolution equals the length of the cutting stroke. The cutting stroke is usually factory-set at the longest stroke that is normally most efficient for sawing wood and similar materials.

The stroke lengths on the Multimax-3 and Polymax-3 can be changed, but they cannot be changed on the Multimax-2 or the Hobbymax machines. (Illus. 135–138 on pages 87 and 88 contain specifications on the stroke lengths of the various machines.) Cutting speed and efficiency are reduced with shorter stroke lengths, but control and precision are more easily maintained; this can be easily observed when comparing the newest and the least expensive Hegner saw, the Hobbymax, to other Hegner saws. Consequently, set the Polymax-3 at the shortest stroke and slowest speed (700 csm) for the best performances when veneer-sawing and doing marquetry.

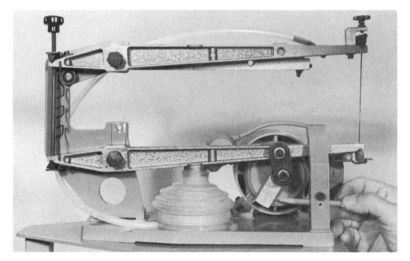

Illus. 154. This view of the Multimax-2, with the table removed, shows the arms in almost full upstroke position. Note the drive connector and the counterbalance for smooth operation.

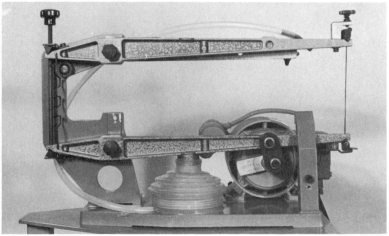

Illus. 155. The same saw in almost full downstroke position. Note how the movement of the lower arm works the plastic bellows, which provide dust-blower air that is piped conveniently to the upper arm.

Illus. 156. A view of the four-step belted drive of the Polymax-3. Note the machined steel pulleys with the speed set at its highest adjustment, 1,600 rpm (1,600 cutting strokes per minute).

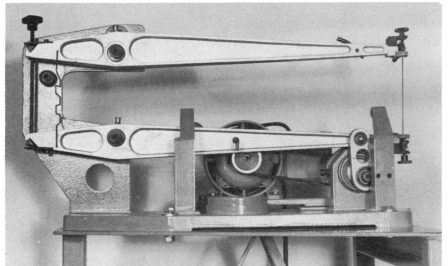

Illus. 157. View showing the eccentric side of the Polymax-3.

Illus. 158. The Polymax-3 at full downstroke.

Illus. 159. The Polymax-3 at full upstroke. The cutting stroke length can be reduced to get more accuracy and to reduce bottom tear-out when cutting thin materials. This is accomplished by shifting the connector to a location that is nearer to the center of the bearing rotation.

Miscellaneous Features

Some miscellaneous features of the Hegner saws, as noted in AMI literature, include: all-cast warp-resistant ribbed construction, accurate and easy-to-adjust tilting tables with full-to-the-edge blade slots, and solid I-beam arms for maximum strength. Also noteworthy is their unique three-legged welded stand that is always steady regardless of ground level or irregular flooring.

Hegner also places strong emphasis on the importance of their motors, which are continuously being rated on their performances, and are the totally enclosed, fan-cooled, induction types. They are very reliable over a long period of time. Variable-speed systems are available, as are extra blade clamps with oversized slots for sawing with extra-thick scroll-saw blades or band-saw blade scraps. Metric wrenches must be used, which is sometimes an inconvenience for American users. However, the necessary sizes are included with each machine as standard equipment.

The hold-down (Illus. 160) is an important safety feature, especially for beginners and for saws used in schools or institutions. When sharp turns are made or thin materials are cut, the work can chatter or flutter up and down on the worktable. A hold-down alleviates these problems. (Illus. 160 and 161.) However, some professionals prefer to work without a hold-down. If you want to work without one, be very careful and apply downwards pressure when you need it. I have removed the hold-down arm completely so I have more room to maneuver when making regular sawing cuts and bevel-sawing (cutting with a tilted table). (See Illus. 162.) The Hobbymax does not come with a workpiece hold-down arm or dust blower, although both are options.

On some Hegner saws, one option is to use a self-made wooden wrench rather than the allen wrench (Illus. 163) if you decide to use the plastic thumbscrews on the blade clamps, because it can be difficult to torque-up thumbscrews sufficiently without assistance. The simple wooden wrench is cut out to fit over the plastic thumbscrew. When using it, provide just slightly more than finger-tight pressure.

Illus. 160. The hold-down is a safety device that ensures a chatter-free operation.

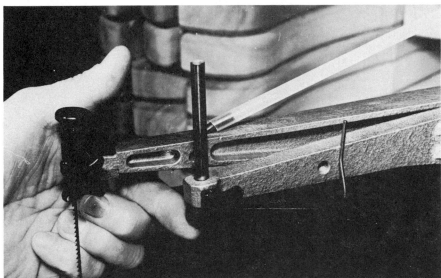

Illus. 161. The hold-down swings up and clamps out of the way when it doesn't have to be used.

Illus. 162. The hold-down arm can be easily removed, if desired.

Accessories

Hegner has several accessory items available. Electronic variable-speed control for the Multimax models is advised when using the Hegner saw for cutting steel or when using extremely thin blades to make jewellery, miniatures, and marquetry projects, where slow speeds are often advantageous. (See Illus. 164.) AMI also sells standard lamps and illuminated magnification lamps that are useful for very precise cutting. Foot-operated switches, replacement blades, and a series of patterns round out the AMI scroll saw line.

A completely new Hegner saw design is being prepared for introduction late in 1986 by AMI, Ltd. No further details are available at this time.

Illus. 164. The Multimax-2 with variable-speed control and adjustable lamp.

8
EXCALIBUR SAWS

Canadian inventor Tom Sommerville developed and perfected a number of mechanical devices that eventually paved the way for the Excalibur saws that first appeared in the early 1980s. Today, there are two models carrying the Excalibur brand name. (See Illus. 165 and 166.) The two machines are considerably different from each other in their basic mechanical functions, but the tables and blade-mounting features are similar. Some of the design features found on these machines are exclusive only to the Excalibur machines, and are unique to the "family" of constant-tension machines.

The Excalibur saws are manufactured in South Pickering, Ontario, by Tom Sommerville Design and Manufacturing, Inc., in a joint venture with J. Philip Humfrey, Ltd., of Scarborough, Ontario. The exclusive worldwide distributorship of Excalibur saws is held by Humfrey's company, J. Philip Humfrey International, Inc. The leading affiliate and distributor in the United States is

Seyco Sales Co., 2107 South Garland Ave., Garland, Texas 75041.

Illus. 165. The Excalibur 24-inch saw on its stand. The machine shown has the variable-speed option. All of the machines have a 24-inch throat and a ¾-inch cutting stroke. The saw can cut stock 2¼ inches thick with a top speed of 1,650 cutting strokes per minute (on the standard machine), 1,800 csm with a variable-speed motor.

Illus. 166. The Excalibur II is the less expensive one of the Excalibur machines. This one has a 19-inch throat, ¾-inch cutting stroke, and can saw stock up to 2 inches thick. It has a belted drive from a ¼ hp motor with optional speeds of 400, 800, and 1,400 cpm.

EXCALIBUR 24-INCH SAW

The Excalibur 24-inch saw (Illus. 165) is the larger and more expensive of the two machines. This machine has a 2¼-inch thickness-cutting capacity and 24-inch throat. (See Illus. 167.) A standard ¼ hp, totally enclosed variable-speed motor drives the parallel arms through a crankshaft and connecting rod system, producing a ¾-inch stroke length. The variable-speed motor (Illus. 168) will deliver an infinite range of speeds from cutting strokes of just 4 or 6 per minute to a top speed of 1,800 cutting strokes per minute. In late 1986, another version of this machine will be available that will accept any ¼ hp motor. It will be mounted below the machine and will generate a single speed of 1,650 cutting stokes per minute.

The Excalibur 24-inch saw has an impressive, integral-cast channel-like housing. This forms the base and sweeps around to enclose about half of the upper arm, the rear tensioning mechanism, and almost three-quarters of the lower rocker arm. (See Illus. 169.) Consequently, most of the moving parts are safely within the casting. Although clean, neat, and safe on the outside, this makes internal repairs and some occasional adjustments somewhat inconvenient. The two cast arms are identical in size; they are shaped like an I-beam when seen from a cross-section. The two arm pivots are on sealed bearings supported in the cast housing by through bolts. (See Illus. 170.) The blade-tensioning knob is located at the upper rear of the machine. The tensioning rod or knob has about seven turns with stops on each end. Unless the knob is threaded to the optimum position when the blade is installed, you might not be able to obtain the desired tension if you are unfamiliar with the tensioning rods.

Located under the lower arm is an arm-activated air pump. This pushes an air supply via a hose to an adjustable position alongside the upper arm to keep cutting dust clear of the layout lines.

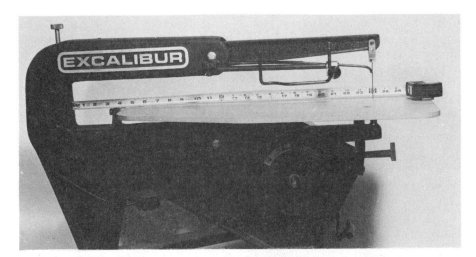

Illus. 167. The Excalibur has a large throat capacity of 24 inches.

Illus. 168. Blade speed changes can be made quickly and simply just by turning the dial on this variable-speed motor control.

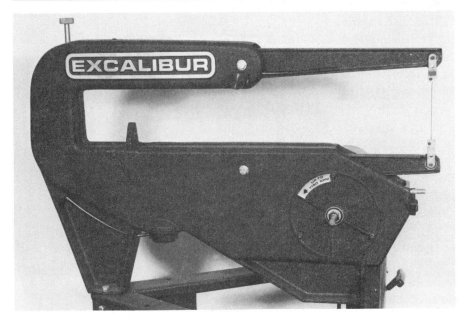

Illus. 169. A massive hollow casting encloses the rear ends of the pivoting arms and covers the tensioning mechanism at the rear. The casting also forms an integral base and motor-mounting housing for the machine.

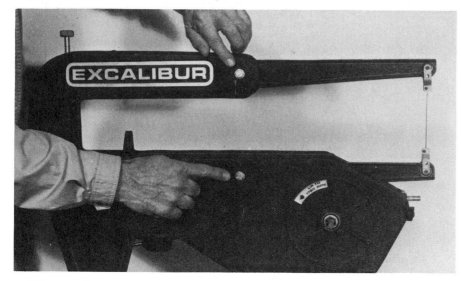

Illus. 170. The arm pivots. Notice the power takeoff shaft at the lower right. This is the end of the crankshaft. It is intended for a flexible shaft connection used when drilling starting holes when making inside cuts.

The machine comes with a steel stand with one hollow leg that can be sand-filled for weighting. In fact, the manufacturer strongly recommends filling the back leg, especially if the unit will not be bolted to the floor. Filling the leg and bolting it to the floor produces a vibration-free operating machine. (See Illus. 171.) When the machine is properly adjusted, the results will be a saw that runs so smoothly that a coin will stand on edge on the worktable even with the power on.

The table, measuring 14 inches × 24 inches, is one of the largest available. It tilts 45° to the left side and approximately 20° to the right, where the table edge strikes the side-mounted motor. One important feature is the long table slot. (See Illus. 172.) This makes it easy to thread the blade through the work when making inside cuts.

The blade-mounting system consists of identical upper and lower gimbal-type blade clamps (chucks) that pivot freely; they are supported in ball bearings at the forward ends of the arms. (See Illus. 173.) This arrangement allows the blade to move and flex effectively while under continuous tension.

One distinct advantage of these blade clamps is that they are always where they should be—attached to the machine. However, blade installation requires the use of a separate "locking key" to hold the blade clamp steady. (See Illus. 174 and 175.) The design of the blade chucks permits the instal-

lation of anything from an 8/0 blade size to .25 inches. This includes the use of different types of cutting tools that do not have flat ends like regular scroll saw blades. A good example is the carbide- and/or diamond-coated rod saws that are used for cutting glass, ceramics, and other extremely hard materials.

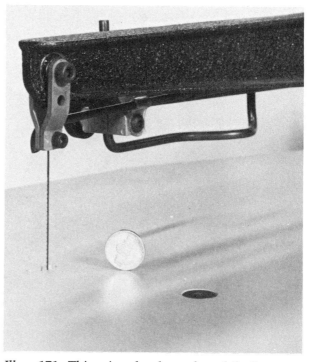

Illus. 171. This coin, placed on edge while the saw is running, is a spectacular testimonial to the smooth operation of the Excalibur saws.

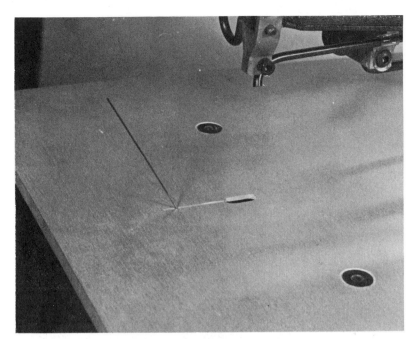

Illus. 172. The long table slot is advantageous when installing blades to make inside cuts.

Illus. 173. Gimbal-type blade clamps pivot on ball bearings in the ends of the arms.

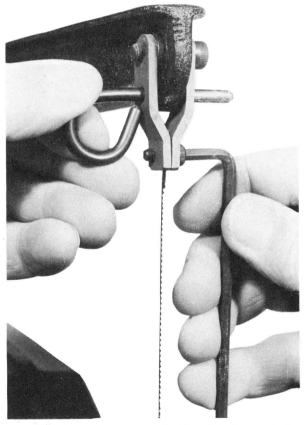

Illus. 174. An accessory, a locking key, is required for blade changes. It goes through holes in the clamp and arm so the clamp will stay steady as the screw is turned to close the jaws against the blade.

Illus. 175. A stop pin registers the optimum distance the blade should be inserted into the chuck.

Illus. 176. Tightening the blade after threading it through the work. The long T-handle allen wrench makes blade changing easy, especially when trying to reach the lower blade clamp.

The Excalibur variable-speed "constant-torque" drive motor has a consistent power supply at both high and slow speeds. Apparently, there are some variable-speed motors of lesser quality with "dimmer"-type devices that decrease their motor power when the motor is adjusted to lower speeds. Illus. 177 shows the saw in use. Note the hold-down and dust blower. Both are adjustable.

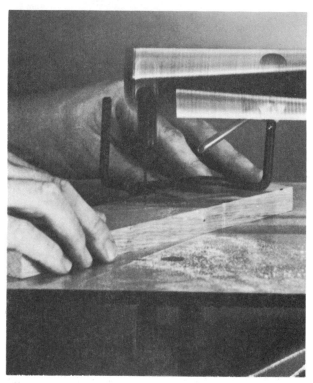

Illus. 177. An action shot of the Excalibur 24 in use. Note the combination fingerguard and hold-down, with the adjustable dust blower hose directed to the cut.

EXCALIBUR II

The Excalibur II (Illus. 166 and 178) is sold without the motor, but the motor pulley is provided. You have to provide your own motor or buy one from the manufacturer as an extra. A ¼ hp, 1,725 rpm motor is recommended, although the constant-torque, variable-speed motor like the one available, as an option, for the Excalibur 24-inch scroll saw can also be used.

With a 1,725 rpm motor and the step pulleys provided, blade speeds of 400, 800,

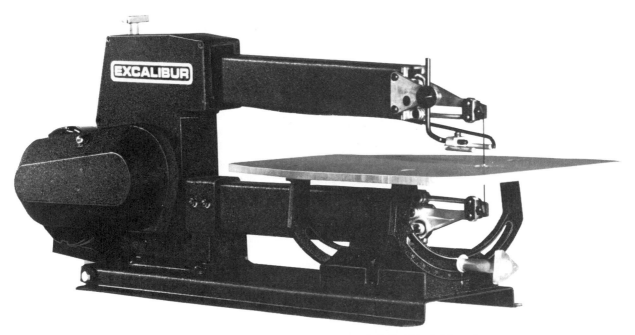

Illus. 178. The table-tilting trunnions on the Excalibur II permit full 45° right and left adjustment.

and 1,400 cutting strokes per minute can be selected. (See Illus. 179 and 180.) A tilting type of motor mounting plate at the back of the machine will accept most motor frames, or it can be drilled as needed for a particular motor. V-belt tension is adjustable with two wing nuts located close to the mounting plate. The machine does not require a special stand. In fact, it is portable; it weighs only 45 pounds without the motor. The manufacturer states that "The Excalibur II works equally well on the tailgate of a truck, on a workbench, or on any table." (See Illus. 181.)

The table is 12 inches × 17¼ inches and tilts a full 45° right and 45° left. (See Illus. 182.) The blade-tensioning knob is located at the top rear of the machine's main cast housing.

The type of drive system that gives the blade its reciprocating motion is quite complex. Competitors call it a "push-rod" system. The manufacturer calls it a "double-parallel link" system. It does have two push rods or drive links that move back and forth inside the hollow top-arm channel and two more below, inside the hollow lower-arm channel. This motion is extended forward from a vertical main rocker arm. They "link" to each side of struts or rocker arms that pivot on bearings at the ends of both arms, as shown in Illus. 183. This motion causes the blade holders to move up and down. Only the struts or rockers extending out of the stationary hollow arms visibly move during operation. This type of drive system is found only on the Excalibur II machine.

The blade, under constant tension, oscillates slightly forward on the downstroke and back slightly on the upstroke, producing essentially the same cutting action as other constant-tension saws. Even though there are many moving parts in rockers, linkages, etc., the machine is exceptionally quiet, and surprisingly smooth running. The blade clamps are somewhat similar to those on the Excalibur 24-inch saw, but they are not of the same pivoting gimbal mounting. The blade is installed to the full depth of the clamp jaws, so that it is against the clamp screw. (See Illus. 185.) The blade is then tensioned as usual. A U-type work hold-down functions similarly to those on all other saws. It is shown in Illus. 186.

Illus. 179. A view with the table, trunnions, and belt guard removed. Note the three-step pulleys.

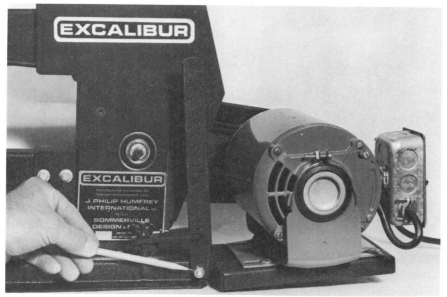

Illus. 180. Changing blade speeds is fairly easy. A pivot-type motor-mounting plate with a wing nut adjustment provides the desired belt tension.

Illus. 181. Mr. J. Philip Humfrey with his Excalibur II.

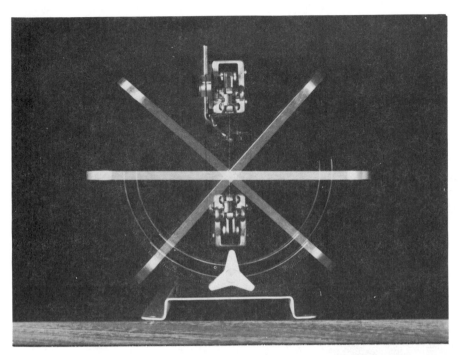

Illus. 182. A demonstration of the table-tilting range of the Excalibur II.

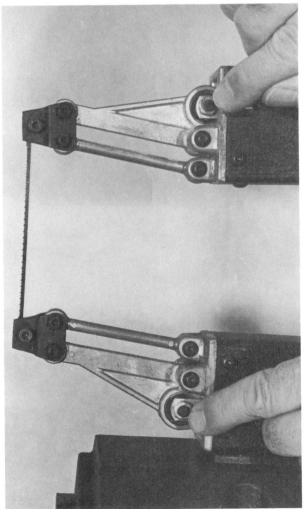

Illus. 184. The ends of the two upper drive links are just visible. They extend slightly out of the hollow top arm where they are fastened to each side of the upper strut.

Illus. 183. Shown are the bearings and major pivot points of the drive links connecting the cast-aluminum struts, which move in unison via a complex linkage system from a crankshaft and connecting rod.

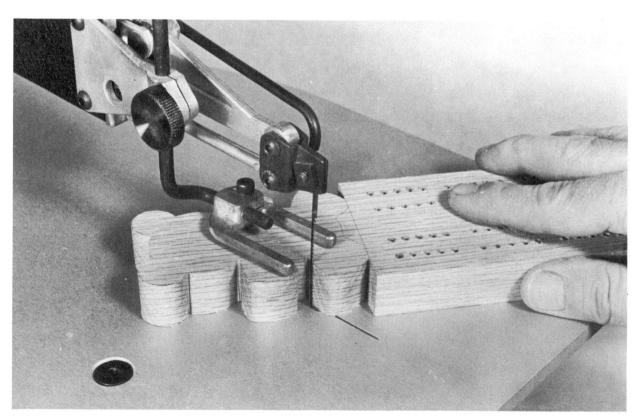

Illus. 186. The hold-down in use.

110

9
RBI SCROLL SAWS

RBI scroll saws are the products of R.B. Industries, Inc., 1801 Vine Street, Harrisonville, Missouri 64701. It is the first United States company to develop a complete line of modern constant-tension scroll saws. The saws can be easily identified by their familiar bright fire-engine red colors. The "R" and "B" in the RBI are the first two initials of Mr. R.B. Rice, the father of the company's owner, Verle Rice.

R.B. Industries also manufactures jointers, planers, drum sanders, dust collectors, roller stands, sharpening tools, and other woodworking items. It entered the scroll-saw business in 1982 with the introduction of its first scroll saw, The Eagle, a constant-tension machine in the C-frame or C-arm design. (See Illus. 187.) Since 1982, its line has grown quickly; design changes and improvements have been made on a consistent basis.

Two scroll saws followed the Eagle. The Falcon was a bench top unit with a 12-inch throat; the Condor was a parallel-arm machine with a 26-inch throat. Both models have since been improved and renamed to fit into RBI's popular Hawk line. The Falcon has become the Hawk 12, and the Condor has become the Hawk 26. In addition, RBI offers the SS-14, the Hawk 14, the Hawk 16, and the Hawk 20.

All RBI scroll saws are the constant-tension parallel-arm type with the exception of the Eagle, which was the company's first saw and the only one in the C-arm mode. The Eagle was phased out of production due to the success of the other parallel-arm machines.

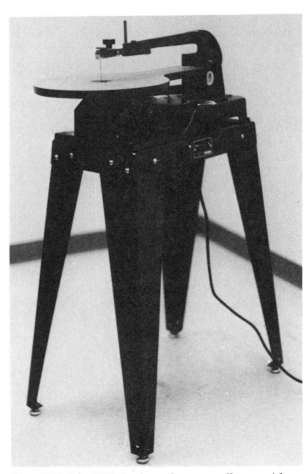

Illus. 187. The RBI Eagle, a C-arm scroll saw with a 16-inch throat, 1⅛-inch stroke, two-speed belted drive, 2-inch maximum-cutting thickness, and tilting table, was discontinued in August of 1986 due to the success of the company's other parallel-arm machines.

111

THE HAWK SCROLL SAWS

As mentioned, all of the Hawk scroll saws have a parallel-arm, constant-tension design. Structurally, almost all of the major functioning parts on the saws are the same. The major differences among the machines are their throat capacities, stroke lengths, speed options, and, of course, their overall weights.

All Hawk saws have ⅛ hp motors except the Hawk 26 and the SS 16; the Hawk 26 has a ⅓ hp motor, and the SS 14 comes without any motor. The SS 14 is designed to be either powered by a Shopsmith unit or bench-mounted and belted to another motor.

The Hawk 12

The Hawk 12 (the "12" refers to its 12-inch throat capacity) is a single-speed saw. It makes 1,725 cutting strokes per minute; these strokes are ⅝ inch in length. (See Illus. 188.) This tabletop machine is portable (it weighs only 48 pounds) and can be stored in a small area. It carries standard 5-inch blades. Even though it is small, the Hawk 12 has a 2-inch-maximum stock-cutting-thickness capability. The table does not tilt. This machine has essentially the same tensioning system and hold-down overarm, and blade-mounting devices as the Hawk 14 and other Hawk models.

The Hawk 14

The Hawk 14 (Illus. 189 and 190) has a cast-aluminum, 10-inch-diameter banjo-shaped table that tilts 45° left and right; it also has a ¹³⁄₁₆-inch stroke length, a 2-inch thickness-cutting capacity, a single-speed ⅛ hp drive motor, and delivers 1,725 cutting strokes per minute. Although this unit is not equipped with a dust blower, one is available as an option. The Hawk 14 stands freely on formed steel legs with leveling feet that are adjustable for uneven surfaces. The total weight of the machine is 67 pounds.

The Hawk SS 14

The "SS" identifies this scroll saw model as a Shopsmith-type attachment unit. Because

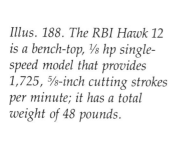

Illus. 188. The RBI Hawk 12 is a bench-top, ⅛ hp single-speed model that provides 1,725, ⅝-inch cutting strokes per minute; it has a total weight of 48 pounds.

Illus. 189. The RBI Hawk 14 has a $^{13}/_{16}$-inch stroke, a csm of 1,725 and will cut 2-inch-thick hard or soft wood. The table tilts 45° left or right, and the machine comes with a stand.

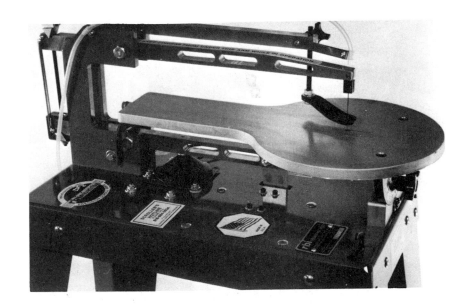

Illus. 190. A closer look at the Hawk 14. Note the banjo-styled table.

the power source is provided by the Shop-smith-type multiple-function woodworking machine itself, the SS 14 (not illustrated here) comes without a motor. Individuals who have their own motors can also mount this machine to a workbench. The cutting speed in terms of strokes per minute will vary, depending on the motor rpm and pulley sizes used. Otherwise, all of the essential features are the same as those on the Hawk 14. However, this model weighs only 40 pounds.

The Hawk 16

Like the Hawk 14, this machine (not illustrated) has a 10½-inch banjo-shaped aluminum table that tilts 45° left and right. It has a 2-inch-hard- or soft-wood thickness-cutting capacity and a stroke length of ⅞-inch. It can be used at three speeds (375, 750 or 1,550 strokes per minute), just like the larger Hawk 20. The speeds can be quickly and easily changed with a "rollover" V-belted three-step pulley-drive system. (See Illus. 194.) To change speeds, simply transfer the belt to a different combination of pulley sizes. The variable speeds, when combined with the saw's 16-inch throat and ⅞-inch stroke, make the Hawk 12 a versatile machine that can cut a variety of materials efficiently. A dust blower is standard. The saw's total weight, including the stand, is just 69 pounds.

The Hawk 20

The Hawk 20 is RBI's most popular machine. (See Illus. 191–194.) It has a stock thickness-cutting capacity of 2⅛ inches and a 1⅛-

Illus. 191. The Hawk 20 will cut hard or soft wood up to 2 inches thick and features a choice of three speeds of either 375, 750, or 1,400 cutting strokes per minute.

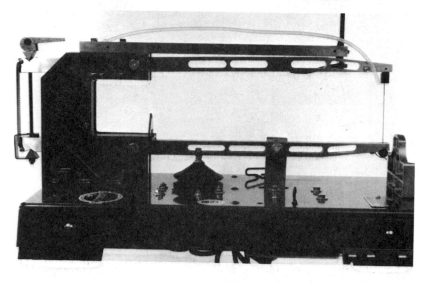

Illus. 192. This photo of the Hawk 20, with the table removed, clearly shows the arms milled from aircraft-grade aluminum. Note the pitman connected to the lower arm ahead of the bellows for the dust blower.

Illus. 193 (left). This bottom view shows the gear box with the pulley shaft and pitman attached to it at the right. Illus. 194 (above). A closer look at the motor pulley, gear box pulley, and drive belt. To change speeds, first roll the belt from the large pulley over to the smaller one, and then roll the belt onto the appropriate second pulley.

inch cutting stroke. Like the Hawk 16, this machine can be used at three different speeds (375, 750, or 1,400 strokes per minute) when you use its "rollover" belt-changing system. An optional variable-speed unit is available for those who need more precise control of the cutting action. The 14-inch diameter banjo-shaped table is similar to those on RBI's other saws. The dust blower is standard; so is the safety stop and spring that control and limit the vertical motion of the upper arm in the event of blade breakage. The machine weighs 87 pounds.

The Hawk 26

The Hawk 26 (Illus. 195) has the biggest throat capacity (26 inches) in the industry. It also has a maximum thickness-cutting capacity of 2 inches. The structural features of this 130-pound machine are similar to the other Hawk saws, just bigger. It has a ⅓-hp motor and can be used at speeds that range from 450 to 1,450 cutting strokes per minute.

Illus. 195 (right). The Hawk 26 features the largest throat capacity in the industry, a 2-inch maximum-cutting thickness, and a variable-speed range of 450 to 1,450 cutting strokes per minute.

Essential Features

With the exception of the fixed steel table on the Hawk 12, almost all of the other structural components of the Hawk saws are very similar to each other. The important functioning parts such as the arms, blade suspension, tensioning system, cutting action, etc., are essentially the same.

Construction The machine bases are made of heavy-gauge stamped metal, as are the four attached legs on the freestanding units. The stands have adjustable leveling feet on each leg. The motors are mounted under the machine, and the switches are conveniently located in the base. The connecting rod (bar linked to the lower arm) on the pitman-type drive system protrudes through an opening in the base of the machine. (See Illus. 193 and 194.)

The arms are not die- or molten-cast, but are all machined individually from aircraft-quality aluminum. (See Illus. 192.) The bronze bearings provided at the arm pivot points are oil-impregnated; conventional ball bearings are provided on all rotating parts, such as at the pitman connections.

The tables of all the Hawk saws (except the 12-inch unit) are made of cast aluminum and have narrows slots that aid in blade threading and mounting.

Blade Suspension The blade-suspension system on all Hawk scroll saws have a parallel-jaw blade clamp of flat steel blocks that pivots on the upper arm. (See Illus. 196 and

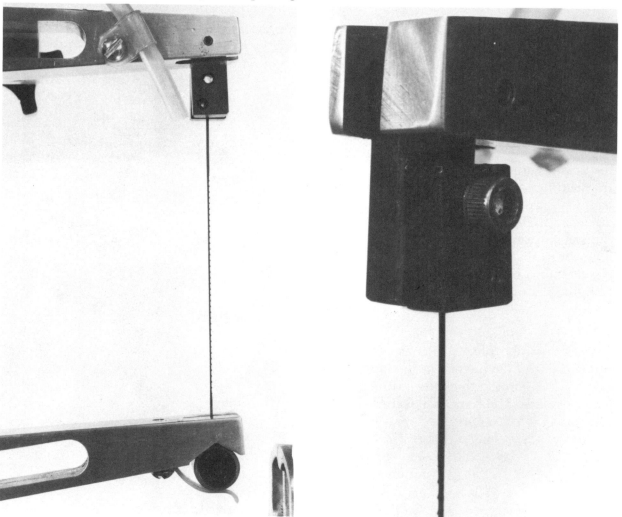

Illus. 196 (above left). The blade suspension on the RBI Hawk saws. Illus. 197 (above right). A close-up look at the upper blade clamp.

197.) These blocks have stops that properly position the blade in the holder at exactly the same location every time a blade is reclamped or a new blade is installed.

The lower blade holder incorporates a uniquely simple bearing-and-clamp combination. (See Illus. 198–200.) The manufacturer claims that this design "gives a 100–300% increase in blade life, based on the user's sawing experience."

Illus. 201–203 show how to install blades or make blade changes. A special combination wrench, when used with the milled slot in the base of the machine, tightens the blade in the lower blade clamp. The same F wrench is used to steady the upper blade clamp while the blade is being secured with the allen wrench. The wrench cradles the jaws of the blade clamp, making it rigid for blade installation.

Tensioning One of the most advantageous features on the Hawk saws is the patented Camover Tensioning Mechanism (Illus. 204 and 205), which is very helpful when you are making inside cutouts and pierced cuttings. Once you have established the correct tension for the specific blade size you've selected by rotating the handle on the threaded blade tensioning rod, you can quickly reset the tension

Illus. 198 (above left). A close-up look at the Hawk saws' lower blade clamp. It features an outer oil-impregnated bronze bearing shell that provides greater blade life than previous systems. Illus. 199 (above right). The lower blade clamp in place on the lower arm.

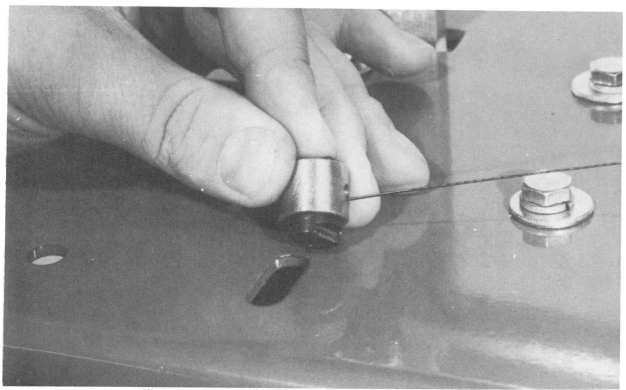

Illus. 200. Shown here is the slot in the base of the machine which matches the "flats" on the lower blade clamp to facilitate blade installation.

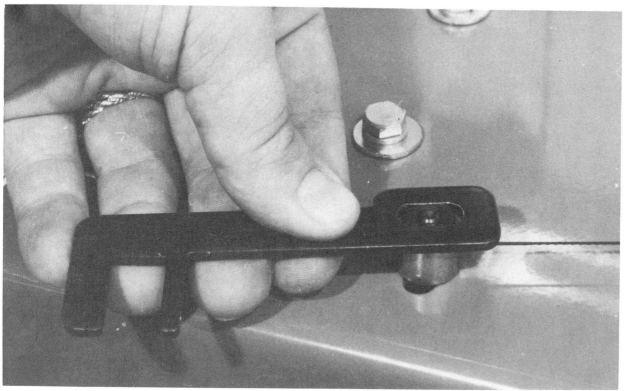

Illus. 201. This F wrench is used with the aid of a slot in the saw base to tighten blades in the lower blade holder, as shown.

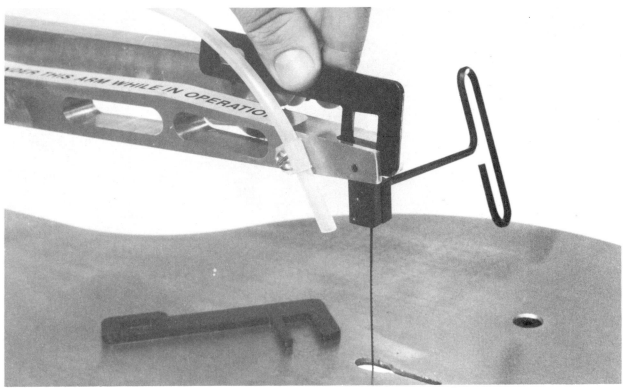

Illus. 202. Here the combination F wrench is being used to steady the upper blade clamp.

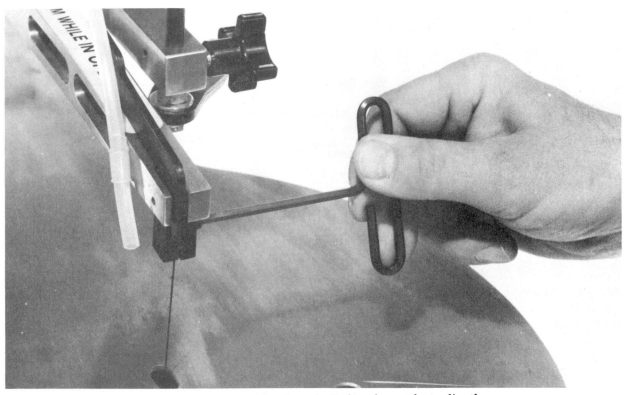

Illus. 203. Tightening the upper blade clamp. Note how the F-shaped wrench steadies the otherwise pivoting clamp.

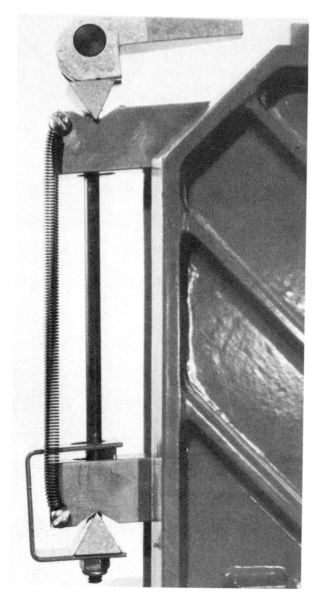

Illus. 204 (left). The tensioning system on all RBI Hawk saws features the camover lever shown above. Illus. 205 (above). With the camover tensioning handle, you can quickly reset the correct tension.

to precisely the same point by simply flipping the camover handle. There is no need to pluck the blade while rotating a tension knob.

Cutting Action The Hawk saws have stroke lengths that range from $^{13}/_{16}$ to $1^{1}/_{8}$ inch; a saw with a $1^{1}/_{8}$-inch stroke length can more effectively carry out the sawdust from thicker material. The blade on all RBI Hawk saws cuts by moving slightly forward on the downstroke (the cutting stroke) and then moving slightly back on the upstroke. This produces a very smoothly cut surface. At all times, the blade's cutting teeth remain in a true vertical position, in relation to the saw table, throughout the complete stroke. (See Illus. 206 and 207.)

RBI hold-downs are now made of "Zytel"

nylon, which is flexible and can expand or contract when holding materials of varying thicknesses. (See Illus. 208.) R.B. Industries also offers lamps (Illus. 209), magnifier lights (Illus. 210), foot switches, blades, etc. The company keeps RBI scroll saw users and customers up-to-date with plans and project ideas through newsletters and a subscription pattern service called the *RBIdeas*. (Illus. 211-214.) The *RBIdeas* publication comes free the first two years to new Hawk owners. Thereafter, the subscription is $9.00 for three issues per year.

Illus. 215–219 show the RBI Hawks used in different cutting situations.

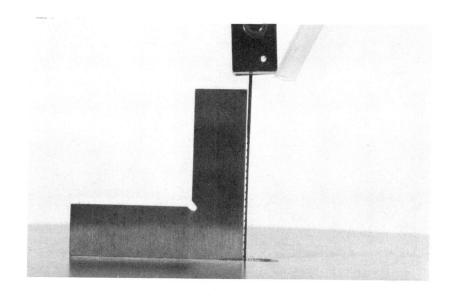

Illus. 206. The blade action is perfectly vertical on the downward stroke.

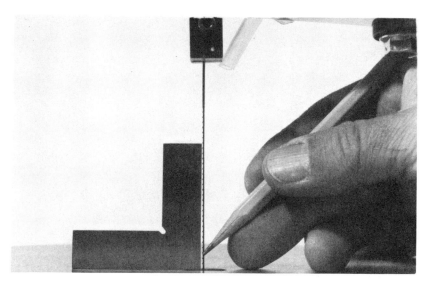

Illus. 207. At the peak of the upstroke, the blade backs away slightly.

Illus. 208. The hold-downs are made of a special nylon (Zytel) that flexes over flat pieces or pieces that may be of irregular thicknesses.

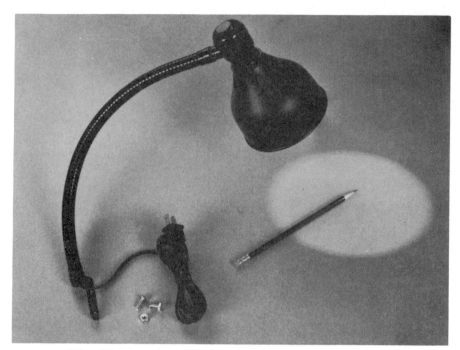

Illus. 209. Optional inexpensive lamps are available for RBI machines.

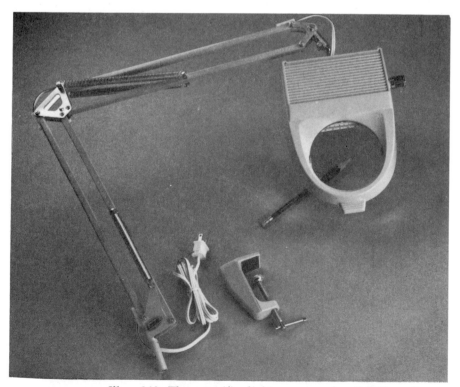

Illus. 210. The magnifier light accessory for all RBI scroll saws.

Illus. 211. Scroll sawing projects and the latest techniques are provided in RBIdeas, a subscription publication from RB Industries.

Illus. 212. A typical project offered in the RBI Pattern Pack.

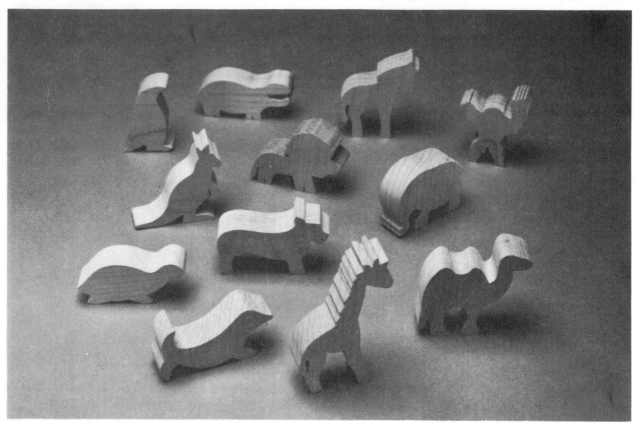

Illus. 213. The Corn Crib's zoo animals.

Illus. 214. Copyrighted plans provided by Dick Powel of The Corn Crib Workshop for hobbyists, as shown in the RBIdeas newsletter.

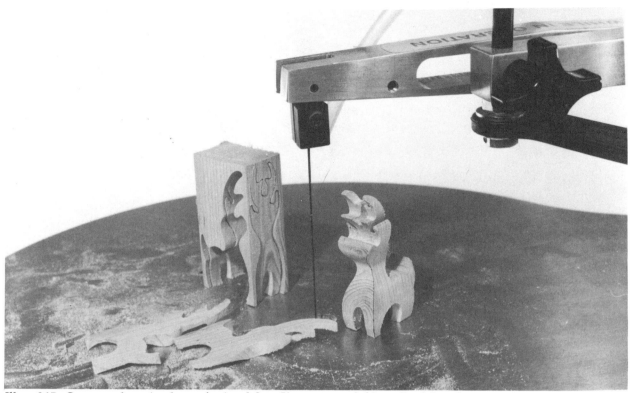

Illus. 215. Compound-sawing by professional Sam Keener created this stylized deer from 2-inch-thick stock on the Hawk 20 in approximately 1 minute and 15 seconds total sawing time.

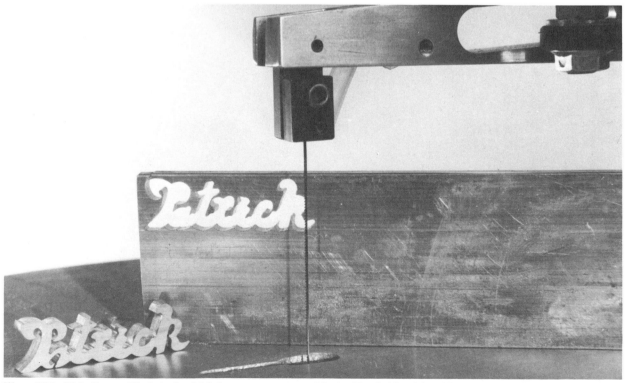

Illus. 216. This three-eighth-inch-thick brass was sawn with the Hawk 20 with a No. 5 jeweller's blade at 750 strokes per minute.

Illus. 217. This delicate fret-work by professional John Polhemus was also made with a RBI Hawk.

Illus. 218. A closer look at John Polhemus's incredible sawing accuracy with ¾-inch-thick oak, backed with ⅛-inch birch.

Illus. 219. This pierced scroll-sawn sign work was created by professional John Polhemus with a Hawk saw.

10

WOODMASTER AND STRONG SCROLL SAWS

WOODMASTER SAW

Since 1983, Woodmaster Tools, Inc., 2849 Terrace, Kansas City, Missouri, 64108, has been manufacturing a 16-inch scroll saw. (See Illus. 220–222). The Woodmaster saw has many features comparable to the RBI and Hegner scroll saws. It is a parallel-arm, constant-tension saw. Woodmaster also makes planers, drum sanders, and band saws.

The essential specifications of the Woodmaster scroll saw include a 16-inch throat, a 2-inch-maximum-thickness cutting capacity, and a $^{15}/_{16}$-inch stroke length; it cuts at 1,725 strokes per minute and is powered by a ⅛ hp direct-drive motor with pitman arm linkage to the lower arm.

The cast-aluminum table is approximately 9¾ inches × 15½ inches. It has a full-to-the-edge blade slot and will tilt 45° right and left. The machine base and worktable are made of stamped metal; the saw table height is 39½ inches. The overall machine weight, including the stand, is 65 pounds.

The standard 5-inch-long-blade-suspension clamps are very similar to those on Hegner machines and the RBI Eagle. The first models had a knife-edge blade clamp (Illus. 223) like the Hegner saws, but round- or barrel-type blade clamps like the RBI (Illus. 224) were eventually used. The blade clamp design is now being changed to a clevice- or gimbal-type design, which will be standard on machines purchased from late 1986 on. A typical tensioning knob is located at the rear of the upper arm.

Woodmaster also has an optional work lamp that fits into predrilled holes in the stand, and a dust-blower accessory. This mounts to the rear of the machine, with the air supply directed to the cutting area via a PVC hose clamped to the hold-down arm. (See Illus. 225 and 226.)

Illus. 220. The Woodmaster 1600 model has a 16-inch throat, 2-inch maximum-material cutting depth, and a ⅛ hp, direct-drive motor, with a pitman linkage that provides 1,725 cutting strokes per minute.

Illus. 221. The Wood-master and a bevy of project cuttings.

Illus. 222. This shelf bracket is a typical example of work done on the Wood-master scroll saw.

Illus. 223. A view of the upper arm and knife-edge blade clamp, which are similar to those on the Hegner saws.

Illus. 224. The Wood-master saw with barrel-type blade clamps similar to those used on RBI scroll saws.

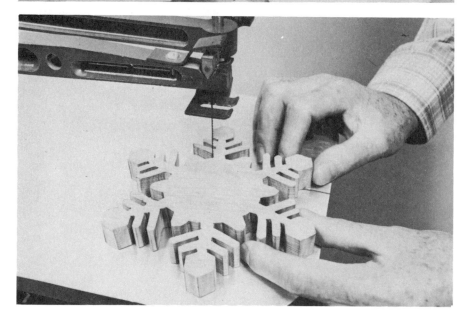

Illus. 225. Cutting without the hold-down.

STRONG SCROLL SAW

The Strong scroll saw (Illus. 227–229) was introduced to the market in the spring of 1986. This machine was developed by Donald Strong (Illus. 228), inventor and originator of several specialty woodworking machines. Manufactured by Strong Tool Design Co., at 20425 Beatrice in Livonia, Michigan, this scroll saw has many of the typical specifications of other machines, but employs an unusual drive system. The major parts are essentially all cast-aluminum construction.

The saw has a 20-inch throat, a 2¼-inch-maximum-thickness cutting capacity, and a large tilting table that measures 15 inches by 25 inches. A blade-changing device similar to that on the Hegner saw is located to the rear side of the table, but it is not visible in the illustrations.

A typical ⅛ hp motor drives the lower arm with an unusual linkage. (See Illus. 229.) A belt-driven system works a multiple-piece linkage device that the manufacturer calls a "patented chain action blade drive," but no chains are actually involved.

The design is such that this machine has the potential to deliver two strokes with every revolution of the motor. However, when this happens, the stroke length, normally 1⅛ inches, is shortened to approximately ⅜ inch.

Conventional or standard operation will usually require the longer stroke length (1⅛ inches) for more efficient cutting. The longer stroke length works at either 728 or 1,028 cutting strokes per minute. The speed can be changed simply by shifting the belt to another combination of pulleys.

When set to the doubled-up stroke position (with the shorter stroke length), the speed choices are 1,456 or 2,056 cutting strokes per minute.

The upper blade suspension is a one-piece pivoting-clamp jaw that pinches the blade with a thumbscrew action. The lower end of the blade pivots on a "ball-nose" radius clamp somewhat similar to the barrel-blade clamps found on the RBI scroll saws.

Illus. 227. The Strong scroll saw has a 20-inch throat, 2¼-inch thickness cutting capacity, four speeds ranging from 728 to 2,056 cutting strokes per minute, and a variable-stroke adjustment.

Illus. 228. Donald Strong with his "Vari-Stroke" scroll saw.

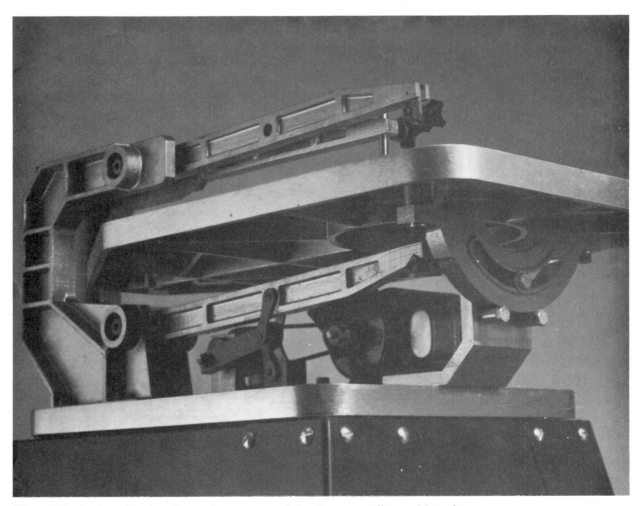

Illus. 229. A view showing the understructure of the Strong scroll saw. Note the belted motor drive and the unusual chain-like linkage driving the lower arm.

11
AMT AND JET SCROLL SAWS

Illus. 230 and 231 show two inexpensive, parallel-arm saws with different trade names that have all or at least some of the same parts. They are probably made by the same Taiwanese manufacturer. The saws are very similar in appearance, as are the designs of the essential functioning parts. These machines, with almost identical specifications, are sold by several different companies, including: American Machine & Tool Company, P.O. Box 70, 4th Ave. and Spring St., Royersford, Pennsylvania 19468; and Jet Equipment and Tool, 1901 Jefferson Ave., Box 1477, Tacoma, Washington. These two machines have many of the design elements of the Hegner saws. Sun Hill Enterprises Co., 414 Olive Way, Suite 205, Times Square Building, Seattle, Washington, sells a similar machine. Woodcraft Supply Co., 41 Atlantic Ave., Woburn, Massachusetts, sells AMT saws.

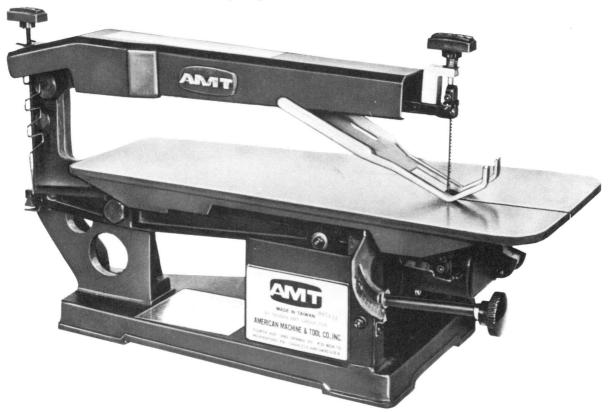

Illus. 230. The AMT 15-inch scroll saw has a 2-inch thickness cutting capacity, a ¾-inch stroke length, and a direct-drive ⅛ hp motor with 1,725 cutting strokes per minute.

Illus. 231. The Jet 15-inch scroll saw has a 2-inch thickness cutting capacity, a ¾-inch stroke length and a ⅛ hp, direct-drive motor with 1,725 cutting strokes per minute.

The 15-inch saws shown in Illus. 230 and 231 have 2-inch-thickness-cutting capacities, ¾-inch stroke lengths, carry standard 5-inch blades, and have ⅛- or ⅒-hp, direct-drive motors linked by a pitman arm to the lower arm that produce 1,725 cutting strokes per minute. The saws have cast-iron bases and tables; the tables have full-to-the-edge blade slots and only a 45° full-left tilt. The tables are 7⅞ inches × 17 inches with identical mountings on the base castings. The weights of these two machines are very close to each other, approximately 44 pounds.

Illus. 232 and 233 show the AMT saw with the table and upper sheet-metal arm-shield removed. The rear tensioning device is similar to the rear tensioning device on the Hegner saws. (See page 92.) The blade suspension system (Illus. 234) is also similar to the blade suspension system on the Hegner saws. Illus. 235 and 236 show the upper blade clamps on the AMT saw.

The AMT saw does not have a convenient blade-clamp device attached to the saw table—a feature Hegner saws have. This means the blade clamps (especially the lower one) must be held in a vise or with pliers as the blade clamp is tightened with an allen wrench. The upper blade clamp can be held steady by turning the upper lock knob downwards until the screw puts sufficient vertical pressure on the blade clamp. This will hold the clamp and allow the blade to be secured in the blade clamp with an allen wrench. Before using the saw, back the upper lock knob off slightly; this allows the upper clamp to pivot freely. Illus. 236 shows the upper blade clamp in position, with the upper lock knob turned slightly back to allow the blade clamp to pivot. Tension is applied with the typical adjustment at the rear of the machine.

Illus. 237 shows the plastic blade guard in use. Notice how similar it is to the Dremel guard shown on page 75. These machines do not have dust blowers.

Illus. 232. The AMT 15-inch saw is shown here with the upper arm shield and table removed, and at almost full downstroke.

Illus. 233. The AMT saw at full upstroke. Note the arm pivot points and the rear tensioning mechanism.

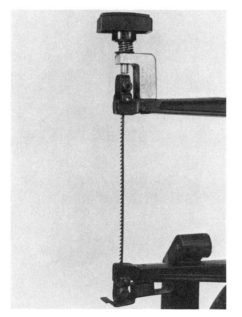

Illus. 234. The blade suspension on the AMT 15-inch scroll saw is similar to the blade suspension on the Hegner saws.

Illus. 235. The upper blade clamp has been slightly modified, but still has a pivoting action similar to that of the Hegner upper blade clamp.

Illus. 236. The lock knob above keeps the blade clamp in position, but it is loose enough to permit a pivoting action.

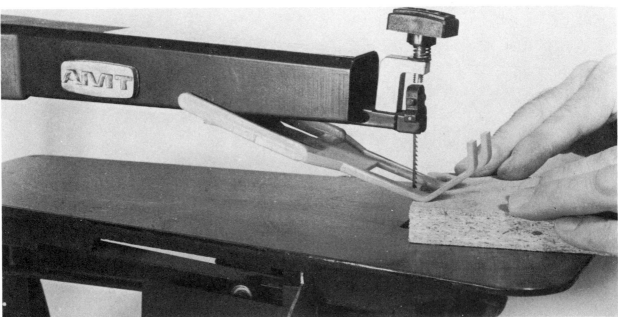

Illus. 237. A spring, plastic blade guard attaches to the arm cover.

12

DELTA C-ARM SCROLL SAW

In 1985, Delta International Machinery Corp. (formerly Rockwell Power Tools), 246 Alpha Drive, Pittsburgh, Pennsylvania 15238, entered the constant-tension scroll saw market with their C-arm, electronic variable-speed machine (See Illus. 238–240.) This has an 18-inch throat and a 2-inch-maximum-thickness cutting capacity. The Delta C-arm machine carries the standard 5-inch-long blades and has a stroke length of ⅞ inch.

This saw's most novel feature is the digital,

electronic, solid-state controller that automatically adjusts the blade speed and torque to maintain the desired level of cutting performance. The speed range is from 40 to 2,000 cutting strokes per minute. (See Illus. 241 and 242.) The digital readout tells the operator the speed in strokes per minute, which is helpful when he is sawing a variety of materials. The switch can be either a rotating on-off switch or a push-pull, on-off switch.

A 16-inch diameter table is adjustable to

Illus. 238. Delta's 18-inch C-arm variable-speed machine will cut 2-inch stock.

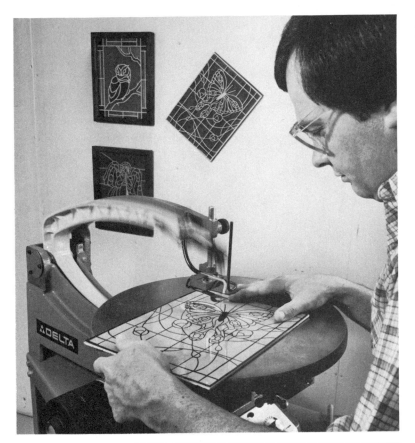

Illus. 239. The Delta C-arm machine in use.

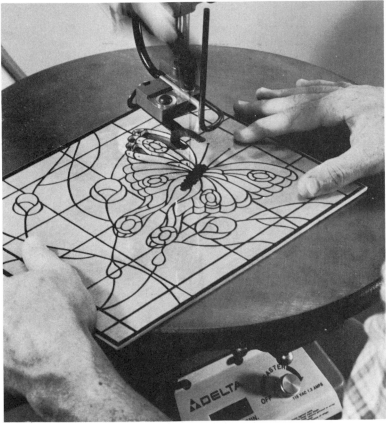

Illus. 240. The internal cutting of delicate fretwork.

Illus. 241. Delta's electronic variable-speed control. Its digital solid-state controller maintains blade speed and torque to suit varying cutting conditions. The operator can adjust the speed according to the digital display, which gives the cutting strokes per minute.

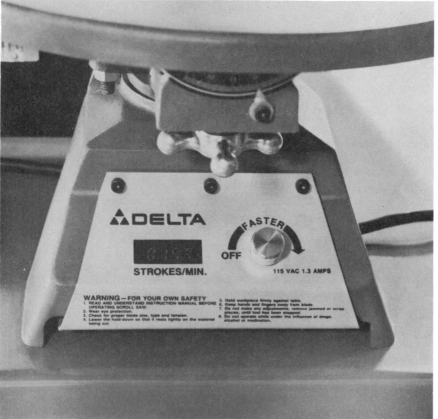

Illus. 242. The variable-speed digital read-out allows the operator to adjust the speed accordingly.

30° left and 45° right, and 15° to the back and 30° down to the front. (See Illus. 243 and 244.) It can also be rotated 90°. The table is made of heavy cast iron, with an aluminum center insert. The total machine weight, including stand, is 132 pounds.

The blade suspension system is somewhat different from the systems on other machines, but it does have features similar to those on the RBI Hawk saws and the Excalibur 24-inch saw. One design exclusively Delta's is its tension lever, which is located on the left side of the upper C-arm. Simply pulling it forward releases a preadjusted tension; pushing it back returns the same amount of tension. (See Illus. 243 and 245.)

Illus. 243. The round table has a removable center insert. Note the front blade guard and two hold-down fingers. The quick-release tensioning lever is to the left of the upper C-arm.

Illus. 244. The table adjusts to the right and left, and to the front and back.

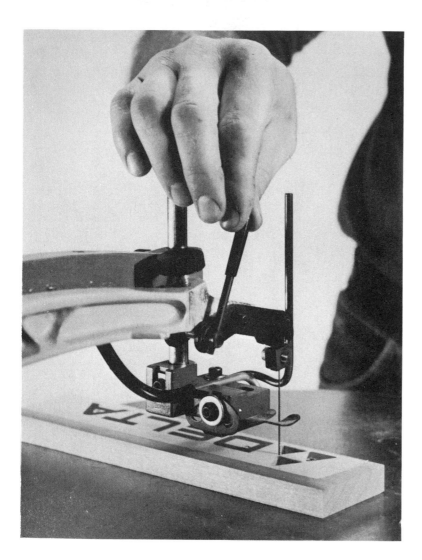

Illus. 245. The blade tension is conveniently located up front. A forward pull of a lever releases blade tension.

The blade clamps or chucks are of the flat-jaw, swivel type. Pressure against the jaws is provided with a screw and T-wrench. (See Illus. 246.) The lower blade chucks also swivel, which allows the blade to tilt forward. This feature makes it easy to thread the blade through a workpiece for inside cutting. (See Illus. 247 and 248.) For very fine work with thin blades, the owner's manual recommends the use of an auxiliary blade guide. The V-slot device is similar to those sold as accessory items for the old Delta rigid-arm saw shown on page 64. The blade guide for this machine supports the blade from the rear and helps to maintain vertical blade position. Feeding pressure will push the blade back against the guide during cutting.

This Delta scroll saw is the only constant-tension machine that incorporates the use of a rear (or other type of) blade-supporting guide of any kind. The blade guide and hold-down assembly are very similar to that of the older Delta 24-inch rigid-arm saw shown on page 62. The hold-down fingers are of spring steel and straddle each side of the blade. A vertical blade guard consisting of a simple vertical rod is positioned to the front of the blade as a safety feature. A dust-blower nozzle comes in very close to the blade at the cutting area.

Also available from Delta are a variety of blades, 90° blade holders that permit a ripping cut similar to that made on a band saw, and a flexible gooseneck lamp that attaches to the hold-down arm, shown in Illus. 249.

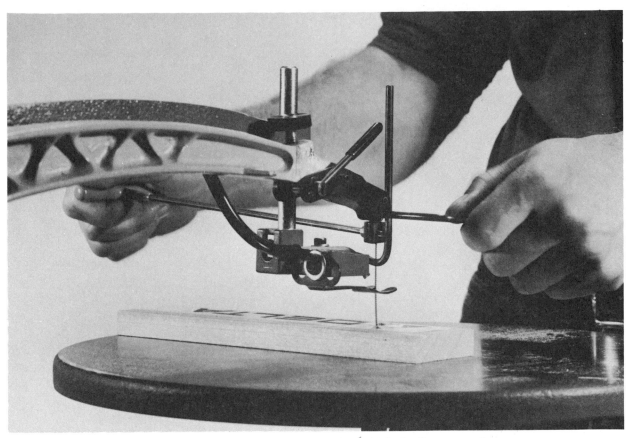

Illus. 246. The blade chucks (clamps) require the insertion of a special pin (in operator's left hand) that goes through the chucks and the arm to hold the chuck steady as it is tightened (or loosened) with the T-wrench.

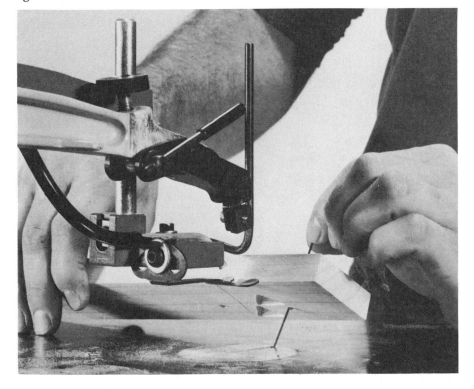

Illus. 247. Threading the blade through the work for making inside cuts.

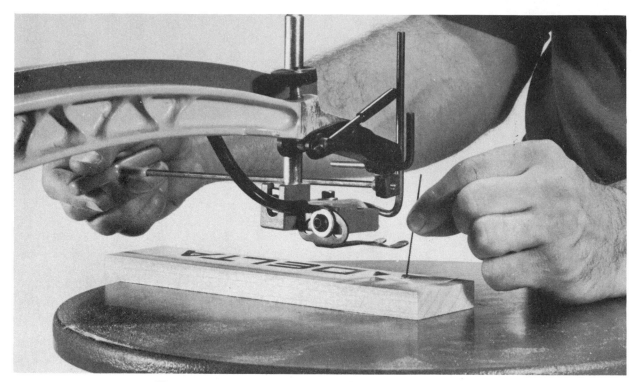

Illus. 248. With the blade clamped in the lower chuck, clamp the blade in the upper chuck as it is usually done; then simply set the tension by returning the lever to its back position.

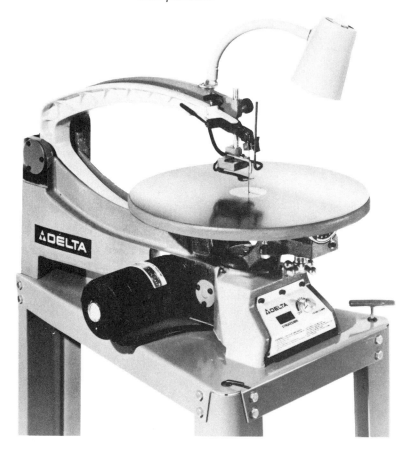

Illus. 249. This saw has a flexible goose-neck lamp attached to the hold-down arm. Note the T-wrench and the blade-chuck holding pin stored at the front corners of the table.

13
SEARS "WALKING BEAM" SCROLL SAW

The Sears "Walking Beam" scroll saw (Illus. 250 and 251) has some design elements that separate it from all other machines. However, the Walking Beam saw is still essentially a parallel-arm, constant-tension machine like many other saws available today.

The general specifications include an 18-inch throat, a 2-inch-maximum-thickness cutting capacity, a ⅞-inch stroke length with 1,700 cutting strokes per minute, and a direct-drive, rear-mounted motor with linkage to the lower arm. The machine will accept 5- to 6-inch plain-end blades and 5-inch pin-type blades. The worktable measures 9 inches × 14⅜ inches, and it has grooves for a mitre gauge attachment. The table also features two blade-holder "pockets" cast into the surface to ensure that the blade clamps are always attached with precisely the correct spacing from each other. (See Illus. 252.) The machine weight without the stand is only 26 pounds.

Illus. 250. The Sears 18-inch Walking Beam scroll saw on a four-leg stand.

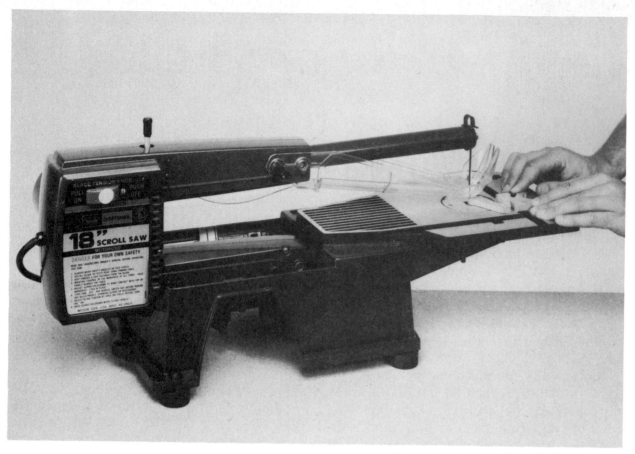

Illus. 251. The Sears saw bench-mounted.

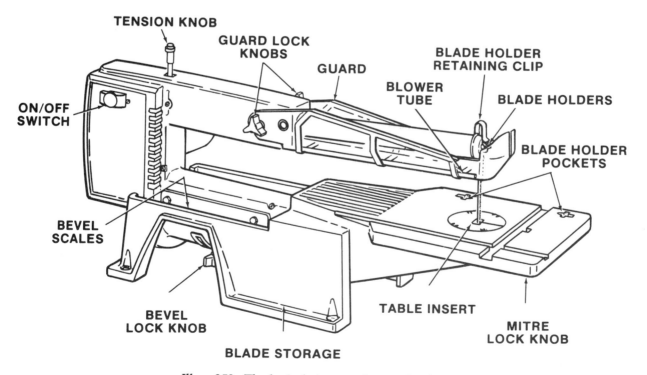

TENSION KNOB

GUARD LOCK
KNOBS

GUARD

BLADE HOLDER
RETAINING CLIP

BLOWER
TUBE

BLADE HOLDERS

ON/OFF
SWITCH

BLADE HOLDER
POCKETS

BEVEL
SCALES

BEVEL
LOCK KNOB

TABLE INSERT

MITRE
LOCK KNOB

BLADE STORAGE

Illus. 252. The basic features and controls of the Sears Walking Beam scroll saw.

The fan-cooled induction motor is mounted not below but in the rear housing, between the upper and lower arms. Illus. 253 and 254 show the housing and arms removed from the integral die-cast table and base. (See Illus. 255.) The table does not tilt. The entire motor-housing unit, with the arms, tilts in a sliding-bracket trunnion, that fits into the base casting. Illus. 256 depicts bevel-sawing with the blade tilted instead of the table or workpiece being tilted. Illus. 252 and 257 show the tilt-control knob located under the base. Tilting of up to 45° in either direction is possible. The two arms consist of tubular construction with bearing pivot points at the ends of the main housing. (See Illus. 258.)

A plastic key locks the on-and-off switch. The key must be inserted correctly in order to activate the switch. This is an important safety feature that prevents unauthorized use of the machine. (See Illus. 259.)

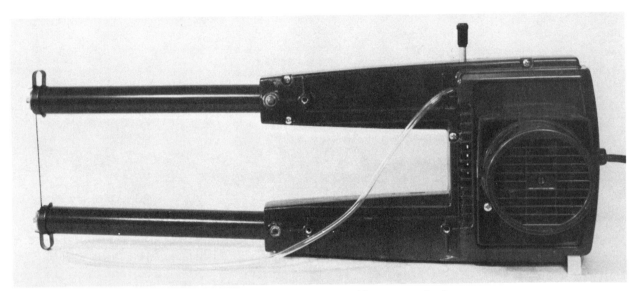

Illus. 253. *The right side of the machine without the base, table, or guard; shown are the housing, motor cover, and air tubing.*

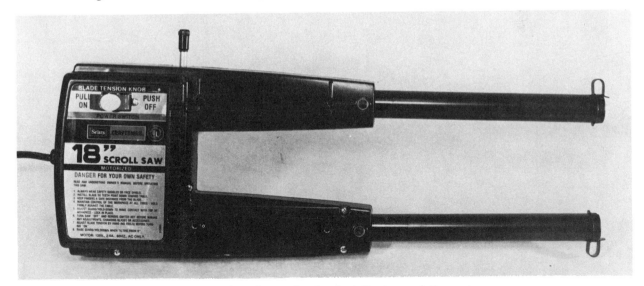

Illus. 254. *The left side of the saw. Note the tension knob at the top and the motor switch.*

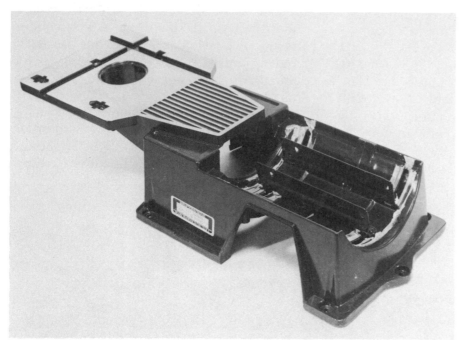

Illus. 255. Die-cast aluminum forms the integral base and non-tilting table.

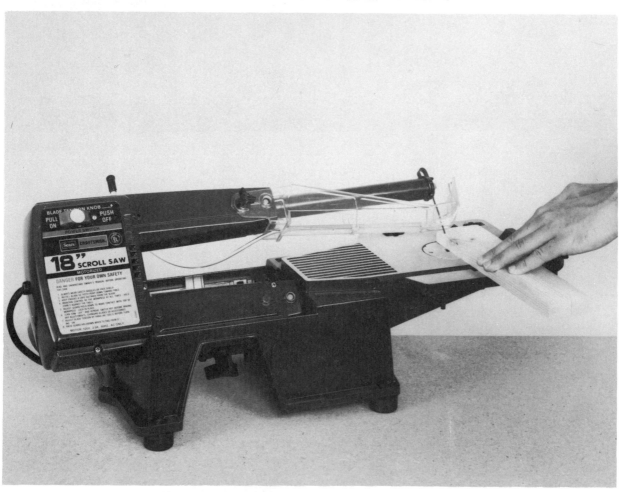

Illus. 256. The table surface and workpiece remain horizontal during bevel sawing. Instead, the blade is tilted.

Illus. 257. The tilt control knob is located under the base.

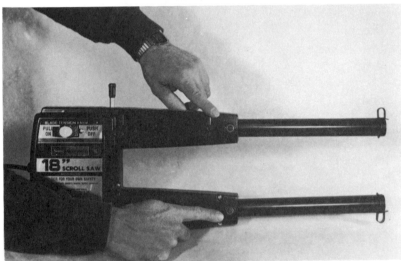

Illus. 258. Arm pivot points.

Illus. 259. To operate the machine, a plastic key has to be inserted.

The blade suspension system is based upon the action of the blade clamps that pivot on the ends of the hollow tubular arms. (See Illus. 260.) The versatile blade holders are designed to carry either plain-end blades or pin-type blades. (See Illus. 261.) As stated earlier, the blade holder pockets in the table verify correct blade length and positioning. A setscrew tightens plain-end blades. (See Illus. 262.) The blade holders are also of the four-position type, which means the blade can be installed with any one of the 90° orientation positions desired. "V's" cast into the blade holders actually permit pivoting on the "edges" of the slots in the end caps of the upper and lower arms. (See Illus. 264 and 265.) The retaining clips (See Illus. 252 and 265) do not touch the blade holders. Their purpose, supposedly, is to keep the blade holders in place if or when the blade breaks. Tension is provided by the tensioning knob with a clockwise turning direction. (See Illus. 266.) This saw has one serious limitation: The operator cannot make convenient and fast blade changes.

The operator's manual recommends the use of pin-end blades for cutting inside openings and piercing work. In order to allow for the pin of the blade, it is necessary to "drill an oversized hole in a scrap section of the workpiece." Pin-type blades do not come in the very fine sizes. Consequently, the ability to saw fine detail and make "on-the-spot" turns when doing interior or inside cutting is seriously limited. Plain-end blades can be used, but it is more difficult to fasten the blade holders to the blades.

Straight line cuts can sometimes be performed successfully using wide blades and slow feeds with the accessory mitre gauge. (See Illus. 267–269.) Sometimes the "burr" that exists on scroll saw blades during manufacturing interferes with a true straight-line cutting direction that's parallel to the blade direction. (See page 169 for more information.) The Sears Walking Beam saw is best used for cutting curves in thinner materials. (See Illus. 270.)

The Sears Walking Beam saw must be bolted to the workbench or table if the metal stand is not used. Use rubber vibration-absorbing bumpers between the saw base and workbench. If this saw is not secured by bolting, it is almost impossible to use as it moves at random ("walks") from just its own operating vibrations.

Illus. 260. The blade suspension of a Sears Walking Beam saw.

Illus. 261. Blade holders (above) will carry plain-end blades (left) or pin-type blades, as shown at the right.

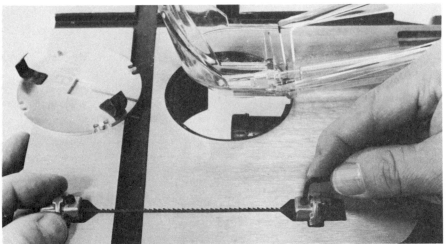

Illus. 262. Here a blade is being clamped in the blade holders, which have been properly located by the "pockets" in the table.

Illus. 263. The lower blade holder is attached. Note the teeth pointing downwards.

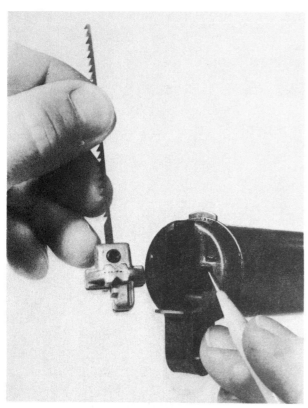

Illus. 264. The lower arm end. Note the slot in the end cap and "edges," which correspond to the "v's" of the blade holder and permit a pivoting action during the operation of the saw.

Illus. 265. The upper blade holder (clamp) in pivoting position on the edges of the arm's end cap. Note the inverted U-shape spring-retaining clip above the arm.

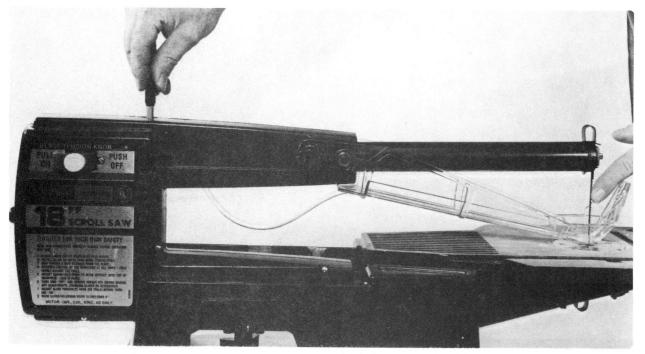

Illus. 266. Blade tensioning.

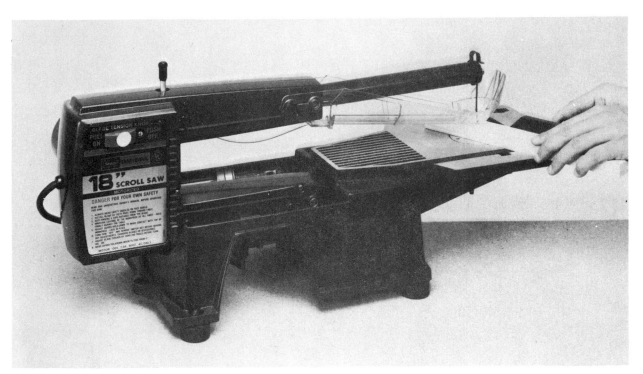

Illus. 267. Making a mitre cut.

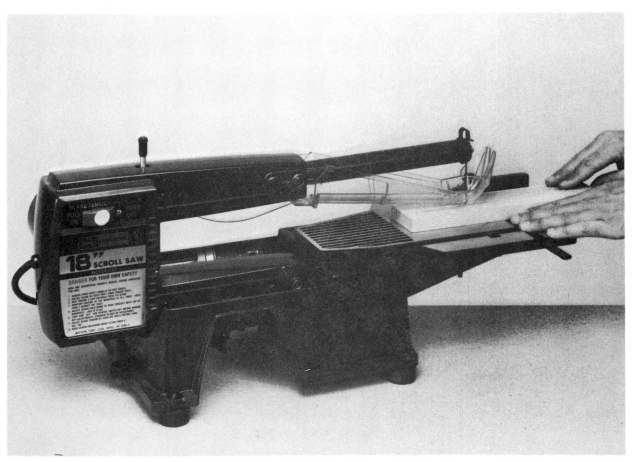

Illus. 268. Ripping, using the mitre gauge clamped to the table as a fence.

Illus. 269. Another view of the ripping procedure, with the guard removed for an easier operation.

Illus. 270. Making outside, curved cuts in thin material produces a smoothly cut surface. Thick materials cut proportionally slower. Note the use of the plastic hold-down guard.

SAWING TECHNIQUES

14
SAFETY

A scroll saw is probably the least hazardous power tool to use. However, this does not mean accidents cannot occur. A scroll saw is a machine tool, which means that everyone—beginners and professionals alike—should use it with respect and caution.

A scroll saw is ideal, however, for anyone starting woodcrafting. If youngsters are using it, supervise them carefully. In addition to instructing them about the benefits gained from scroll saw woodcrafting, teach them safety procedures and emphasize a respect for all tools and equipment. (See Illus. 271.)

Some adults may not take these safety procedures seriously, probably because manufacturers and sales personnel emphasize the comparatively safe and simple use of scroll saws. However, they too should pay careful attention to all safety guidelines.

There can be some potentially hazardous

Illus. 271. Here 11-year-old Jessica demonstrates some good safety habits. Note the goggles, the hair drawn back, the snug clothing, the use of the hold-down guard, and that the hands are well to each side of the blade.

situations when using a scroll saw. One is the unlikely probability that a blade might pierce your hand or fingers when it breaks. (See Illus. 272.) However, a good machine will have a mechanism to stop the motion of the upper arm the instant a blade breaks, which can only happen on a certain area of the blade. As an added precaution measure, however, make sure you do not put your fingers close to the blade action when using smaller blades. Normally, when larger blades are used, you are cutting larger and thicker work; therefore, your hands are, of necessity, farther from the blade. It might be a good idea to find out from the manufacturer or salesman what would happen to your machine if a blade breaks in an undesirable location and at an inopportune time.

A foot switch is a good option because you can immediately shut down the saw without having to first find the switch and move your hand to turn off the power. (See Illus. 272.) The foot switch is also an especially convenient and timesaving accessory. When thin stock is sawed or highly detailed cuts are being made, the saw blade may lift the material on the upstroke. A foot switch allows you to use both hands, with confidence, to help hold the work down against the table.

The scroll saw user will learn ways to pre-

Illus. 272. *The way this broken blade damaged the project before the power could be stopped should be sufficient warning to keep your fingers at a safe distance from the blade. (Note: On some machines, the arm is designed to kick up and stop reciprocation immediately when the blade breaks.)*

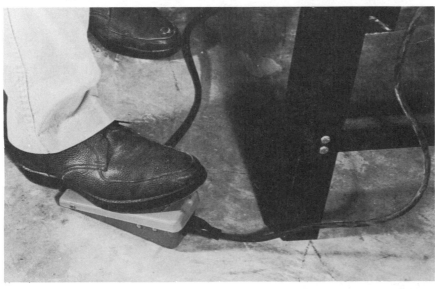

Illus. 273. *A foot switch frees both hands for full control of the workpiece. If a blade snaps, you can shut down the saw immediately without removing your hands from the workpiece.*

vent the workpiece from lifting and fluttering on the table as he gains experience. Hold-downs sometimes work, but are not always practical because of the size or nature of the workpiece. If the work is caught by the blade, the blade will lift the workpiece on the upstroke—it's at that time when your fingers can become pinched between the work and the table, or between the work and a hold-down that isn't adjusted properly. When constant-tension saws are used to make sharp turns, the workpiece is turned faster than when band saws or rigid-arm scroll saws are used. You have to learn how to make quick turns while applying pressure downwards on the workpiece, a skill that takes some practice to develop the right coordination. As you practice, the blade may catch in the workpiece and chatter up and down. With experience, you'll soon overcome this problem.

Another potentially dangerous situation exists when sawing thick stock. It's easy to become so mesmerized by the action of the blade that you forget where your hands and fingers are. If they are on top of the workpiece as they guide it around and under a moving overarm, they may get pinched. (See Illus. 274 and 275.)

Magnifying lights help some people follow the cutting line. (See Illus. 276.) They are also highly recommended for extremely detailed and precise cutting jobs. However, be careful when using a magnifying light on a constant-tension saw. Make sure it is adjusted properly; that is, that it is safely away from the up movement of the upper arm so it doesn't get banged when you turn the power on. Also, don't attempt to adjust a light and/or a magnifier with the power on. Magnification distorts the image under the glass and you might inadvertently move the light into a position where it can be hit by the oscillating arm. It is also important that the lamp be positioned so the safety spring device that lifts and stops the arm movement will not cause the arm to strike the lamp the instant a blade breaks. (See Illus. 277.)

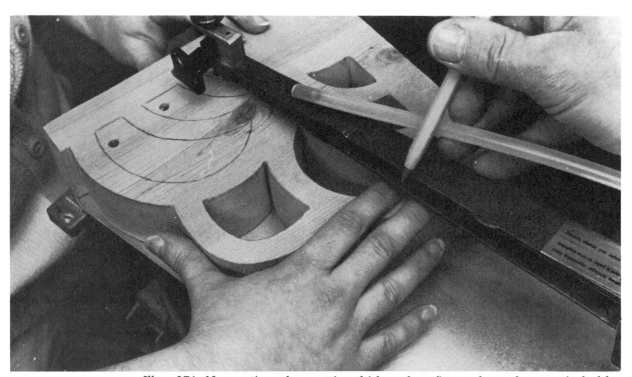

Illus. 274. Use caution when cutting thick stock so fingers do not become pinched between a moving saw arm and the workpiece.

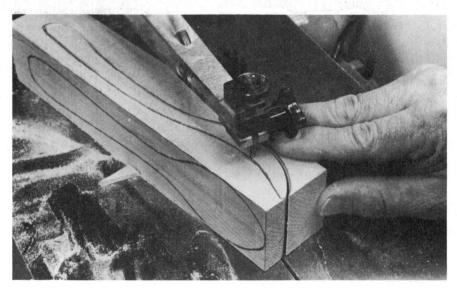

Illus. 275. A similar situation with thick wood. Here, fingers are pinched under the thumbscrew of the blade clamp.

Illus. 276. A properly positioned magnifying light is a great accessory. However, distortion is such that it may take some practice to work out safe eye-to-hand coordination.

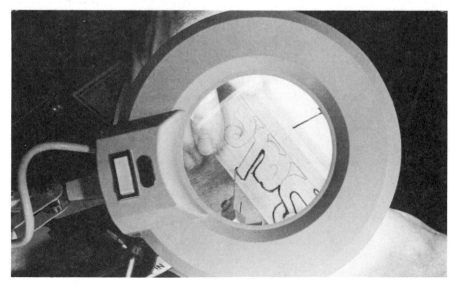

Illus. 277. Though things look bigger under magnification, they are also distorted; also, the normal hand reference points are somewhat different.

Here are some general safety rules that apply to scroll saws and power tools in general:

1. Know your machine; read and study the owner's manual carefully. You have to know the machine's capacities, limitations, and any special operational conditions that might be hazardous.

2. Caution: Most machines *should not* be lifted by the upper arm when they are being carried or moved. Lift by the base or stand.

3. Make sure the machine is properly grounded with a three-prong plug that is plugged into an appropriately grounded electric receptacle.

4. Always keep hands and fingers out of the line of cut; that is, away from the front of the blade.

5. Do not operate the scroll saw in dangerous environments, such as in damp or wet basements and workshops.

6. Dress appropriately; pull back long or loose hair and do not wear loose jewellery or clothing that could get tangled up in the moving parts of the saw.

7. Wear goggles or approved safety glasses. A dust mask is recommended during extensive use.

8. Make sure the workshop is child proof. Lock master switches, remove starter keys, and make sure that unauthorized individuals cannot obtain entry to or use of the machines.

9. Disconnect the power when servicing, installing accessories, lubricating and changing blades, etc. Avoid accidental start-ups; make sure the switch is off when plugging into the power supply.

10. Do not leave a machine unattended with the power on and running.

11. Use all appropriate guards.

12. Remove all adjusting keys, wrenches, blade chuck stiffeners, and similar devices before turning the power on.

13. Use extra precautions when cutting small pieces. (See page 198 for some tips on cutting small pieces.)

14. Do not operate tools while under the influence of drugs, alcohol, or medication.

15. Use approved accessories. If in doubt, consult with the manufacturer.

16. Keep floors and work areas clean so you don't trip on scraps, cords, or other items.

17. Do not rush by forcing the machine. If it isn't cutting as fast as you think it should, something needs correcting. Perhaps the blade being used is not the correct one or is dull; maybe something in the machine needs investigation.

18. Keep observers and visitors at a safe distance.

19. Do not exceed the specified capacities of the machine.

20. Slow down the feed rate before the work is suddenly freed at the completion of a cut.

21. Use sharp blades. Dull blades slow cutting efficiency and require extra feeding pressure.

22. Avoid cutting stock that does not sit flat on the worktable. Cutting dowels and similar objects requires special precautions and special work-holding fixtures.

23. Lubricate and maintain machines as recommended by the manufacturer.

24. Clean and remove accumulation of sawdust from moving parts. Remove deposits of pitch from the worktable immediately with a solvent, and then apply a coat of paste wax.

25. Slack off the blade tension at the end of each day or when the machine will not be used for a period of time.

26. Think and practice safety at all times.

15

SAWING BASICS

Elementary scroll-sawing techniques can be quickly mastered, but performing them accurately is essential to becoming a skilled scroll saw craftsperson. Following is a discussion of these basic but essential techniques.

PRE-CUT PREPARATIONS

Preparing the Machine

Getting the machine ready for use includes many of the obvious details, such as selecting the best blade, and installing and tensioning it. (See Illus. 278.) Review the particular chapter that describes the kind of saw you plan to use. That chapter and the owner's manual should provide all the necessary information about blade installation, tensioning, and other necessary operating adjustments and instructions.

Squaring the Saw Table

Square the saw table to the blade. All of the basic jobs discussed in this chapter will be done with the table adjusted precisely at 90° to the blade. One way to do this is to read the tilt scale and tighten the clamp at the zero setting. However, you can trust the scale markings on very few machines.

There are two other ways that are much better and more certain. Simply align the table to the blade with a good square, as shown in Illus. 279. Another, very quick method is done with a piece of thick scrap wood. Make a shallow cut, just deep enough to mark the wood, as shown in Illus. 280. Turn the stock end for end and bring it up behind the blade. If the blade lines up with the cut, the table is square. (See Illus. 281.) If it does not, adjust the table *slightly* (about half of what is off) and repeat the procedure.

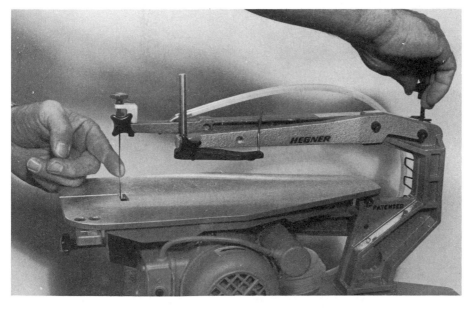

Illus. 278. Prepare the machine for sawing. Make sure the blade is retensioned before starting.

Illus. 279. Using a square to check table adjustment.

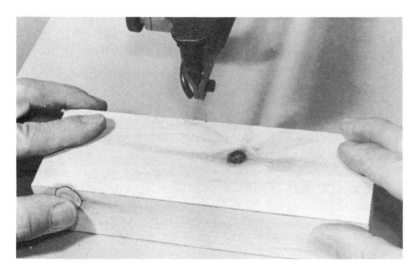

Illus. 280. A shallow cut is the first step in checking table squareness with thick scrap stock.

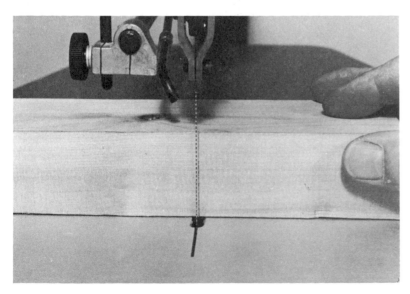

Illus. 281. Turn the stock around and bring it up behind the blade next to the shallow kerf. If the table is square, the back of the blade will slide easily into the kerf (cut).

CUTTING TECHNIQUES

Sitting Versus Standing

Is it best to sit or stand when cutting? Sitting is generally recommended, especially for long-term sawing. This requires a stool of an appropriate or adjustable height so you do not have to hunch over your work. (See Illus. 282.) One of the problems in sitting is that you're not always well-balanced or mobile. Also, when sitting on a stool close to the saw, it is difficult to swing large pieces around without striking your body. (See Illus. 283.)

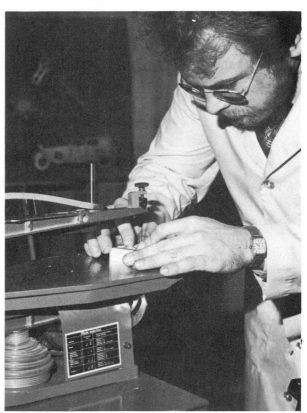

Illus. 283. Standing for long periods while bent over a scroll saw can make you very tired.

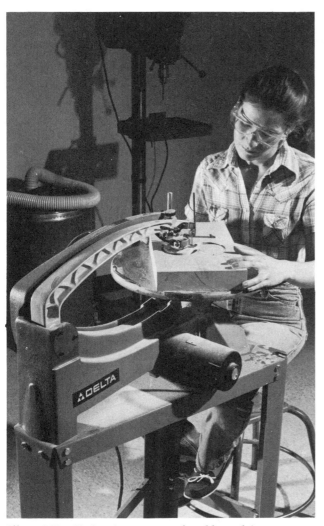

Illus. 282. Sitting is more comfortable and is recommended, provided you have a stool the right height.

Starting Points

The best starting point in cutting out any design is at a point or corner. Take a simple heart shape, for example; begin the cut so you come into the pattern at the point of the heart. (See Illus. 284.) This is a much better starting point than beginning the cut on the side. (See Illus. 285.) When you come around and meet your starting point, it is difficult to make that part of the cut a flowing curve that intersects smoothly with the start. (See Illus. 286.)

When cutting out a circular shape like a disc or a toy wheel, it's best to come into the pattern layout line in a crosscutting (across the grain) direction, rather than a ripping (with the grain) direction. Also, it is far better to have a starting point on an outside curve, as in Illus. 286, than an inside curve. It's easier to sand away any knobs or wavy lines that result when "coming around," and meeting up with the starting point.

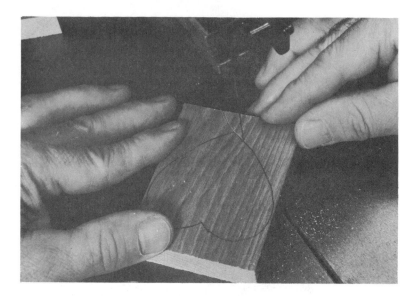

Illus. 284. Starting cuts at a point or corner is better than starting them on a curve.

Illus. 285. This is not the best starting point for making this cutout. This is a "ripping" starting point that's cut with the grain.

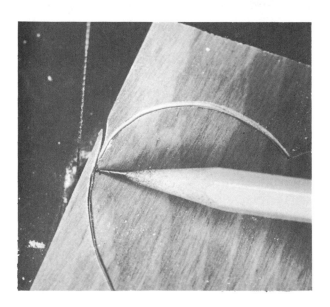

Illus. 286. Coming around to smoothly intersect with your starting point is more difficult when the cut is started in a direction that's with the grain, as shown.

Layout Line

Should you save the layout line (Illus. 287) or cut on it (Illus. 288)? The answer depends upon the type of project being made and the smoothness or quality of the saw cut. With most projects it will not make any difference.

Illus. 287. Following a layout line and "saving-the-line" by sawing on the waste side.

Illus. 288. Sawing right on the line.

If you are cutting with a conventional rigid-arm saw, or with a blade that does not provide a smooth-enough cut surface, save the layout line and sand down all cut edges. Constant-tension saws usually cut so smooth that no or little sanding is needed. Therefore, you can usually cut right on the layout line, removing it as you saw along. This eliminates the need to sand off the layout line later.

If very precise cutting is required, the thickness and accuracy of the layout lines become more important, and the cut is normally made very close to line, but not so close that you cut it away. With practice you'll be able to split layout lines if you wish.

On-the-Spot-Turns and Cornering

On-the-spot turns and cornering are also skills that require practice. They can only be done on constant-tension saws. An on-the-spot-turn is the ability to actually spin the workpiece 360° on a very small radius that is actually just ½ of the blade width. This can be done when cutting thick or thin stock.

Spinning the workpiece around on the blade is a new experience and technique for woodworkers accustomed to conventional rigid-arm saws or band-sawing techniques. Instead of making the "spin" (turn) slowly, which is the usual way, hold down on the work while turning it as quickly as you can. Don't become alarmed if the first time or so the blade catches in the workpiece and chatters up and down on the table.

Practice 180° on-the-spot-turning as shown in Illus. 289–291 until you can do it with confidence. The ability to make on-the-spot turns permits sawing sharp inside or outside corner cuts nonstop.

An example of a job requiring two sharp inside corner cuts is shown in Illus. 292. The cuts are made nonstop from start to finish. Illus. 293 is a good example of a cutout made utilizing to full advantage the on-the-spot cornering capabilities of a constant-tension scroll saw.

Illus. 294–296 show how the project depicted in Illus. 293 would be cut if you used a wide blade. As you can see in the illustrations, an on-the-spot turn is impossible with a wide blade. Notice how the outside corners are cut in Illus. 294; Illus. 294 also shows how to start an inside corner cut. Backing up, rounding the corner, and continuing the cut are shown in Illus. 295. The rounded corner is "cleaned-up" later. (See Illus. 296.) A good practice project is the "magic belt hook" shown in Illus. 297.

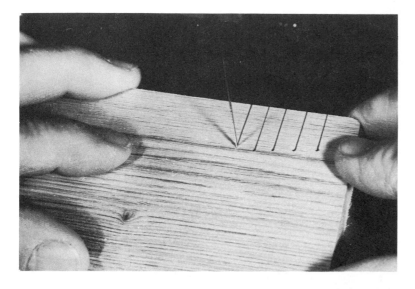

Illus. 289. Practicing "on-the-spot" turning on a constant-tension saw. To do this, saw partway into the board, spin it quickly around, and exit in the same cut (kerf).

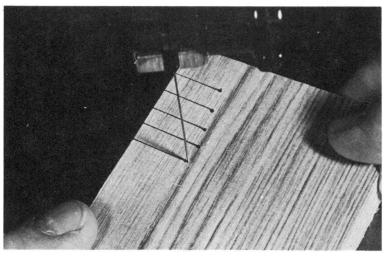

Illus. 290. Making an on-the-spot turn, about halfway through a 180° turn.

Illus. 291. When the turn is completed, the blade should exit through the "inbound" kerf.

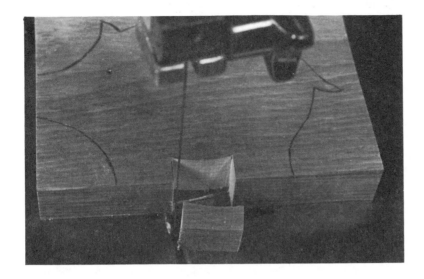

Illus. 292. The ability to make perfect 90° turns and other sharp cornering cuts accurately is the key to quick, precise and pleasurable sawing.

Illus. 293. Sharp, accurate, and quick cornering completes this cutout in just seconds.

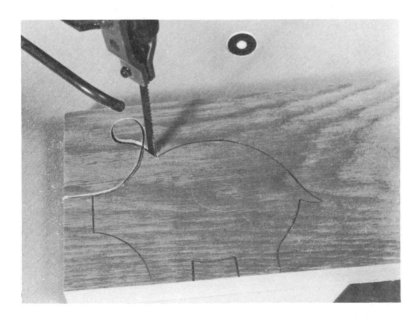

Illus. 294. Wide-blade cornering. Looping around to cut a sharp outside corner makes only the point of the ear. The blade will not make the required sharp inside corner.

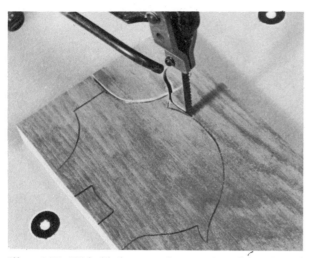

Illus. 295. Wide-blade cornering continued. Back up and "round out" the inside corner, as shown.

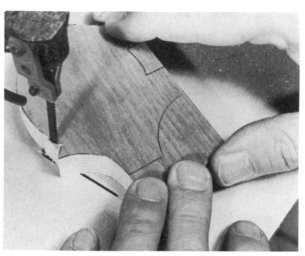

Illus. 296. Later, the inside corner is completed by cutting in from the opposite direction.

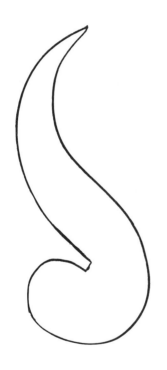

Illus. 297. This full-size pattern of the "magic belt hook" is a good practice project. Use ¼- to ⅜-inch thick material.

168

Straight-Line Cutting

Straight-line cutting across the grain and with the grain takes practice; also, a couple of factors have to be taken into consideration. First, almost all scroll saw and fret saw blades don't saw straight or cut parallel to the blade; they often cut a few degrees more towards one side than the other. This is because when the teeth are formed in manufacturing by milling, punching or filing, there is a material flow in one direction only, leaving a little burr remaining on one side of the teeth. This burr is much like the burr you get when grinding a new chisel or plane bevel. It makes the saw grab slightly in one direction. There is nothing the manufacturers can do about it without adding substantially to the price of blades.

When you stand facing the direct front of the saw, you will note that the angle of normal feed is off approximately 2 to 4 degrees to compensate.

You can verify this for yourself. Draw some lines across a board with a square. (See Illus. 298.) Now cut each one on the line; you will soon determine that it's easiest to follow the line with the work feed slightly angled into the saw blade. When you understand the concept and compensate correctly, straight-line sawing freehand is surprisingly easy—even when using very narrow blades.

Straight-line ripping (sawing with the grain) is done in essentially the same way. (See Illus. 299.) However, be alert because the blade may follow the grain rather than the layout line, as you expect. In such cases, slow the feed and compensate by changing the feed angle slightly more in the appropriate direction. The toaster tongs shown in Illus. 300–302 are a good project on which to practice straight-line ripping. Use ¾-inch-thick straight-grain hardwood and finish it with peanut oil.

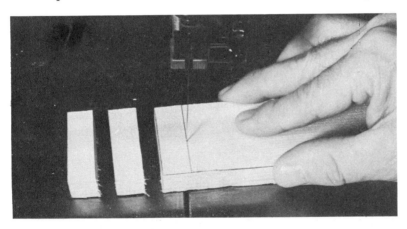

Illus. 298. Straight-line crosscutting requires a compensating, slightly angular feed direction.

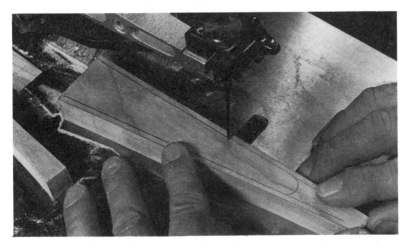

Illus. 299. Straight-line cutting with the grain (ripping).

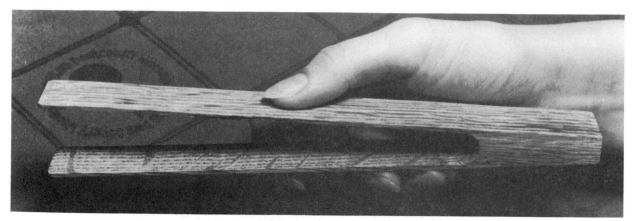

Illus. 300–302. These toaster tongs make a good straight-line sawing project.

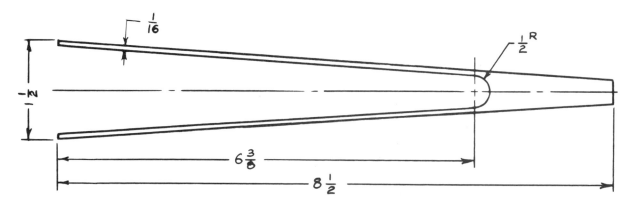

Illus. 301.

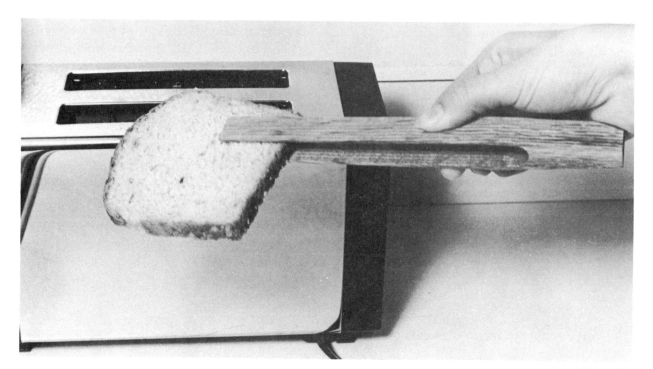

Illus. 302.

Stack Cutting

Stack cutting saves lots of time when two or more pieces need to be cut from the same pattern. Simply stack the pieces together and cut all the layers together at one time, just as you would saw one piece. The pattern only has to be marked out on the top layer. The layers of individual pieces can be held together easily with double-faced tape (Illus. 303), or you can nail into the scrap area.

It's important that the saw table be set perfectly square to the table. If it is not, some pieces will turn out larger or smaller than the others. Also, you cannot stack to a height that exceeds the thickness-cutting capacity of the saw. If the stock thickness capacity is 1½ inches, then you can stack six pieces of material ¼ inch in thickness (Illus. 304–306), but only two pieces that are ¾ inch thick.

Illus. 303. Layers are held together with small pieces of double-faced tape.

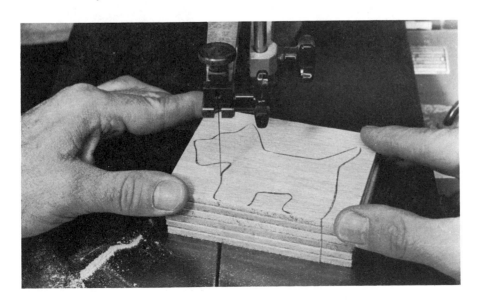

Illus. 304. Whenever two or more identical pieces are required, stack them together and cut them as one piece. Here six pieces are cut at once. (See Illus. 305 on the next page.)

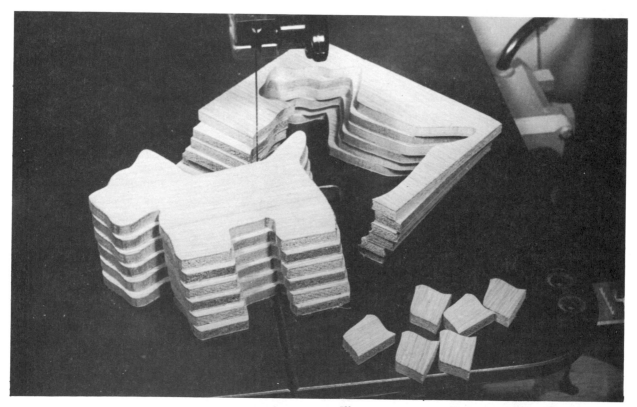

Illus. 306. All six identical pieces made in one cut.

16
PATTERNS AND PROJECTS

Good scroll saw work requires patterns of interesting and varied designs and projects. Therefore, we have put together a companion book, the *Scroll Saw Pattern Book*. This volume contains more than 400 traceable project patterns designed for most areas of scroll saw woodcrafting.

Some of the scroll saw manufacturers provide a selection of project plans and patterns. Almost all of the woodcrafting magazines frequently feature project plans for scroll saw owners. A number of mail-order companies and catalogue houses also sell commercially produced patterns. Even full-size trace-around template patterns made of plastic are available.

COPYING AND TRANSFERRING PATTERNS

Good scroll-sawing skills hinge on the careful and accurate development of the design or pattern and the transfer of it to the wood. Most plans in magazines and project books are not full size. They are usually printed, considerably less than full size, on a two-dimensional, squared grid.

Drawing talent is not required to develop a good pattern by enlargement (or reduction) and transferring it to the wood. Even pictures and designs from books, magazines, newspapers, coloring books, napkins, wallpaper, etc., can be converted rather easily to a scroll saw pattern. Any design is possible to copy, even it is not drawn with a two-dimensional squared grid over it.

To copy and enlarge designs from such sources, begin with some transparent tissue paper. Accurately rule it out making small, uniformly sized squares all over it in the ¼-inch or ½-inch size. The greater the detail and the smaller the design being copied, the smaller the size of the squares should be drawn. Next, on a larger piece of paper, about the size that you want the eventual project design to be, divide the space up with exactly the same number of squares as occupied by the design under the transparent tissue paper. The size of the larger set of squares can also be determined by the enlargement ratio desired. If you want the design twice the size, then draw the big squares twice the size of the smaller ones.

Now, copy the design square by square. Copy each point of the original pattern onto the graph squares. Curves may be drawn by "eye" after locating them with reference to their surrounding square. However, it is more accurate to mark the points where the line of the curve strikes each horizontal and vertical line, as shown in Illus. 307. The example shown in Illus. 307 has a 1 to 4 ratio, which means the design is enlarged four times larger than the original.

This technique can be modified so that the design is drawn directly onto the surface of the wood if so desired. Usually, however, the pattern is drawn onto paper first. It's easier to erase, refine, and smooth out contoured lines. When the full-size paper pattern is made, you have several choices of how to transfer the pattern to the wood.

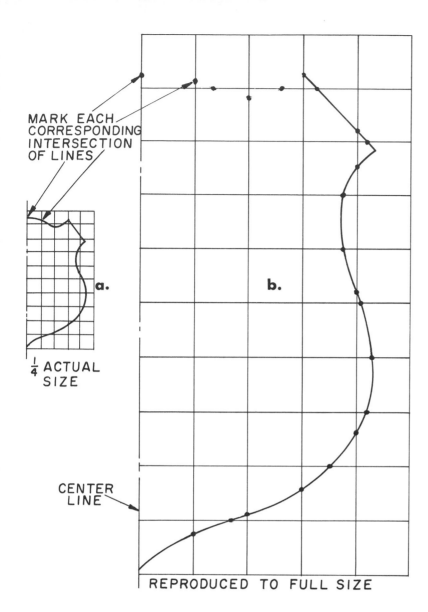

MARK EACH CORRESPONDING INTERSECTION OF LINES

a.

b.

¼ ACTUAL SIZE

CENTER LINE

REPRODUCED TO FULL SIZE

Illus. 307. Enlarging a design pattern with the graph square or grid system. A is the original design; B shows the method of locating the points for the enlarged pattern.

Sometimes you might decide to paste the entire pattern directly onto the workpiece. Rubber cement seems the best for this because it does not wrinkle the paper and rubs off fairly easily. For highly detailed precision-cutting, as when making jewellery, miniatures, gears, etc., scissor-cut the pattern out and glue it to the workpiece with rubber cement. This gives a very crisp, sharp line that's highly visible, accurate, and much easier to follow than any other line. The disadvantage of this technique is that you must sacrifice the pattern; it cannot be reused. Also, it's not always fast or easy to remove the pattern and rubber cement from the work surface.

The design can also be transferred to the workpiece with carbon paper, as shown Illus. 308 and 309. Still another method is to enlarge the pattern onto a piece of heavier paper (like a file folder) or lightweight cardboard (like a writing tablet "backer"). Then, cut out the pattern with scissors. Place it on the workpiece and trace around it with a pencil, as shown in Illus. 310. This method is probably the best in that it least dirties or soils the surface, thus requiring less subsequent sanding.

Another method that has some applications is the transfer of the pattern to the wood with a pounce wheel. (See Illus. 311.)

On light wood, you can put carbon paper underneath. On softwoods you can just exert enough pressure to track in the wood. This method is not recommended for projects requiring accuracy. It's best to cut the wood with the blade, actually removing the depressions left by this marking tool.

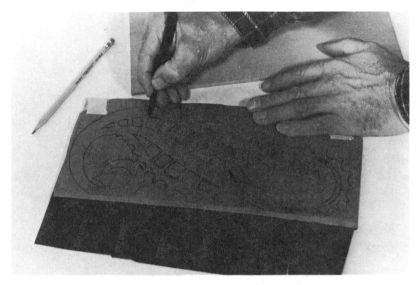

Illus. 308. The enlarged design is drawn on heavy paper and transferred to the wood with carbon paper.

Illus. 309. The pattern transferred to the wood. Since two pieces will be required, one ¼ inch wider than the other, for a butt corner shelf joint, the pieces are offset and secured with double-faced tape so they both can be cut to the same shape at one time.

Illus. 310. Tracing around a scissor-cut pattern made of heavy paper.

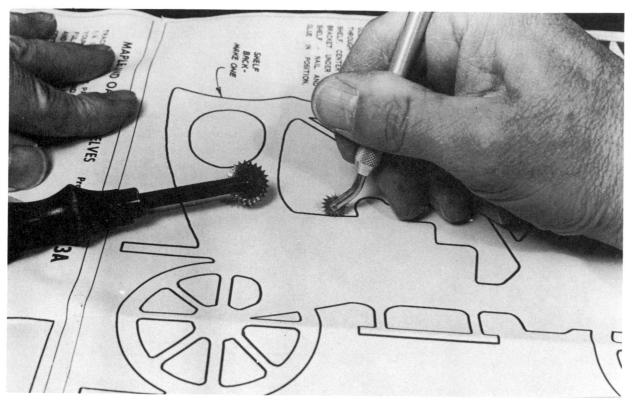

Illus. 311. Transferring a pattern with a pounce wheel or tracing wheel.

Using a Pantograph

A pantograph is still another way of copying any two-dimensional or flat profile shape. (See Illus. 312.) The enlargement (or reduction) can be drawn directly onto the workpiece or onto paper. The follower point is guided along the original design as the pencil end automatically recreates the outline in the exact size and desired proportions.

Office Copy Machines

Office copy machines are also very useful to the scroll saw craftsman. Some even have the capabilities to enlarge or reduce, which, for the cost of one copy, is certainly very reasonable. Usually, the simplest designs are easy to visualize in terms of a scroll-saw project. With experience, you will be able to visualize more and more potential project designs. Illus. 313–316 depict a project developed simply from a 1 to 1 copy taken from a book on birds.

COMMERCIAL PATTERNS

Commercial patterns have been around for a long time. (See Illus. 317–319.) A look at the advertising pages in the popular woodcraft magazines will uncover many sources for plans and patterns. Dremel and Sears sell a fairly inexpensive sign layout pattern kit. (See Illus. 320–322.) The kit contains 100 patterns in script, Old English, and block letter styles in 2-, 3-, and 4-inch letter sizes. To use, transfer the patterns to the wood with carbon paper. The patterns are designed so proper spacing is easy to achieve as the wording is progressively developed. (See Illus. 321 and 322.)

Since sign work is a popular activity for scroll saw owners, I recommend my two books on wooden signs, *Making Wood Signs* and *Alphabets and Designs for Wood Signs*; both are published by Sterling Publishing Company, Two Park Avenue, New York, New York 10016.

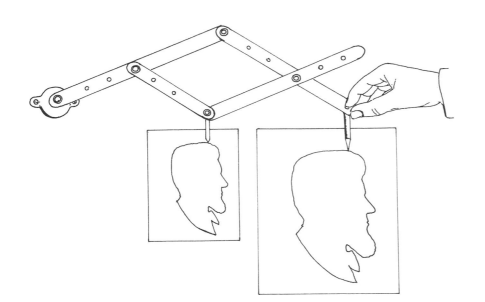

Illus. 312. An inexpensive pantograph (less than $7.00) enlarges a pattern to over 10 times its original size or reduces it to ⅒ its original size.

Illus. 313. This book page was copied on a Xerox machine.

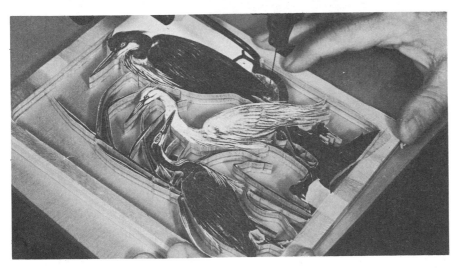

Illus. 314. The copy was pasted to the back of ¼-inch veneer plywood with rubber cement. Two layers of plywood were secured face to face with just two small pieces of double-faced tape near the edges. Here is the cutting in progress.

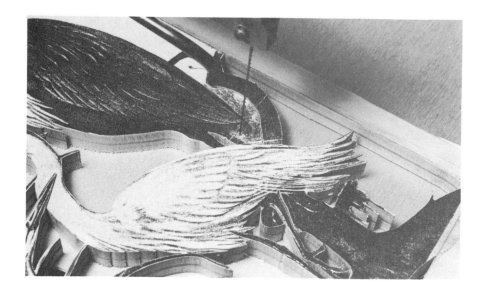

Illus. 315. A close-up look at the cutting. Remember, the copy (pattern) is pasted to the back side of one workpiece.

Illus. 316. The resulting delicate silhouette projects. Anywhere from three to six silhouettes can be made at one time if a precision saw is used.

Illus. 317. The "Pattern Pack" is a rather expensive subscription service provided by RBI, a scroll saw manufacturer.

Illus. 318. A typical full-size pattern provided by RBI.

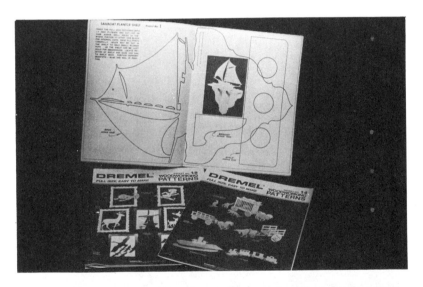

Illus. 319. A typical full-size scroll-saw project packet sold by Dremel.

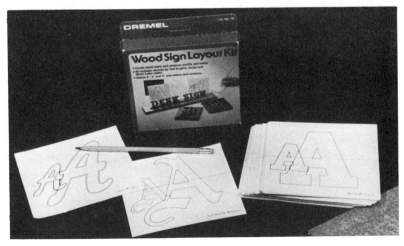

Illus. 320. The sign layout kit sold by Dremel and Sears consists of two-, three-, and four-inch patterns for alphabets in script, Old English, and block letter designs.

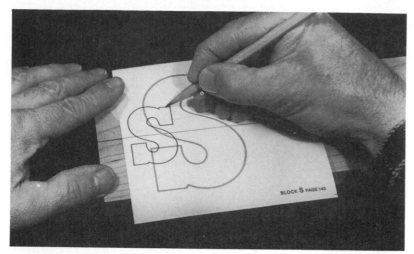

Illus. 321. The board needs a length-wise center line.

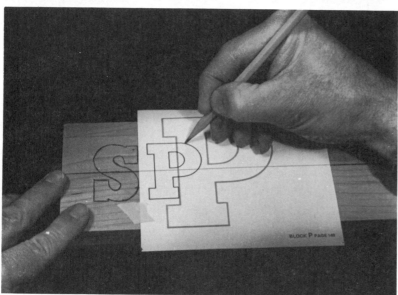

Illus. 322. If the letters are to be connected, like those used for a desk sign, the spacing between them is the distance the letter is from the left edge of the paper.

Illus. 323. Some basic sign project ideas.

TEMPLATES

Templates are ideal when two or more identical layouts are required. (See Illus. 325.) A template is nothing more than a full-size pattern cut from a stiff, rigid material that can be easily traced around. Almost any thin, inexpensive sheet material can be used for making templates. One-eighth-inch tempered hardboard, thin plywood, sheet aluminum, thin plastics, etc., can all be used. *Tip*: If you have already made a paper pattern or the design is already transferred to the wood, and you decide that it would be nice to have a permanent template, cut one on your saw simultaneously as you cut out your project. Use double-faced tape to attach the template material under the workpiece. It takes just a little effort to produce a perfect copy template while cutting out the first project(s).

Plastic letter templates, in a variety of different styles and sizes, are available from Seyco Sales Co., 2107 So. Garland Ave., Garland, Texas 75041. (See Illus. 326 and 327.) They are made of clear, see-through plastic and are simply traced around when used.

PROJECT IDEAS

Jigsaw Puzzles

Jigsaw puzzles are very easy and fun to make. (See Illus. 328.) Simply find a suitable picture, perhaps from a calendar, magazine, or poster shop. Bond it to ⅛-inch-thick hardboard with rubber cement. Apply two coats to each surface; allow the first coat to dry completely before applying the second coat. (See Illus. 329.) With chalk, roughly mark out the sizes of the pieces desired. If you want a more complicated puzzle, plan to cut it into more and smaller pieces. Cut bigger and fewer pieces for younger children's puzzles. Make the typical interlocking puzzle cuts freehand, using the chalked guidelines for piece and size reference only. (See Illus. 330.) Make all the cuts in one direction first, as shown in Illus. 330. Lay the cut strips, assembled together, onto a piece of corrugated box cardboard. Then make the second run of cuts in the opposite direction, as shown in Illus. 331. The cardboard supports the pieces until they are cut away.

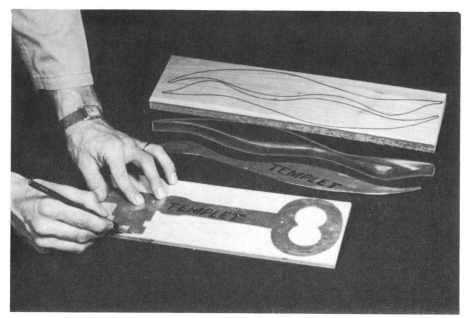

Illus. 325. Marking the wood with templates cut from an aluminum sheet. As you may notice in the illustration, the word template can be spelled two different ways.

Illus. 326. These commercial letter templates of clear plastic come in a variety of styles and sizes. They are available from Sevco Sales Co.

Illus. 327. Tracing around the plastic letter templates.

Illus. 329. A suitable picture, ⅛-inch-thick hardboard, and rubber cement are needed to make a jigsaw puzzle.

Illus. 328. A jigsaw puzzle is a fun, easy-to-make project for beginners.

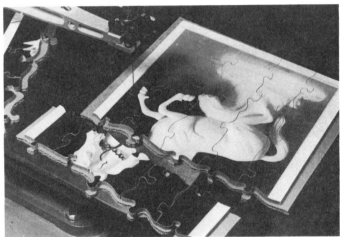

Illus. 331. Once the vertical puzzle cuts are made, assemble them on a piece of cardboard. Hold the puzzle stock and cardboard together with hand pressure and make the horizontal, interlocking cuts.

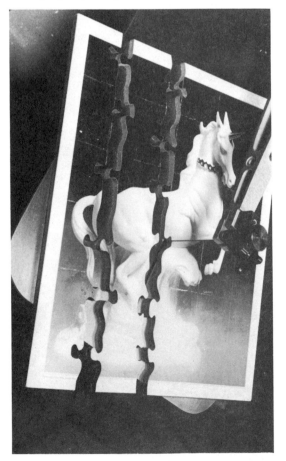

Illus. 330. Light, grid chalk lines are used to indicate the relative sizes and maintain some uniformity during cutting. The interlocking cuts are made freehand without any precise layout lines.

Decorative Wall Puzzles

Decorative wall puzzles are also fun to make with the scroll saw. (See Illus. 332.) Pictures, photos, etc., are stylized and reduced to represent simple pictorial lines and shapes. The puzzle shown in Illus. 332—"Lovers in the Moonlight"—is from a commercial plan and is available from Advanced Machinery Imports, Box 312, New Castle, Delaware 19720. However, you can create your own patterns for stylized works of scroll-sawing art. Cut out individual pieces on the layout lines. Use ¾-inch or thicker stock. Cut out an uninterrupted border piece and glue it to a thin plywood backing. (See Illus. 333 and 334.) Sand every individual piece on the top edge, just to round the edges slightly. Individually stain or paint all of the cutout parts in contrasting colors or tones; combining stain and pigmented colors in the same project leads to a very nice-looking puzzle. Then, either leave the parts free or glue them to the backing. The stock lost from kerf made by the fine blade makes a shadow line, giving a feeling of depth to the project.

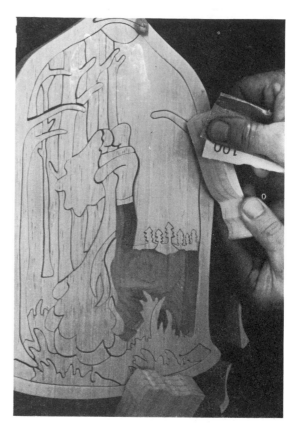

Illus. 333. The border is glued to a backing and the edges of all cut parts are softened and slightly rounded with sandpaper.

Illus. 332. AMI's "Lovers in the Moonlight" is a decorative wall puzzle.

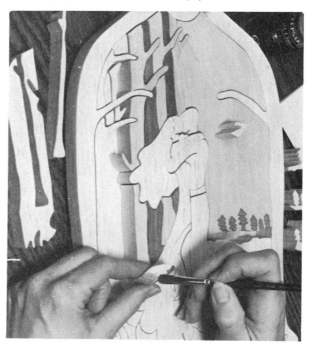

Illus. 334. Individually stain and paint all cutout pieces in contrasting colors. Glue them to the backing.

Illus. 335 shows this concept taken a few steps further. Jay Beck cuts individual pieces for his designs from different kinds of wood that also vary in thickness. This gives the picture a three-dimensional look. He also rounds over the corners more on the thicker pieces. If thicker wood is not available, plywood shims can be cut and glued to the pieces that are to stand out further. In addition to using wood and stains of contrasting colors, Jay also carefully combines high gloss and duller surface coatings to selected pieces.

Miscellaneous Projects

Projects and designs made with the scroll saw are shown in Illus. 336–344. The full-size patterns for them are published in the companion book, the *Scroll Saw Pattern Book*.

Illus. 335. Jay Beck's plaques are made of different woods and with pieces that vary in thickness. This, coupled with a combination of different-colored stains and a tasteful selection of glossy and flat top coat finishes, makes a truly dramatic work of art.

Illus. 336–344. Examples of the basic projects that can be found in the Scroll Saw Pattern Book.

Illus. 337.

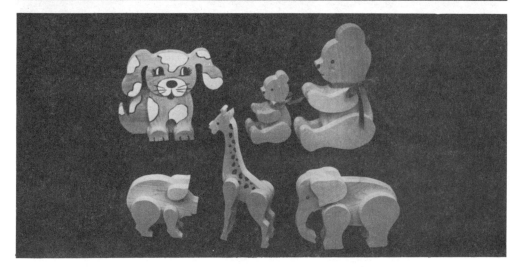

Illus. 342.

Illus. 341.

Illus. 343.

Illus. 344. *Interesting letter and number patterns, some in the cut-through style shown here, can be found in the* Scroll Saw Pattern Book.

17
SAWING INSIDE OPENINGS

Sawing inside openings—sometimes called piercing work, pierce cutting, or internal cutting—is not only a common procedure, but a frequently utilized one as well. (See Illus. 345–349.) In this class of scroll-sawing work, the blade is threaded through a hole drilled into the workpiece. The detail or design of the pattern is cut as usual, and then the blade is unclamped and removed. This is a relatively uncomplicated sawing procedure.

The complexity of the overall project and the number of openings that must be cut, dictate the time involved and the number of blade threadings required for a given project. [For example, fretwork, which is often more highly detailed, with a very large percentage of delicate cutouts making up the overall design, takes relatively more time and blade threadings than other projects.] Illus. 345 and 346 represent two typical extremes. The seahorse designs in Illus. 345 will require a great number of blade manipulations. The cat cutouts in Illus. 346 do not.

To saw out each opening, repeat the following general steps: 1) release the blade tension, 2) unclamp the blade, 3) thread the blade through the predrilled workpiece, 4) reclamp the blade, and 5) retension. Some scroll saws require a great deal more time and effort to complete these simple steps than do other saws.

The essential differences between making internal cutouts with constant-tension and the rigid-arm saws are shown in Illus. 350–354. Highly detailed work is much more suited to the capabilities of the new constant-tension saws. Internal cutting can be made

with rigid-arm saws, but their efficiency diminishes progressively as the stock thickness increases, and as the complexity of detail becomes more intricate.

One obvious advantage of the constant-tension saws is that extremely narrow, fine blades can be used. The cutting capability of these blades is potentially so fine that as little as a line's width can be cut away. (See Illus. 354.) Conversely, rigid-arm machines require wider blades when cutting stock that is ½ inch thick and heavier. Wide blades require more time to make sharp curves and they cause more difficulty when attempting 90° cornering.

Illus. 345. Here is a sample of work that requires a high percentage of inside cutouts.

Illus. 346. When an inside pattern is cut on a constant-tension saw with a thin, narrow blade, useful "positive" and "negative" pieces can be made.

Illus. 347. These narrow cutouts are being made with a constant-tension saw.

Illus. 348. The completed project. Designs like this can be used for signboards or other projects.

Illus. 349. A small, inexpensive spiral drill.

Illus. 350. Threading a blade for an inside cut on a rigid-arm scroll saw. Note the blade width.

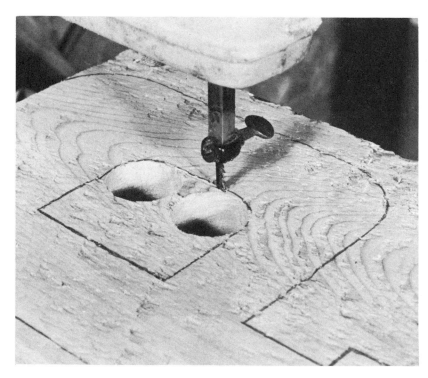

Illus. 351. Making an inside cut on thick stock with a rigid-arm saw. Remember, the size of the "turning holes" equals the outline of the cut.

Illus. 352. Heavy brackets cut from 1¾- and 2-inch-thick stock in cedar and oak challenge the maximum capabilities of the scroll saw.

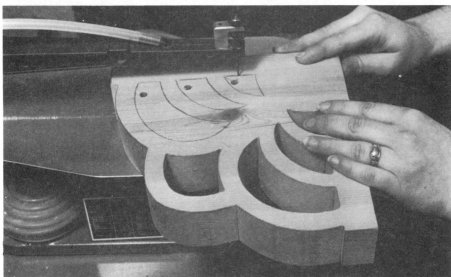

Illus. 353. Making inside cuts on 1¾-inch-thick stock with a constant-tension saw.

Illus. 354. A very narrow blade was used to make the inside cuts on the line comprising this signature; the cuts were made through ¾-inch oak.

Perfect, unblemished cutouts, as shown in Illus. 346, also are only possible with constant-tension saws. Constant-tension saws permit the sawing of clean, unobstructed positive and negative internal cutouts, also shown in Illus. 346. Only very small blade entry holes are required. This becomes an even greater advantage when scroll-sawing solid wood inlays and doing marquetry in thin veneers. (See Chapters 21, 22 and 23 for more information concerning those operations.)

Illus. 355–358 show typical blade-threading operations involved with the Excalibur and Hegner scroll saws. Before buying any saw, determine how difficult it will be to thread blades to make inside cutouts.

The hanging lamp projects shown in Illus. 359 and 360 were made by combining stack-sawing and internal cuts into one operation. This is a technique that is convenient and saves a great deal of time. (Illus. 361–363.) Illus. 364 and 365 show some assembly tips for fabricating the hexagon hanging lamps.

Illus. 355. Here a blade is being threaded on an Excalibur saw so an inside cutout can be made. Note the use of the slot in the table.

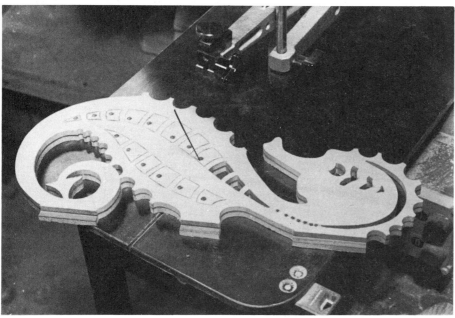

Illus. 356. Blade threading on a Hegner saw. Note that the blade slot runs to the edge of the table.

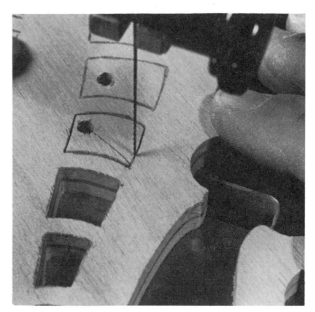

Illus. 358. Making a cut. Note the saw path from the hole to the first corner. Each successive corner was cut sharply, as approached, all around, nonstop.

Illus. 357. Anchoring the blade in the upper clamp on a Hegner saw. The blade clamp is held rigid with the upper thumbscrew. Once the blade is clamped, the pressure is released so the blade clamp will pivot freely.

Illus. 359 and 360. Hanging lamp projects require a combination of techniques: namely, stack cutting and sawing inside openings. Full-size patterns for these projects are found in the Scroll Saw Pattern Book.

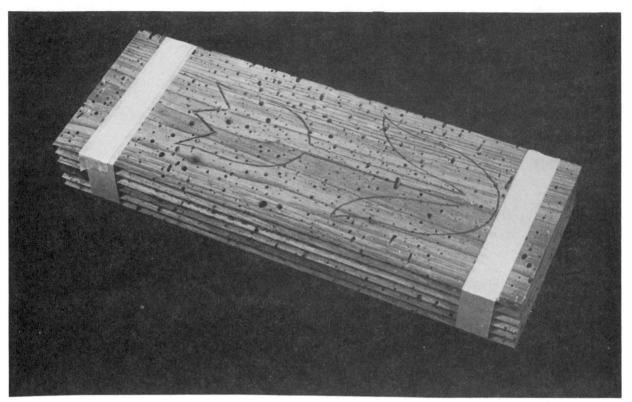

Illus. 361. These six pieces, stacked and taped, are ready to be sawed so the tulip design can be cut out.

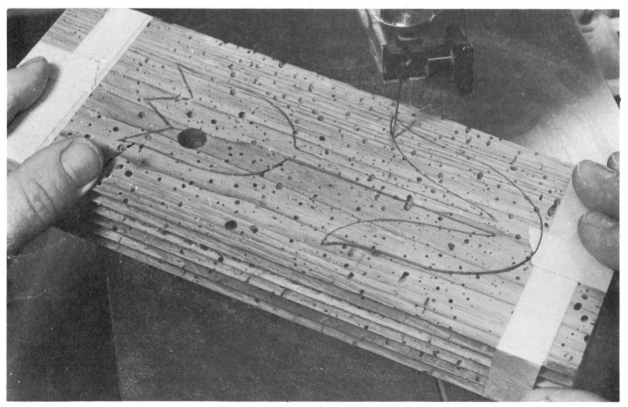

Illus. 362. Sawing the inside tulip design in six pieces simultaneously.

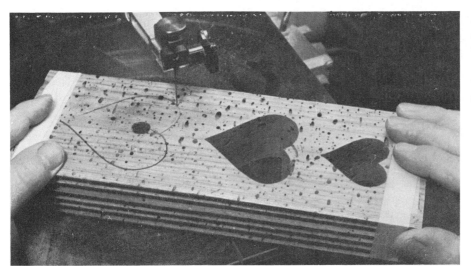

Illus. 363. The same time-saving operation for a lamp with heart designs. Only three blade threadings make a total of 18 heart cutouts.

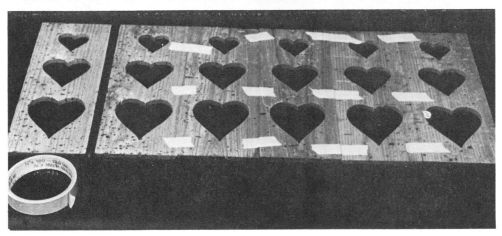

Illus. 364. The easy assembly of cutout parts begins with all the pieces taped together face-sides up, as shown.

Illus. 365. Flip the taped pieces over, spread glue, and then "roll" the assembly to form the hexagon cylinders. The tape acts as both hinge and clamp. See the Scroll Saw Pattern Book *for more details.*

18
SAWING SMALL PIECES AND THIN STOCK

Sawing thin wood or soft metallic pieces, as done in jewellery making, is work that can be perfectly handled with a good scroll saw. Illus. 366–369 show the essentials of do-it-yourself jewellery making. Pieces even smaller than those depicted can be cut on the scroll saw. Minute items for miniatures and scale-model projects are also easily handled on the scroll saw.

This class of work can best be done more safely on a scroll saw more than any other machine. However, anytime you are working very small pieces on a machine, extra precautions should be taken. Very small cuttings often dictate that you get your fingers in very close to the blade. (See Illus. 368.) You'll most likely be working with thinner and narrower blades, which break more frequently. So, be aware of potential hazards and don't let your concentration lapse. Select the appropriate blade and tension it accordingly.

Fine and highly detailed designs might be more easily cut with a slower speed setting to reduce the number of cutting strokes per minute. If sawing a considerable amount of thinner material, adjust your machine to a shorter-than-usual stroke length if your machine is able to do this. Shorter cutting strokes increase efficiency and accuracy when cutting thin materials.

Illus. 366. Do-it-yourself jewelry can be easily made on the scroll saw. See the Scroll Saw Pattern Book *for designs.*

Illus. 367. Rubber cement is used for pasting scissor-cut patterns to the workpieces. Double-faced tape is used for multiple stack cutting.

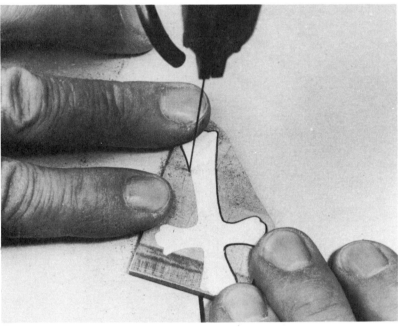

Illus. 368. A close-up showing the sawing of soft brass. The paper pattern glued to the material makes a precise cutting line.

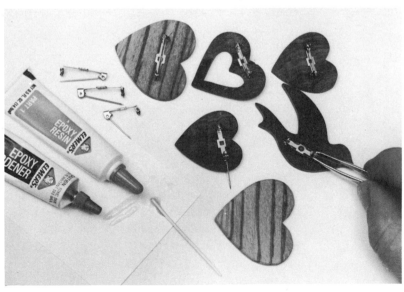

Illus. 369. Jewelry findings are simply glued on with epoxy.

SAWING EXTREMELY SMALL PIECES

Illus. 370 and 371 show how to saw extremely small pieces. One of the problems associated with cutting out very small pieces is the table opening around the blade. (See Illus. 370.) Some machines have larger blade openings than others. The openings must be at least a certain size to permit the table to be tilted without the blade striking the table. Thus, when cutting small pieces, there is a lack of support in the opening. This causes small pieces to tip in or fall through; thin material can bend, tear, or break because it is not supported at the blade area.

This problem can be overcome in one of two ways or a combination of both. One technique is to saw the material while it is supported on another piece of waste material. Cheap plywood or a flat piece of corrugated cardboard may do the trick. (See Illus. 371.) The other method is to use an auxiliary table made of thin plywood or hardboard. This is cut to an appropriate size, and a very small hole is drilled for the blade opening. Thread the blade through the small hole and secure the auxiliary table to the original table with double-faced tape. (See Illus. 372.) Sometimes the nature of the job is such that both methods are utilized. An example would be cutting out a small design from thin veneer.

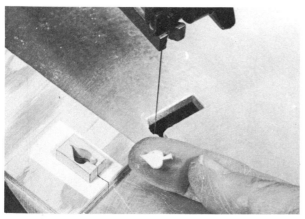

Illus. 370. This mini-cutout was sawn while supported on a piece of scrap plywood. You can visualize the problem presented by the blade opening on the table unless some auxiliary support for the work is provided.

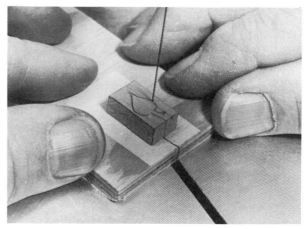

Illus. 371. Making a very small cutout. The workpiece is secured to a scrap piece of plywood with double-faced tape. This way, the work is supported and your fingers do not have to be close to the moving blade.

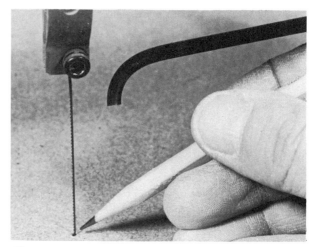

Illus. 372. This auxiliary table of hardboard is attached to the existing table with double-faced tape. Note the small hole at the blade so that the workpiece will have sufficient support.

Some very delicate and unusual projects can be made with mini-cutouts. Various designs for overlays, jewellery, miniatures, and model-building of extremely small profile shapes can be cut from a variety of thin materials. One project idea is to make little "stick-on" designs from veneer scraps. Apply double-faced tape to the back before sawing out the part and you can adhere little veneer cutouts to almost any surface, including very smooth plastic and glass. Or simply use the new "peel and stick" veneers that already have adhesive applied to one side.

SAWING VENEERS

Use a very fine-toothed blade—such as a 2/0 or one slightly heavier—so there is minimal splintering or tear-out on the bottom side. (See Illus. 373 and 374.) Even though you have an auxiliary table mounted so the blade-opening hole is at a minimum, you'll find cleaner cuts are made with the work supported on a piece of corrugated cardboard during cutting. Tension the blade correctly. Remember, excess tension will most likely cause premature blade breakage. You need just the right amount of tension. Without sufficient tension, the blade will be "spongy," and you will have a hard time controlling the cutting direction. If blades keep breaking in the center, it indicates a tension problem.

If possible, the speed should be slowed to a range of several hundred cutting strokes per minute or less. If you have a machine with an infinitely variable speed control, you'll be able to dial the optimum speed for the work at hand. If you are cutting a highly detailed design, you may want to bring the speed down to even less than 100 strokes per minute. If you have a single-speed machine, you'll just have to work with that speed. Lower the feed rate and make some trial cuts before undertaking a major project to make sure you can do the work at that cutting speed.

Illus. 375–377 show how to cut a design out of a thin piece of veneer.

Illus. 373. An enlargement of the bottom or exit side made by different cutting situations. The cut at left was made with a No. 5 blade, which was obviously too wide and didn't have enough teeth. The center and right cuts were made with a fine 2/0 blade, but the cut on the right was made with the veneer supported on corrugated cardboard.

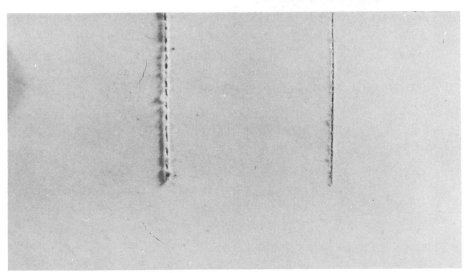

Illus. 374. An enlargement of the bottom or the blade exit side of the very thin (1/64-inch) peel and stick veneer. Both cuts were made with a 2/0 blade, but the cut on the right was made with the veneer supported on corrugated cardboard.

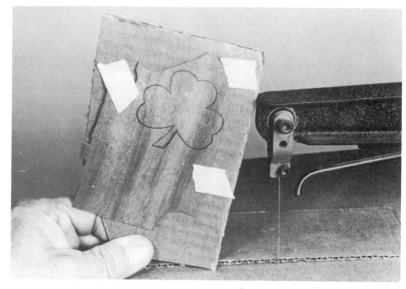

Illus. 375. Preparations for sawing veneer cleanly. The auxiliary table "minimizes" the blade opening. The workpiece is taped to a piece of waste corrugated cardboard for added support.

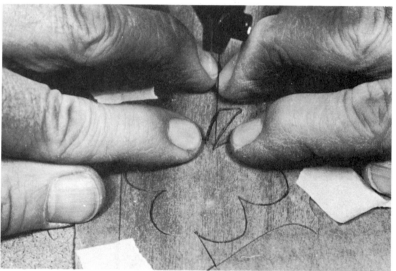

Illus. 376. Sawing the veneer. Pressure must be cautiously applied close to the cut to prevent "fluttering" of the workpiece.

Illus. 377. The resulting cut is clean and splinter-free on the exit side.

19
SAWING JOINTS

The capabilities of a good scroll saw can be exploited to make a number of precise woodworking joints. In fact, some kinds of joints are surprisingly ideal as scroll-sawing jobs. The dovetail joint is a good example. Dovetails can obviously be made very easily using a router with or without the aid of special dovetail jigs. (Various methods of dovetailing are described in the *Router Handbook*, Sterling Publishing Co.) However, the scroll saw even has some great advantages for dovetailing that the router doesn't have. It does a much cleaner and a quieter job. Also, a router kicks up lots of dust. Finally, you don't need any commercial jigs or fixtures for the scroll saws.

However, as in most areas of scroll-sawing, the quality of the cut depends a great deal upon your ability to make and follow precise layout lines. The ability to cut to a layout line (or even split it) is important. Accuracy is more essential when sawing two parts that must fit together than when sawing out, for example, a pig-shape cutting board, which will not be seriously affected if you cut a little to one side of the layout line.

CORNER LAP JOINTS

Good joint-making hinges upon the proper application of scroll-sawing fundamentals. If the table is not set square you'll have difficulty making many joints, such as corner lap joints. (See Illus. 378 and 379.) As a matter of fact, corner lap joints can be made more easily and accurately on a table saw. However, if you don't have a table saw, the scroll saw is far better than doing the job with just a hand saw. On joint work of this type, use the widest blade possible. You'll be able to apply more tension, which is necessary to prevent bellied surfaces when cutting thick stock.

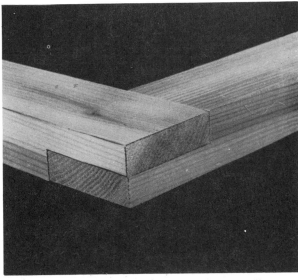

Illus. 378. A corner lap joint cut with a scroll saw.

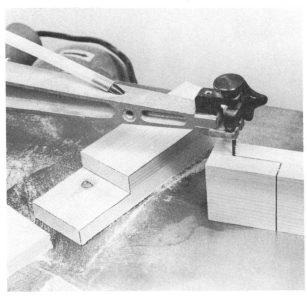

Illus. 379. Joint cutting requires a good machine, good layout, and an ability to follow lines precisely.

SPIRAL DOWEL PINS

Spiral dowel pins can be easily made with a scroll saw. Spiral dowel pins are used in dowelled butt and edge joints, mitre joints, leg-and-rail assembled joints, etc. To make them, use standard dowels and rotate them against the blade with the setup shown in Illus. 380. Use a fairly stiff blade. A number 6 spiral-cutting blade works well for grooving dowels ⅜ inch in diameter and larger. The amount of table tilt will determine the spacing or pitch of the groove. A 10 to 15° table tilt is about right for most dowel sizes.

SLIP JOINTS

Slip joints are relatively easy to saw, and they are used for various projects that require easy disassembly and assembly. Illus. 381 shows a Christmas star ornament that has interlocking slip or slot joints. Illus. 382 shows all of the pieces unassembled, with the slots cut to match (or slip over) the thickness of the material.

COPE JOINTS

The cope joint is one way of fitting mouldings into an inside corner without using a conventional mitre joint. Illus. 383 shows the cut pieces and the assembled joint. To make this joint, only one piece is cut to the profile shape of the moulding. The cut on this one piece is made simply by starting with a 45° mitre cut on the end, as shown in Illus. 384. The profile cut is then easily made by sawing precisely on the mitre line, which gives the exact curve required. This cut is made with the blade and table adjusted square to each other at 90°.

No table tilting is required to make the coped cut. Illus. 385 shows the coped cut in progress. The resulting surface will be the coped end that matches the profile of the moulding. This second piece should now "butt" perfectly against the first piece.

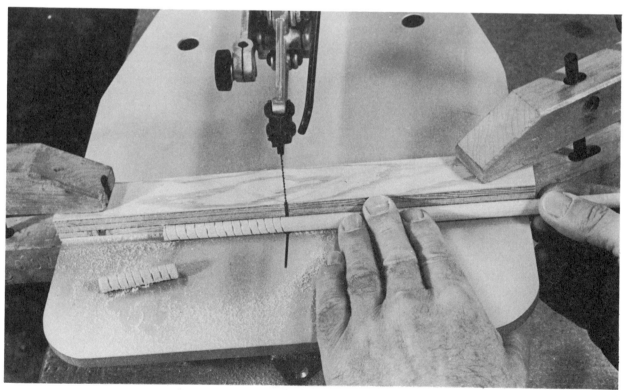

Illus. 380. Cutting spiral grooves in dowels. The table is tilted approximately 10°, and the dowel is rotated against the clamped boards, as shown, which limits the cutting depth.

Illus. 382. The ornament in Illus. 381 disassembled.

Illus. 381. This Christmas ornament is assembled with interlocking slip joints.

Illus. 383. The basic cope joint. The cut pieces shown above and the assembled joint shown below make a non-mitred corner joint.

Illus. 384. One piece (at left) is cut to length with a square cut; the end of the second piece is mitre-cut at 45° before it is cut to the profile, which is shown in Illus. 385.

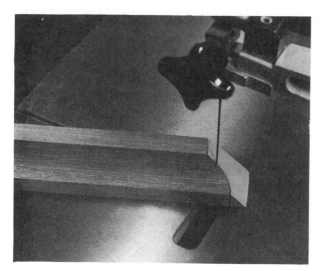

Illus. 385. Here the mitre-cut end is sawn precisely on the mitre line to make the profile of the "coped" cut.

COPE-DOWEL JOINT

Modelmakers often use this joint to join dowels to each other to make various structures. Cabinetmakers can use this joint for making door and drawer pulls or handles. To get good intersections (Illus. 386), saw the ends of the dowels to a profile that equals the diameter of the mating dowel. A simple work-holding fixture makes sawing this type of cut on the scroll saw easy. Simply bore a hole through a piece of scrap wood, as shown in Illus. 387. If you are "coping" the end of a ¾-inch diameter dowel, then bore a ¾-inch hole. It will be difficult to insert and remove the dowel for cutting unless a slot is cut lengthwise or horizontally, as shown in Illus. 387. Transfer layout lines to the top surface of the fixture to indicate the diameter for the end cope desired. The same idea works for making a coped cut into the side of a dowel. The fixture shown in Illus. 387 can be used for sawing both end and side coping cuts.

The cuts on the dowels are made by cutting precisely along the same successive path; be careful not to cut into the fixture material or cut too far away from it, as shown in Illus. 387.

Illus. 388 and 389 show some very easy-to-make drawers for workshop storage of small parts. The pulls are simply side cope cuts on 1-inch dowels that provide a finger grip. The dowels are glued into holes bored completely through the drawer front and secured with a finish nail driven vertically into the dowel.

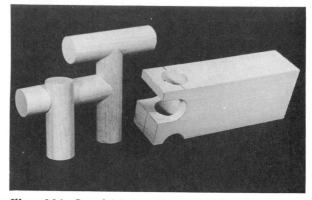

Illus. 386. Coped joints make perfect dowel intersections. The simple cutting jig at the right helps to make these round profile cuts.

Illus. 387. "Coping" the end of a dowel. Note the horizontal slot cut; it makes the insertion and withdrawal of the dowel from the fixture easier.

Illus. 388. The dowel finger-pull on this small-parts drawer for the workshop is made by cope cutting.

Illus. 389. Here is a partial look at workshop drawers used for the storage of small items.

MITRE JOINTS

With the assistance of a very basic and simple fixture, you can make perfect-fitting mitre joints. Illus. 390–393 show the approach. The key is to carefully make the jig or fixture, which is not difficult. Use a piece of ¼-inch plywood about 6 inches × 12 inches. Lay out two lines 90° to each other for fastening two ¾-inch × 1¼-inch guide strips. Glue and nail them in place so they make a perfect 90° inside corner. Don't worry about the quality or fit of the mitred corner on the fixture. It is of no importance, because you'll be running the saw through it anyway. Any miscut mitre (Illus. 390) is corrected by making successive passes and shifting the pieces together after each previous pass, until there are no longer any gaps remaining. (See Illus. 393.)

Illus. 390. With a scroll saw, you can easily correct miscut mitres.

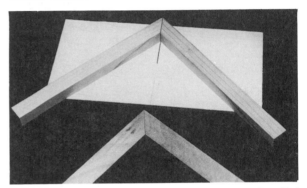

Illus. 391. These two guide strips, glued and nailed to ¼-inch plywood forming a square inside corner, are all that's required for this scroll-saw mitring fixture.

Illus. 392. Hold the workpieces tightly against the guide strips, and the mitres as close together as possible. Make saw cuts through the gaps of the joint. Make as many successive passes as required until the joint closes perfectly without any gap at all remaining.

Illus. 393. With each successive pass, the joint becomes tighter until perfect, as shown here.

DOVETAIL JOINTS

Beautiful corner joints that are the symbol of high-level craftsmanship can be made by dovetailing with the scroll saw. Scroll saw dovetailing is remarkably easy. One advantage of dovetailing with a scroll saw is that no special jigs or fixtures are needed; in fact, all that's needed are a good scroll saw with a table-tilt capability and a sharp, narrow blade with good tension.

Make a practice joint before attempting it on a major project. Make sure that your stock is of uniform width and the ends are cut square. Set the pieces on edge, with the choice surfaces (faces) to the outside. Determine which piece is to be the pin piece and which is to be the one with the tails. In Illus. 394 the tail piece is on the left and the pin piece is on the right. Start with the pin piece first. It is the more complex of the two parts to make. It's far easier to make the tails fit previously cut pins.

Lay out the spacing and angular marks for the pins on the end of the board. Usually angles of 14 to 15° are standard, with 15° recommended here simply because it's easy to find on the saw tilt scale. On the inside face draw a line square across the board to repre-

sent the thickness of the tail or other member of the joint. Then "square-in" lines extending from the end to the line on the inside face. This will now give you the left and right angle of the pins and their length. Study Illus. 395, which clearly shows the pin layout and how to make one of the bevel or angular cuts that forms one side of the pin.

To make the pin "bevel-ripping" cuts, as shown in Illus. 395, tilt the table correspondingly to 15°. You can only cut one side of each pin at this first table setting. Cut the full length of every pin, which is also shown in Illus. 395.

Next, to make the second cut on each pin you must do one of two things: Either reverse the blade so it cuts backwards, as shown in Illus. 396, and leave the table at the same adjustment, or simply tilt the table to the identical degree setting but in the other direction. Illus. 396 shows how to make the

Illus. 394. This through dovetail joint was cut on the scroll saw without the aid of any fixtures. This type of work can be done by anyone with the ability to follow a layout line. The piece on the left is the "tail"; the other piece is the "pin" piece.

Illus. 395. Begin by making the pins first. Here a bevel cut is being made to form one side of the pins. The layout lines are drawn at 15°, and the table is set to the same angle for these cuts. As shown here, the table is tilted left. All cuts are made by saving the layout lines.

Illus. 396. Cutting the second side of the pins. If you look closely at this unique procedure, you can see that the blade is installed backwards, so the teeth point away from the operator. The cut is made by pulling the work towards the operator, as shown. This technique works on all scroll saws that tilt only one way. Otherwise, the operator has the option to tilt the table to the right to make this second angular cut to form the pins.

second bevel cut, to form the pin, on saws that have tables that tilt in one direction only. Simply install the blade so the teeth face away from the operator, and make the cut by pulling the work towards you, as shown in Illus. 396.

Once all of the bevel-ripping cuts have been completed, adjust the table to a perfect 90° setting. Now, cut out the majority of the waste between the pins, as shown in Illus. 397. Carefully follow the layout line so that the pins are all of uniform length. You will have to leave little wedge-shaped waste pieces next to each pin. Study Illus. 397.

Remove the wedge-shaped waste pieces that remain on each side of the pin with a sharp knife. (See Illus. 398.) Practically any knife will handle this job—the only requirement is that the knife is sharp enough to slice off the end-grain fibres, as shown in Illus. 398. The completed pin member is shown in Illus. 399.

Making the tail member is easy, although accuracy in the layout and cutting is essential. Use the finished pin member as a pattern for laying out the tail member. Simply, but carefully, trace around it as shown in Illus. 400. Use a square and "strike off" the depth of the tails so they equal the thickness of the mating pin board.

Illus. 397. Once the pins have been cut on each side with the table tilted, the spaces between the pins are cut with the table set exactly to 90°. The on-the-spot turning capability of the saw is employed to advantage. All but the little "wedges" next to the pins are sawn away.

Illus. 398. The triangular waste next to the pins can be cut away with any sharp knife, as shown here. When this is done, the pins are completed.

Illus. 399. The completed pins. Note that the pencil layout lines (for the most part) have not been cut away.

Illus. 400. Align the mating pieces and very carefully transfer the outline of the pins to the second member, as shown. This is all that's involved in laying out the tails.

Sawing the tails is easy. However, it's imperative that you do not cut beyond your layout lines. It's especially important in cutting out the tails that you try to save the layout lines. Utilize the "on-the-spot" turning capability of the constant-tension saw to make the sharp inside corner cuts required for this job. (See Illus. 401.)

The joint should fit together without much problem provided you saved the line when cutting the tail member. This should create a tight joint that may require some tapping with a hammer and a scrap block to bring the joint together—exactly the type of fit you want!

Illus. 401. With the saw table still set at a perfect 90°, cut out the tails. Again, using the on-the-spot turning capabilities while saving the layout line is all that's involved in making the tails.

20
COMPOUND SAWING

Compound sawing is the process involving cutting on two or more sides of the workpiece. (See Illus. 402 and 403.) This is a popular band saw operation, but many unusual projects can also be made by compound-sawing on the scroll saw. In fact, because the scroll can make inside cutouts, there are some compound-sawing jobs that can only be performed with it. The weed and candle holders with piercing heart cutouts, shown in Illus. 404, are good examples of compound-sawing inside cutouts.

Compound sawing is limited only by the thickness of material you can cut on your saw. All of the projects shown were cut from stock 2 inches or less in thickness. *Caution:* Whenever sawing thick stock that approaches the capacity of the machine, make sure your fingers don't get pinched. (See Illus. 405 and review Chapter 14, Safety.)

Compound sawing simply involves laying out a pattern on two adjoining surfaces. (See Illus. 406–408.) The pattern does not have to be the same shape on both surfaces. In fact, different-shaped designs create some very interesting shapes.

Compound sawing is like *carving* out shapes. In fact, many woodcarvers use compound sawing to rough-out their carvings. And once the carving is formed by compound-sawing, the corners can sometimes be removed by tilting the table and making chamfering cuts, as discussed on page 219. The effectiveness of making chamfering cuts on workpieces that were previously formed by compound sawing depends entirely on the amount of detail and the type of shapes involved.

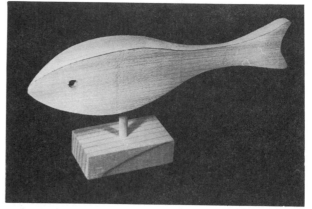

Illus. 402. *This fish project was given its shape by compound sawing with the scroll saw.*

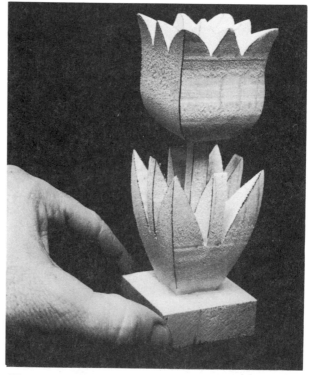

Illus. 403. *This compound-sawn dimensional tulip was cut from just one piece of wood 2 inches square.*

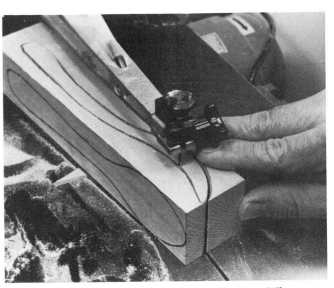

Illus. 405. Compound sawing a spoon project. Whenever sawing thick stock, always be careful that you don't pinch your fingers between the oscillating saw arm and the workpiece or, as shown here, under the blade clamp thumbscrew.

Illus. 404. Heart cutouts that were cut through two surfaces create these interesting projects. The candle is a metal cup insert.

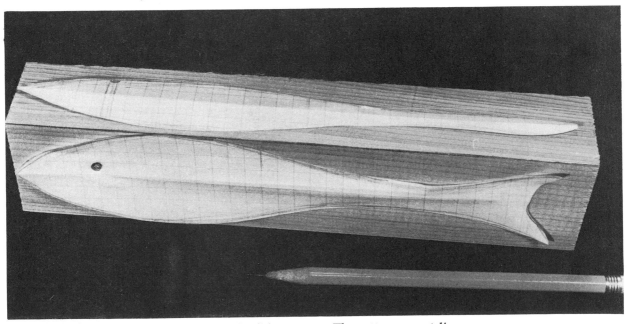

Illus. 406. The top and side profiles for the fish patterns. The patterns must line up at the ends.

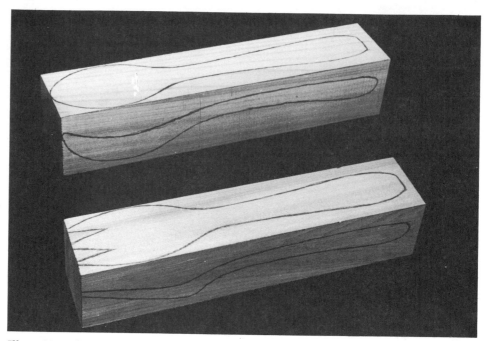

Illus. 407. These fork and spoon salad-servers patterns are ready for compound sawing. Here, the side views should be sawn first. See Illus. 405.

Illus. 408. Identical layouts on both surfaces should be done very accurately. Note the blade threading holes.

Once the workpiece is laid out with the patterns drawn on two surfaces you have to make a choice as to which of the two surfaces to saw first. Usually it will not make any difference, but sometimes you can save yourself some aggravation by thinking about the sawing sequence first. Select the first profile cutting that will have the fewest free scrap pieces once it is cut. After the first profile is cut out, return the scrap or waste pieces to their original locations so you have a fairly complete prismatic shape to safely and effectively cut out the second profile.

In Illus. 409, the top view is being cut first, rather than the side view. The reason the top view was chosen for the first cutting is because the waste piece will come off intact as one complete piece. Illus. 410 shows how the pieces are held together with tape. The pieces have to be held secure without any slippage until the second profile cut is completed. Sometimes it is advantageous to drive small nails into the scrap areas, use a drop of hot-melt as temporary glue, or use double-faced tape to secure the waste pieces while cutting out the second profile shape. In compound pierce-cutting, as shown in Illus. 411, the scrap is not a problem.

Illus. 409. Sawing the top-view profile shape of the fish project shown in Illus. 402. Note that when the entire cut is made, the waste is just one piece that's still totally intact.

Illus. 410. The second cut is made on the side profile of the fish project. Note that the pieces have been taped together; also note the number of scrap pieces that fell away as the cut progressed around the pattern.

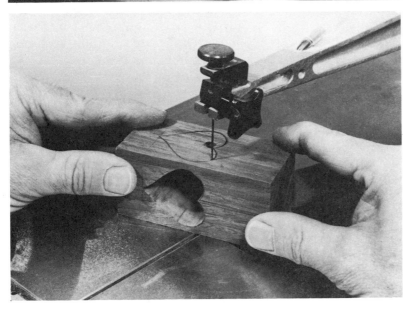

Illus. 411. Compound sawing an internal opening.

21
BEVEL SAWING

Bevel sawing involves any one of the wide range of cutting jobs that are performed with the saw table tilted. Inlays and some forms of marquetry could be included in this category, but individual chapters are devoted to these subjects. Bevel sawing is also done on the scroll saw to make the "pins" of dovetail joints. (See page 206.)

Bevel-sawing operations allow for some creative scroll-sawing projects, but this class of work is not easily performed on all scroll saws. Some saws do not have any table-tilting features. Others have tilting features that may present some serious problems, even preventing some bevel-sawing work from being performed at all. (See pages 36 and 37 in Chapter 2.) Therefore, the bevel-sawing capacities of a scroll saw will be enhanced considerably if the scroll saw has good table-tilting functions and a blade that cuts thick pieces.

One important point to note: when a bevel is sawed with the table tilted, the cut is being made through more material than just the normal thickness of the workpiece. For example, a board that's ¾ of an inch in normal thickness presents about 1⅛ inches of material for cutting when it is fed to the blade at a 45° tilt.

MAKING CUTOUTS

Almost any cutout can be sawed with the table tilted. However, bevel sawing is one area of scroll sawing in which the amount of detail in the shape dictates how accurately and "cleanly" the object can be cut. Increasing the amount of tilt or bevel, coupled with progressively greater detailing that involves sharp inside corners, proportionally reduces the capabilities of bevel sawing.

A relatively simple disc or doughnut shape, such as the letter "o," can be cut easily with 45° edges if desired. This is because there are no sharp inside corners on a letter "o," and the curve is fairly consistent regardless of its size. Any cutouts having an extremely small radius or sharp inside corners will create some very serious problems when cut on-the-bevel. Illus. 412 and 413 show this problem with the example of the Old-English style letter "s" that has been bevel-cut on a tilted table.

Illus. 414 shows random bevel cutting on the sides of a hexagon hanging lamp. With the cuts made at various widths, varying amounts of light shine through the lamp. (See page 192 and the *Scroll Saw Pattern Book* for more information on making hanging lamps with the scroll saw.)

Illus. 412. In bevel sawing, the wood is cut while supported on a tilted table. This produces the bevelled edges on the letters shown here. Inside corners, shown at the right, will not cut cleanly. See Illus. 413.

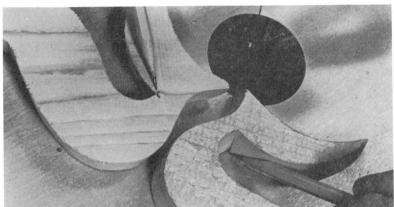

Illus. 413. A close look at the results of sharp inside cornering when bevel sawing. The little kerfs cut into the edges (back and front) cannot be eliminated unless the corners are cut on a radius, rather than sharply—as done here.

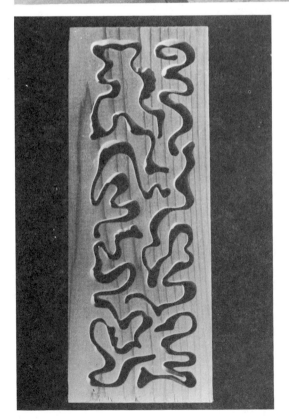

Illus. 414. A side panel for a hexagon lamp. The irregular lines were bevel-cut to varying widths, which permits a variable amount of light to shine through—making this a very interesting project.

ON-THE-SPOT-TURNS

When an on-the-spot turn is made in stock supported on a tilted table, the result is a cone-shaped piece that comes out of the bottom or the downside. (See Illus. 416.) Practice a few of these cuts on scrap pieces, trying both clockwise and counterclockwise turning directions. With the table tilted to the left, you'll probably find it easier to make the turn feeding the stock in one direction rather than the other. The reverse will be true with the table tilted in the opposite direction. This will be helpful to you when bevel-cutting some fairly detailed designs.

INCISED BEVEL-CUT SIGNS

Making incised bevel-cut signs, as shown in Illus. 417, is another unusual application of bevel sawing. This type of cutting calls for skills similar to bevel on-the-spot turning. A certain amount of "kerfing-in" at some corners, along with a little burning, is to be expected on some surfaces. The density of the wood species selected may have some influence on the level of cutting difficulty for this type of bevel sawing. Butternut, ¾ of an inch thick, was used for the sign shown in Illus. 417.

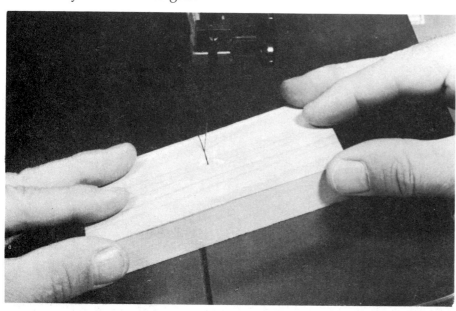

Illus. 415. "Backing out" after making an on-the-spot-turn with the table tilted for bevel sawing. See Illus. 416.

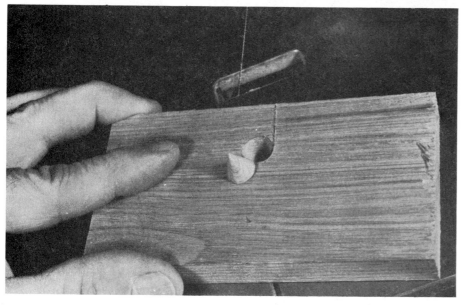

Illus. 416. Here's the result: a perfect cone-shaped dimple cut into the bottom surface.

Illus. 417. An example of the type of incised bevel-cut signs that can be cut on the scroll saw. Note the scraps in the foreground.

Select a fine blade and drill the smallest possible hole at an outside corner of each letter for blade threading. (See Illus. 418.) The angles of the drilling and the sawing must be fairly close to equal. The angle for sawing of stock ¾ inches thick can vary from 14 to 18°. This will give approximately a ½- to ⅝-inch width at the face of the letter when the V cut is made all the way into the thickness of the board. To determine the maximum width for the letters, just make an on-the-spot turn in a scrap piece of the same thickness and measure the diameter at the base of the cone-shaped piece. Lay out the letter patterns on the workpiece with the widest part of any letter not exceeding the diameter of the cone produced by a bevelled on-the-spot turn.

The scrap test piece used for the on-the-spot turn can be cut in half and used as a drilling guide. (See Illus. 418.) This will ensure that the holes are drilled at the same angle the table is tilted to. It's best to drill the blade-threading holes at outside corners rather than inside ones.

When all the holes are drilled, thread the blade through the workpiece and begin sawing. *Caution*: Make sure you feed the stock so that the slant of the letter face is towards the center. With the table tilted left, the letter is cut out by sawing clockwise around the letter. Also, make the cut on very sharp turns by spinning the workpiece in a clockwise direction. Always make every sharp turn (both inside and outside ones) with the stock moving in a clockwise direction. (See Illus. 419.) This means that on some turns you will have to rotate the work almost 360° to stay on the line. (See Illus. 419.)

The techniques will obviously require some study and practice, but the results are impressive and unusual. (Illus. 421 shows a back view of the completed sign.)

Illus. 418. Drilling holes at an angle for threading the blade. The guide block helps to drill at the proper angle. The block itself is half a piece of scrap used for the on-the-spot turn with the table tilted to the desired angle.

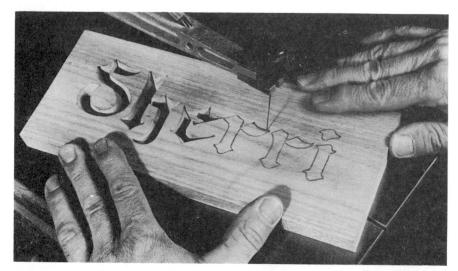

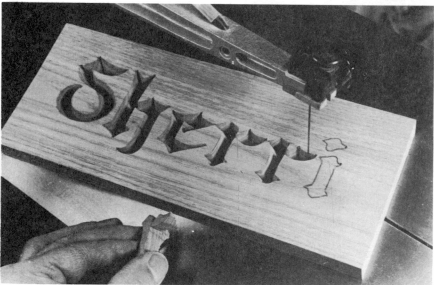

Illus. 419. Making bevel-sawn incise-lettering cutouts. The point of the "r" being cut here is best made with a clockwise feed. That will mean making almost a full 360° on-the-spot turn to go around this "point" of the letter.

Illus. 420. Here is the intact waste from the letter "r".

Illus. 421. A rear view of the sign shown in Illus. 417. Note that all of the cone-shaped cutouts are located where clockwise on-the-spot turns were made to complete very sharp cornering cuts.

SAWING CHAMFERS

Another, much less complicated technique, is bevel-sawing to chamfer edges. (See Illus. 422–424.) This operation is useful on some cutouts, especially small ones that would be impossible to chamfer safely with a router. Scroll-sawed chamfers on any size cutout are not as smooth or uniform as those cut with a router, no matter how skilled one is with a scroll saw. However, if you don't have a router, the scroll saw is the best choice. Also, the scroll saw does do the job with considerably less flying dust. If you want to round over an edge without a router, it's easiest to chamfer first and then file, rasp, or sand the corners off to get a rounded edge. (See Illus. 425.)

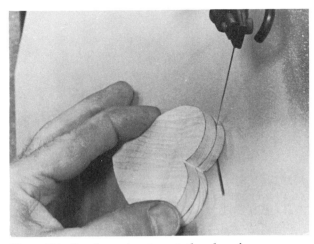

Illus. 424. Bevel sawing to cut the chamfer.

Illus. 422. These corners are cut away to make a chamfered edge.

Illus. 425. Rounding over the chamfer corners with a file.

CONCENTRIC BEVEL CUTS

Concentric bevel cuts made in a flat board make stackable rings that can be utilized for a wide variety of wood-forming jobs. (See Illus. 426 and 427.) There is a very popular specialty machine available that looks somewhat like a headstock lathe; its only function is to cut stackable rings from flat stock. The cost of this machine alone is more than the cost of many of the medium-priced scroll saws, and about one-half to one-fourth the price of the most expensive constant-tension scroll saws available. However, a constant-tension scroll saw can not only do the same work, it can also do a much wider variety of jobs with a greater capacity than this ring-making machine.

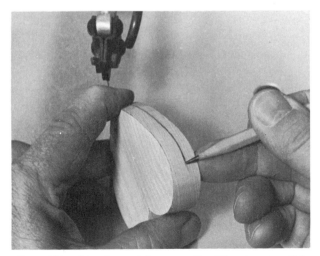

Illus. 423. Gauging with a pencil will put a parallel line along irregular surfaces.

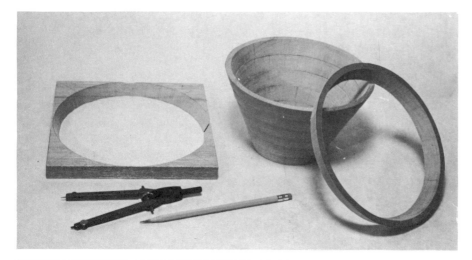

Illus. 426. These concentric bevel-sawn rings, cut from a single, flat board, can be stacked to make hollow vessels, bowls, dishes, etc.

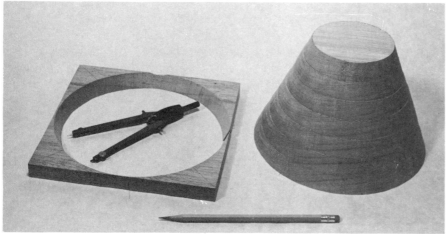

Illus. 427. Hollow forms can be used for various bases or pedestals for art work, lamps, etc.

Bevel-cut rings are easy to make. Some experimentation will be necessary to determine the appropriate combination of bevel angle and the best width to cut the rings. This will vary with the thickness of stock. To give you some idea of where to start, Illus. 428 shows an 8-inch square ¾ inches in thickness. Concentric rings were marked off at ⁵⁄₁₆-inch increments along a radius. When bevel-sawn with the table set to 22°, the pieces line up pretty well. If you want to form a bowl with sides angled at 45°, then rings ¾ inch wide, sawn from material ¾ inch thick, will stack. You have to find the combination of ring width and bevel angle that works best for the material and the slant angle wanted. Once this is determined, lay out and drill the blade threading holes. (See Illus. 429.) A little scrap of wood cut to the bevel angle helps to guide the angle direction of the drill.

Remember, every ring should be cut with the work held in the same relative location to the blade for each successive cut. Usually it's easiest to keep the workpiece to the left of the blade, as shown in Illus. 430 and 431.

To carry the bevel-sawn stacking ring concept a step or two further, consider the same idea, done the same way, but of any one of many different forms other than a perfectly round form. How about stacked oval rings, stacked round rings, or stacked clover pedal, heart, or leaf shapes?

One final note: The sign shown in Illus. 432 has all of the edges bevelled or slanted in one direction. This can only be accomplished with a blade that can cut in all directions without a need for the workpiece to be rotated—that is, a spiral blade. (For more information on spiral blades, see page 46.)

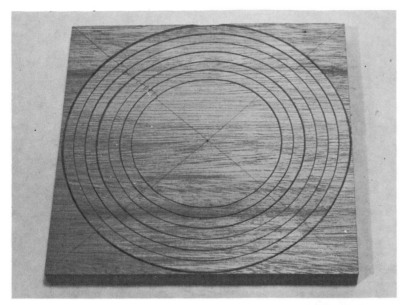

Illus. 428. An 8-inch-square board ¾ inch thick produces stackable rings ⁵⁄₁₆ inch wide with 22° edge bevels. Here all the rings have already been cut. Note the minimum of material lost because of the saw kerfs.

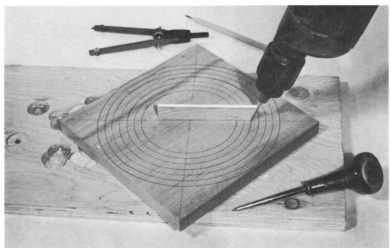

Illus. 429. Here note how the flat board was marked and the blade threading holes were drilled and guided at the bevel-sawing angle.

Illus. 430. A close-up look at the concentric-bevel sawing operation. Cut right on the line.

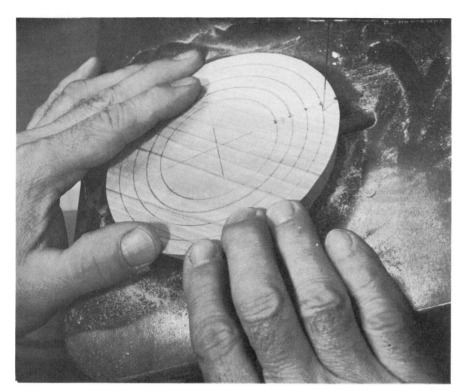

Illus. 431. Every ring should be cut with the stock kept to the left side of the blade, so the rings are tangent to the line of cut.

Illus. 432. All the edges of these letters slant in the same direction. This can only be accomplished with a spiral blade that's capable of sawing in all directions without rotating the workpiece.

22
INLAYS, RELIEFS, AND RECESSING

A lot of exciting projects can be made by employing the basic principles of bevel cutting in scroll-saw inlay work. The potential for inlaying projects is almost unlimited. You can even incorporate inlay work into wood turnings. (See Illus. 433.) And, by taking the basic idea a step or two further, you can make various designs that are raised in relief above the background surface (Illus. 434) or set various designs below the surface, like the object in Illus. 435.

It was only when constant-tension scroll saws were perfected that the inlay work shown in this chapter could be effectively made. Prior to the refinement of scroll saw design, inlay work was pretty well limited to very thin pieces of wood. (In fact, the term "inlay" has almost become synonymous with veneer work and marquetry. Essentially, for some marquetry work, the same concepts do apply. See page 244 for more information concerning inlays in marquetry.) Now the technique can be utilized to make objects with great design detail in thick stock. All of the inlay examples shown in this chapter are done on stock that's ¾ inch thick.

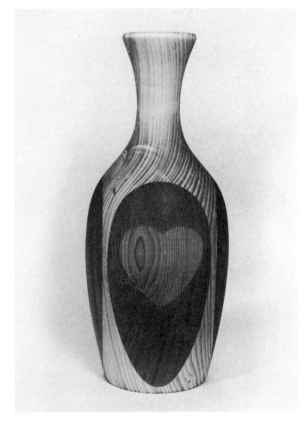

Illus. 433. A simple scroll-sawn heart inlay makes the focal point for this turned vase.

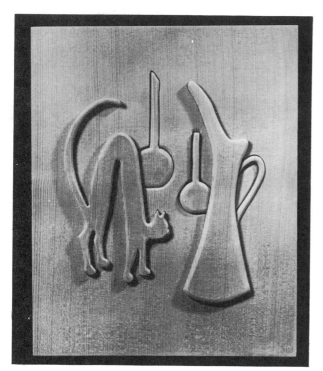

Illus. 434. When slightly modified principles of bevel sawing are used, designs can be raised in relief above the background surface.

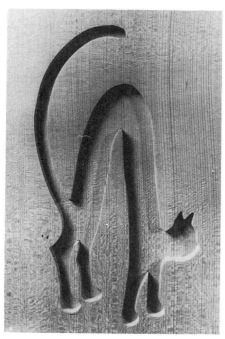

Illus. 435. Designs partially dropped through the workpiece created this engraved look; note that there is no visible trace of the saw cut. It would be difficult to cut detail this fine if a router were used.

SOLID WOOD INLAYS

The objective in solid wood inlay is to fit the pieces so tightly together that no space at all exists in the joint line. Even the thinnest and smallest fret blades will leave undesirable kerf spaces or cracks between the fitted pieces. This space can be eliminated entirely by tilting the table slightly, somewhere between one to eight or ten degrees for making the cuts.

Illus. 436 shows the relationship of the variables involved when solid wood inlays are bevel-sawed. The variables that must be coordinated are the blade width, the stock thicknesses, and the preferred angle of table tilt. Because the background stock and the inlay material are cut simultaneously, as in stack-cutting (page 171, Chapter 15), the two pieces must be temporarily fastened together. This can be accomplished by using a little rubber cement, masking tape, a drop of hot-melt glue, or what I often prefer—small pieces of double-faced tape.

Trial and error is the easiest way to determine the optimum amount of table tilt that is suitable for the blade width and stock thickness being used. If you change blade widths or material thickness between jobs, the saw table will have to be readjusted. For a flush inlay, the opening of the bevel-cut background has to be equal to that of the bevel-cut inlay. This is shown in Illus. 437. The results desired in making the flush inlay are shown in Illus. 438.

Illus. 439–444 show the step-by-step procedures for making a simple flush heart inlay. However, before starting, make sure you have a scroll saw that can produce a perfectly straight and true cut surface in the combined thickness of the two pieces that require cutting. If there is any "belly"-like bulges or the blade drifts and wanders, all of your efforts will be wasted. Also, use fine blades so the threading hole will be as small as possible. The blade must be tensioned sufficiently to obtain a true cut, which means that initially blades will break more frequently. However, eventually you will work out a satisfactory compromise.

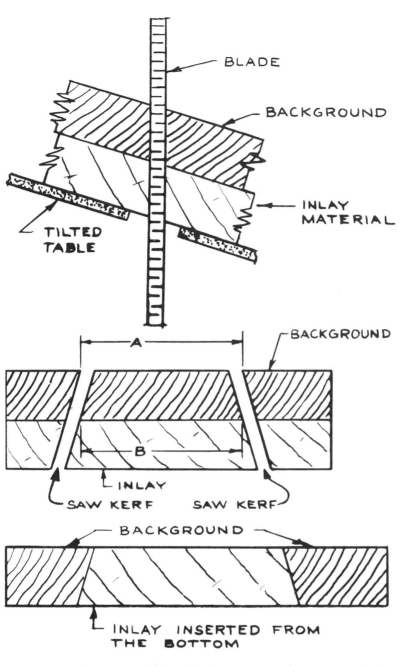

BLADE

BACKGROUND

INLAY
MATERIAL

TILTED
TABLE

Illus. 436. The relationship of the various factors involved in bevel sawing solid inlay material.

BACKGROUND

A

B

INLAY

SAW KERF   SAW KERF

Illus. 437. When the correct table tilt angle is used for sawing, the distance of "a" will be exactly equal to that of "b."

BACKGROUND

INLAY INSERTED FROM
THE BOTTOM

Illus. 438. This flush bevel-cut solid-wood inlay is an absolutely perfect fit; no saw kerf spaces are visible.

Illus. 439. Begin with two scrap pieces of stock equal to the thickness of the proposed workpieces. Tape them together for a test cut to check for the correct table tilt adjustment.

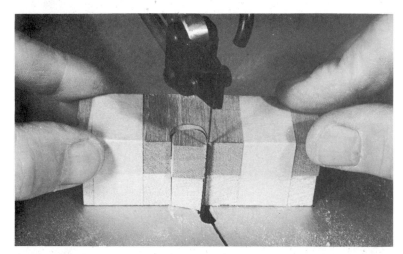

Illus. 440. Making the test cut. A simple circular cut, as shown, is sufficient.

Illus. 441. When the angle of the cut is correct, the upper piece will slip snugly into the lower cutout.

Illus. 442. Use the scrap test piece to help line up the correct drill angle for blade threading. The hole location is selected at a less conspicuous inside corner. The workpieces are arranged for a bottom inserted inlay (Illus. 438), with the light wood going into the background of darker wood. The cut will be made with the workpiece rotated clockwise into the blade. If the cut is made in a counterclockwise feed direction, the slant would bevel outward, and you will have the dark piece inlaying the light piece with a top insertion.

Illus. 443. The sawing is completed and the inlay is in place. Note the small hole, which can be filled.

Illus. 444. The flush inlay on the left is completed. The scrap pieces on the right will be thrown away.

The stacking arrangement of the two pieces and the direction that you feed the workpiece into the blade have to be thought out before you drill the blade hole, as shown in Illus. 442. The way you drill the hole and the way you feed the material into the blade (clockwise or counterclockwise) will determine if the inlay will fit into the background piece the way you planned it to. (See Illus. 443 and 444.)

The inlay can be planned and cut out so it will either be inserted from the bottom or it is inserted into the background piece from the top. Either way is perfectly acceptable as long as you plan it that way. The top insertion is preferred if you're gluing the inlay into the background along the bevelled-cut edges. With a bottom insertion, there is a tendency for the glue to be pushed up and out on to the top face of the project. This is not desirable.

INLAYS FOR WOODTURNINGS

The procedures used for inlays for wood turnings are essentially the same procedures as those just described. (See Illus. 445–450.) Inlays are simply set into boards that are laminated or glued together to make the blank for turning. The inlaid pieces are turned as usual along with the other parts that comprise the turning. The key is careful planning with a pre-established shape and contour that best takes advantage of the inlay design. Although the inlay shown in Illus. 445–450 is on a spindle-turning project, the same idea can be applied to many types and kinds of turnings. Bowls, lidded containers, plates, etc., all can be glued together with stock having flush inlays.

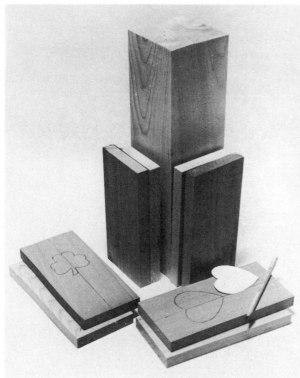

Illus. 446. The test cutting block is used to check the correct table-tilt angle.

Illus. 445. These pieces and layout have been selected for a laminated turning blank with flush inlays.

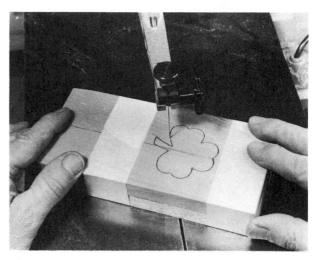

Illus. 447. Bevel sawing the inlay. The background material is on top. The material is fed counterclockwise into the blade.

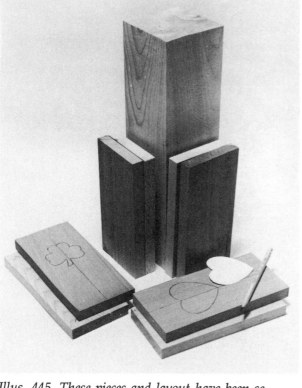

Illus. 448. The inlays are cut and inserted.

Illus. 449. The turning blank glued together.

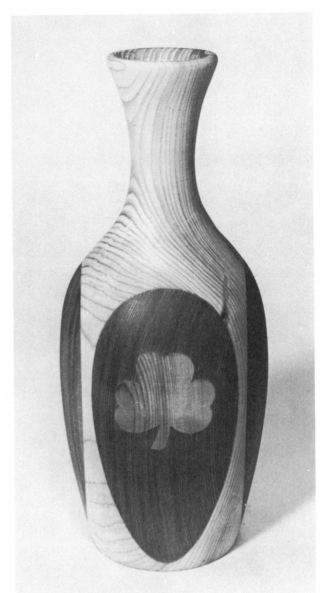

Illus. 450. The completed turning. See Illus. 433.

SILHOUETTES

Bevel sawing to make tight fitting joinery is a procedure that can be applied whenever you want to eliminate a saw kerf. The silhouettes shown in Illus. 451–455 are good examples. The interconnected cuts fit together perfectly because the saw kerf has been eliminated in the same way flush inlays are made. Since both pieces are cut simultaneously, the margin for error has been eliminated.

The patterns for silhouettes can be en-larged from side view photos taken with an instant camera. The enlargement patterns can be made by the graph-square technique or by using a pantograph. The photos can also be enlarged on an office copier that has enlargement capabilities. (Conventional en-largement methods are discussed in Chapter 16.)

The concept of making irregular joints that are gap-free can also be applied to wood bowl and plate turnings, cutting boards, box designs, and many other projects.

Illus. 451. Interconnecting silhouettes are bevel-cut at the joint lines to make tight fits and to eliminate saw kerfs.

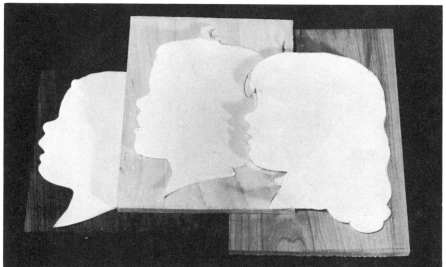

Illus. 452. Paper patterns and wood pieces of contrasting colors are selected and arranged for overlapping.

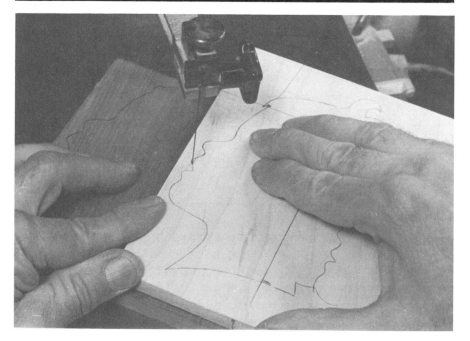

Illus. 453. When bevel sawing with one piece over the other, as in inlay sawing, hold the pieces temporarily together with double-faced tape.

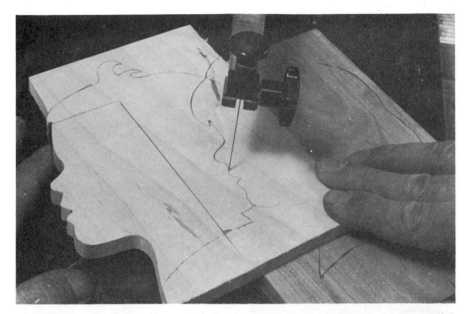

Illus. 454. Cutting the second joint in the same manner.

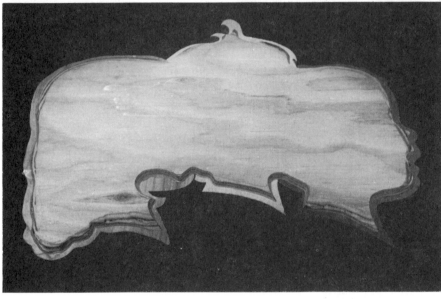

Illus. 455. This rear view shows pieces glued to a piece of plywood for reinforcement.

"SCULPTURE" INLAYS

Inlays that look like sculptures can be made by working the surfaces with contoured carving, texturing, etc. Some of the edges can even be worked or rounded over, as shown in Illus. 456–458. However, inlays with rounded-over edges tend to have deep shadows, and the tight fit produced by bevel-sawing cannot always be fully appreciated visually. For example, compare Illus. 458 and 459.

Because internal cutouts can be made using extremely thin blades that require very small entry holes, projects such as that shown in Illus. 459 are enticing to the scroll saw user. For this class of work, the table *is not* tilted. The rounding over camouflages the kerf-spacing shadow. Interesting and attractive wall plaques similar to the one shown in Illus. 459 are possible even with the most basic design patterns. The one problem with this technique, however, is that some method must be employed to hold the reinserted cutout in place. Usually, it's glued to a thin backing board.

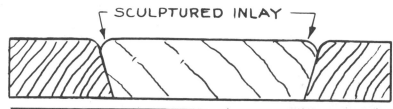

SCULPTURED INLAY

Illus. 456. The essentials of a sculptured inlay.

Illus. 457. Note the rounded-over edges on both parts.

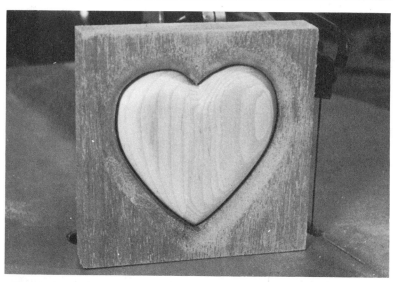

Illus. 458. The inlay is in place, and there is no kerf spacing, just a shadow.

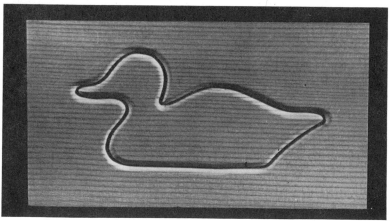

Illus. 459. This is not an inlay. It's simply a cutout with rounded-over edges. The shadow hides the saw kerf spacing. See Illus. 460.

Illus. 460 shows a bevel-sawn cutout with a sculptured look. It is not an inlay. When making a bevel-sawn cutout, select a sawing angle that will not only close the saw kerf space, but also allows the cutout to be pushed out so it's in relief. (See Illus. 461.) Rather than attempting to make a glue line between the two bevel-sawn surfaces, simply run a fillet around the back side. Otherwise, when you glue on the edges, glue could be pushed up with the inserted piece; the result could be a messy job to clean up.

PICTURES IN RELIEF

Some especially interesting picture projects can be made by combining various techniques. (See Illus. 462–468.)

Think carefully about the table tilt and the appropriate feed direction before starting to saw out the parts. Even though the table tilt is adjusted so that the kerf can be eliminated, all of your work will be wasted if the cutout is made with the wrong feed direction of the workpiece. Determine beforehand whether the workpiece must be rotated into the blade with a clockwise or a counterclockwise stock rotation when making the cut.

Illus. 462 shows all of the pieces cut out; some of the pieces will be raised in relief. The end result is shown in Illus. 463. Small router bits can sometimes be used to round over corners. Usually, however, small pieces and parts are too small to be safely cut with the router. Use whatever means available that matches your tooling. The interesting effect of having some pieces in relief and other pieces not in relief can be further dramatized by staining individual pieces different colors. (See Illus. 468.)

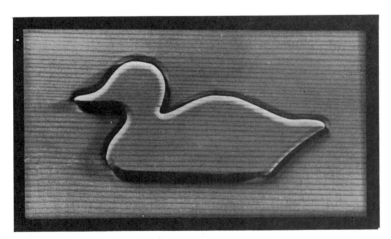

Illus. 460. This is a bevel-sawn cutout, not an inlay. The inlay bevel-cutting technique is employed to close the kerf, and the angle is such that it places the cutout in half relief to the background.

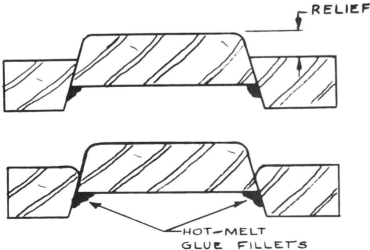

Illus. 461. When bevel sawing for a tight relief fit, you can round some or all of the exposed corners.

233

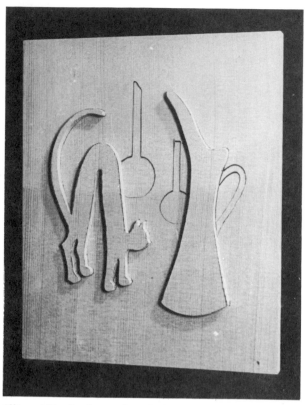

Illus. 462. *A picture in relief. Some elements will be flush, and others will be raised in relief.*

Illus. 463. *Here is the final result: a combination of flush and relief pieces, all with rounded edges, that make an eye-catching project.*

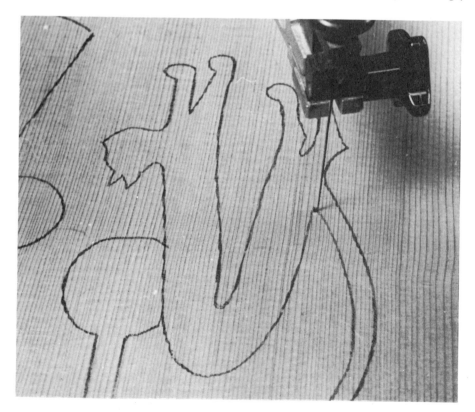

Illus. 464. *This blade has been threaded for sawing. Note that the blade entry is at the sharp intersection of the tail and body. The feed direction will be clockwise into the blade with the table tilted to the left. For a raised bevel, cut in relief.*

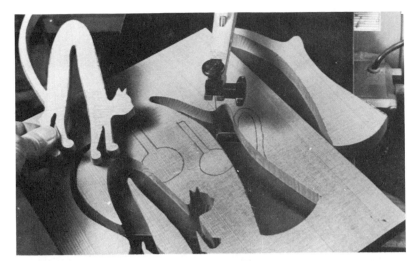

Illus. 465. All of the parts that will be in relief are cut on the bevel.

Illus. 466 and 467 (left and below). Rounding over edges with tools. Follow this procedure with sanding.

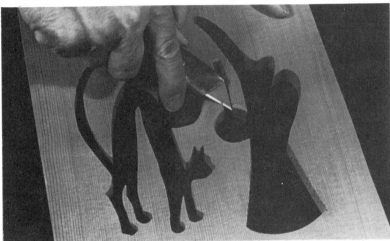

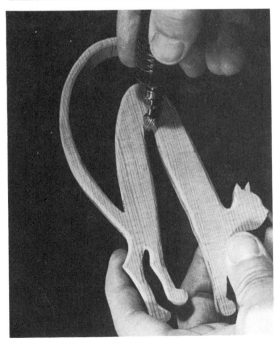

Illus. 467.

Illus. 468. Staining pieces various colors before inserting them adds interest and variety to the final project.

You can also work some designs into the background surface by setting the cutouts inward so they are recessed. This is also achieved by bevel-sawing, as shown in Illus. 469. Illus. 435, page 224, shows a picture with a clean, engraved look. This technique can be used to improve the dimensional effects of signs and pictorial scenes. The recessed pieces can be taken out and stained or painted for sharp contrast and then reinserted. If the material protruding out of the opposite or back side (Illus. 470) is objectionable, it can be removed with a belt sander or hand plane.

COMBINING TECHNIQUES

Flush inlaying, relief projection, sculpturing edges, and recessing surfaces are techniques that can be combined. In addition, you can use contrasting woods in relief or recessed inlays. (See Illus. 471 and 472.) Finally, consider combining unlike materials—such as a brass inlay in some exotic hardwood as a piece of jewellery or a personalized monogram inlaid in bone or ivory on a jewellery box. Use any of the hard plastics or make the inlay from a knot. The combinations of techniques and materials that can be used are almost endless.

Illus. 469. Recessing is also achieved by bevel sawing. Note once more that there is no saw kerf space.

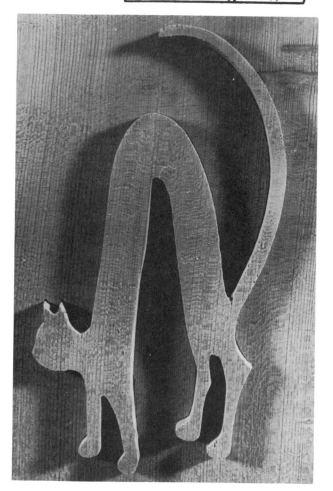

Illus. 470. A look at the rear back-side of the recessed object shown in Illus. 435 on page 224. This extra material can be worked flush to the back with a belt sander or by hand with a plane.

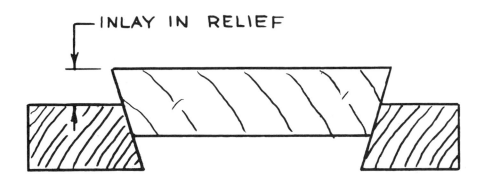

INLAY IN RELIEF

Illus. 471. Using a contrasting material for inlay relief.

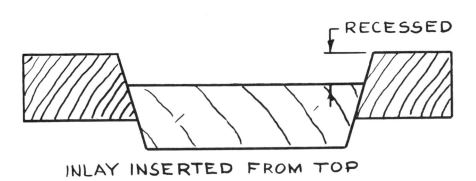

RECESSED

INLAY INSERTED FROM TOP

Illus. 472. Using contrasting material for recessed inlay.

23
MARQUETRY BASICS

Marquetry is the process of cutting and joining different colored veneers together to create a picture or design that can be glued to another flat surface. (See Illus. 473 and 474.) This ancient art form, dating back to the works of early Egyptians and Romans, has grown in sophistication over the centuries.

Marquetry is a vast and fairly complex subject to master, and only the fundamentals can be covered here. There are, however, other sources that will help those who want to learn more about this craft. One book strongly recommended is the *Modern Marquetry Handbook*, published by the Marquetry Society of America and edited by Harry Hobbs and Allan Fitchett. It covers all the fundamentals of marquetry. Membership in the Marquetry Society of America is open to everyone for $15.00 per year. The Society also publishes an informative monthly newsletter and supports a nonprofit pattern library service for members. The address of

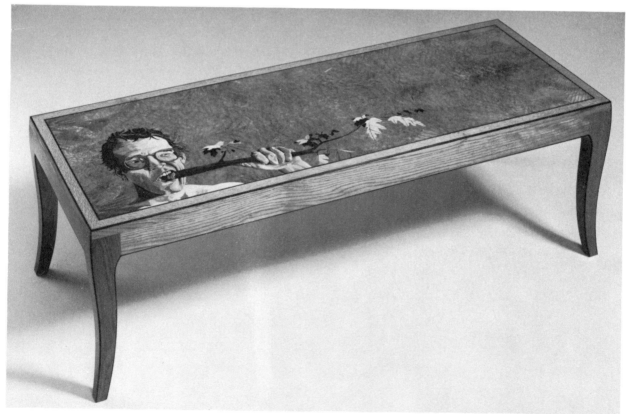

Illus. 473. This marquetry tabletop, entitled Primal Woodworking, *is by Silas Kopf, one of today's premier marquetry experts.*

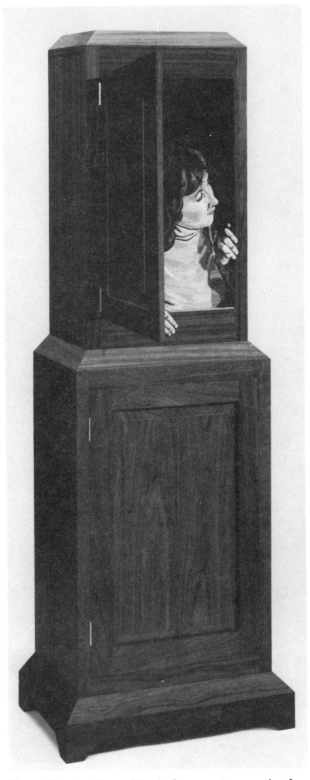

Illus. 474. Another whimsical marquetry creation by Silas Kopf entitled Linda. *The upper door is actually flat with concealed hinges, but the artist has effectively presented a different impression.*

the Society is: P.O. Box 224, Lindenhurst, NY 11757.

Here I will discuss two different techniques utilized by scroll saw users who do marquetry: stack sawing and bevel sawing.

Remember these general guidelines when doing marquetry: slow your saw down considerably (if possible), especially when cutting very intricate designs. A variable-speed saw is a great asset for marquetry because it can slow the cutting strokes per minute so you have better overall control. Also, use a very fine fret blade, such as one in a 2/0 size, for marquetry. (Review Chapter 18, Sawing Small Pieces and Thin Stock.)

The following discussions of marquetry basics focus on two different techniques utilized by scroll saw users who do marquetry: stack sawing and bevel sawing.

STACK SAWING

The stack-sawing method of sawing veneers is referred to by those who do marquetry as the "pad method." This is a fairly easy way to make veneer inlays. The pad system allows you to produce multiple projects all at one time and is fast, easy, and beneficial to production-type marquetry operations. The major disadvantage is that the cut pieces have saw kerf gaps showing in the finished product.

In pad- or stack-sawing, many layers of veneer are cut at one time. The layers are planned to include any number of different species or colors of wood that can be effectively cut in one operation. The saw table setting should be square, at 90° to the blade. An auxiliary table with a small blade-hole opening should be attached with double-faced tape. (See Illus. 475.)

Illus. 476–487 show the steps involved in pad- or stack-marquetry. Illus. 488 shows the saw kerf spacing problem that's typical in this method of veneer marquetry. The filled-in space is always more evident when two darker pieces meet each other. The saw kerf is not as noticeable when a light wood butts next to a dark wood, which is also shown in Illus. 488.

Illus. 475. Use an auxiliary table with a small blade hole for veneer marquetry work.

Illus. 476. Three layers of different-colored veneers will be used to make three identical initial panels, each resulting in a different combination of veneers.

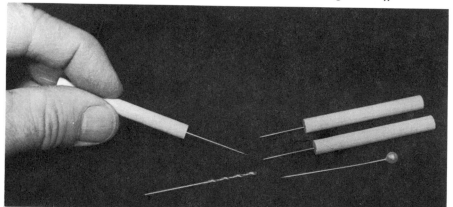

Illus. 477. These tools are used for making blade threading holes in veneers. Needles driven into a dowel work well.

Illus. 478. Here the three layers of veneer are stacked and taped to a piece of corrugated cardboard. A hole is made for the blade.

240

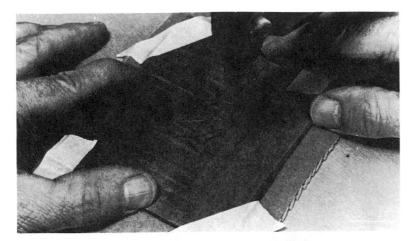

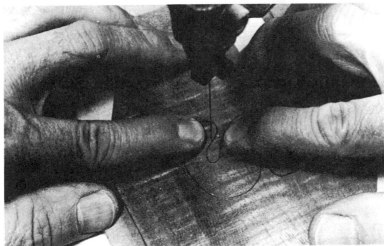

Illus. 479. The blade is threaded and clamped, ready for sawing.

Illus. 480. The feed can be in any direction because the cut is vertical. The pressure has to be close to the blade to prevent chattering and chipping. A foot switch is recommended to keep both hands free to maintain pressure.

Illus. 481. Once all of the pieces are cut out, shift or interchange them with each other for optimum color combinations. Insert the inlay face up into the background piece and apply gummed veneer tape over the face, as shown here. Totally cover all saw kerfs with the tape.

Illus. 482. Glue mixed with wood sanding dust can be used as a filler.

Illus. 483. Work the filler into the saw kerf gaps on the back, untaped side. Remove excess with a putty knife.

Illus. 484. Glue and clamp the veneer assembly to a rigid backer, such as plywood or hardboard.

Illus. 485. After the glue has cured, remove the veneer tape from the face. A slightly dampened rag will soften the tape adhesive. Avoid excess moisture.

Illus. 486. Once the tape has softened, scrape the surface clean with a putty knife.

Illus. 487. Sand and finish as desired. The result is three identical inlays with dark inlaid into light, light inlaid to dark, etc.

Illus. 488. Note the saw kerf visibility that results from the stack-sawn or pad method. It is far more evident with dark-wood-to-dark-wood joints than with light-wood-to-dark-wood joints, as shown below.

BEVEL-SAWING

The bevel-sawing method is based upon exactly the same procedures discussed in Chapter 22. This is the technique preferred by most marquetry veterans because the results look much more professional. The table must be tilted to an appropriate angle so the kerf will be closed when the inlay is inserted into the background. Although this method has the advantage of no visible kerf in the assembly, there are two disadvantages. First, you can only create or saw out one marquetry picture (or inlay) at a time. Secondly, there is more wasted veneer with this method. However, there are "tricks of the trade" professionals use to minimize waste of quality, expensive veneers.

Illus. 489–498 show how to bevel-cut a veneer inlay for an initial and insert it into a background. The same technique is used to make more complicated pictures because each design element is cut out individually, one part at a time. Each successive cutout part becomes another inlay into the background. Work continues until all pieces or parts have been cut out, and inlaid according to the pattern. All pieces are taped to the background. When done, the entire assembly of taped-together pieces of veneer is bonded to a plywood or hardboard panel. This panel then becomes a part for a piece of furniture, a tray, a box lid, a framed wall hanging, or other project.

Marquetry is a very challenging art form with many levels of difficulty and proficiency. It calls for patience, artistry, and a background of basic wood-crafting skills—as well as a knowledge of how to select and handle fine wood veneers.

Illus. 489. The design for the inlay is marked out on the selected veneer.

Illus. 490. Two scrap pieces of suitable thicknesses are cut so the correct table-tilt angle can be checked.

Illus. 491. The correct table-tilt angle is discovered when the inlay fits flush and into the background without any kerf spacing.

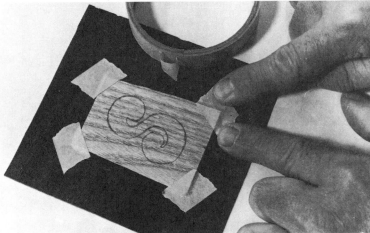

Illus. 492. Position the inlay over the background.

Illus. 493. Make a blade threading hole. See Illus. 478.

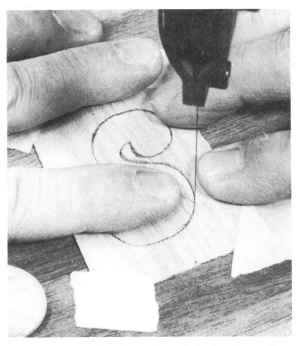

Illus. 494. Bevel sawing through both pieces. Here the table is tilted to the left; the workpiece will be fed counterclockwise into the blade.

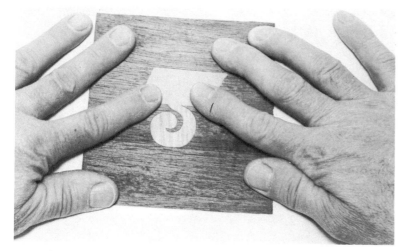

Illus. 495. The inlay is set into the face of the background and secured with veneer tape.

Illus. 496. The reverse (or gluing side) exhibits a nice snug fit with no kerf spacing.

Illus. 497. The waste pieces are at left. The completed inlaid initial is at the right.

Illus. 498 (right). An enlarged close-up of the bevel-cut veneer inlay. Note the tight fit and the fact that there is no trace of the blade threading hole.

24
SAWING NONWOOD MATERIALS

The scroll saw will cut a wide variety of materials other than wood. Many different kinds of metals (ferrous and nonferrous), a variety of plastics, paper, cloth, and even—to some extent—glass and other hard, brittle materials can be cut. A scroll saw can even cut leather, bone, ivory, cork, rubber, and felt.

To cut these materials, you need blades in a variety of different sizes and types. It's also important that you can control the speed, usually to a reduction in cutting strokes per minute, to ensure the proper cutting rate and blade wear. Remember, too, that some saws have adjustments to reduce the length of the cutting stroke, which is an advantage when sawing thinner materials. The scroll-saw-owner's manual should be consulted for the manufacturer's specific recommendations when cutting nonwood or other unusual materials.

Absolute recommendations concerning blade selection, speeds, feeds, coolants, etc., for specific materials are not included in this chapter because there are so many variables that such information will be virtually useless in many situations. Furthermore, such information is so easy to misinterpret. For example, there are so many different kinds of plastics on the market; each reacts differently to various blade configurations, cutting speed, feed rate, and temperature or friction. Though the following advice will prove applicable in many situations, it's always best to experiment with a specific material with your own saw.

SAWING PLASTICS

The word "plastic" refers to everything from low-density Styrofoam® to high-density phenolic and thermosetting plastics such as polyester and epoxy that's reinforced with fibreglass. Generally, the harder and denser plastics will often be cut like the hardwoods. Always select blades with teeth as coarse as possible, but that do not cause chipping on the lower surface as the blade exits through the material. (See Illus. 499.) Remember to always have two or three teeth in contact with the material thickness at all times. Thinner material will require a blade with more teeth. In general, the medium-hard plastics such as acrylics like Plexiglas™, Lucite™, and Acrylite™ should be cut with blades that have some set for clearance so the blades do not heat up so quickly. For sawing material ¼ inch thick and thinner, the blades should have 9 to 12 teeth per inch. (See Illus. 500.) Six to nine teeth are recommended when sawing acrylics over ¼ inch thick.

If sufficient clearance is provided in the design of the blade, 1,000 strokes per minute should be satisfactory. Blade friction coupled with short cutting strokes are the usual, major problems. When the blade heats up, the plastic softens and fuses itself together. (See Illus. 501–504, which compare cutting capabilities of sawing plastics with and without a protective covering or mask.) This thin layer of adhesive-backed paper or even an application of masking tape has a definite cooling effect. When stack-cutting, much

Illus. 499. Clear acrylic plastic ¼ inch thick cuts clean on the scroll saw. Two requirements when cutting are that you use slow cutting speeds and a coarser blade.

Illus. 500. A comparison of surface qualities of cuts on ¼-inch acrylic. Above: a scroll saw cut with a No. 7 skip-tooth blade, 12 teeth per inch. At center: a band saw cut. Below: a circular saw cut. Note the chipping at the surfaces on the center and lower pieces.

Illus. 501. Sawing without the protective paper masking. Plastics have a tendency to soften and fuse together when being sawed. Here you can see the molten plastic gumming the blade and hardening on the underside; this causes difficulty in feeding.

Illus. 502. The result of heat during cutting. The cut edge has "globs" of melted plastic clinging to it. See Illus. 503 and 504.

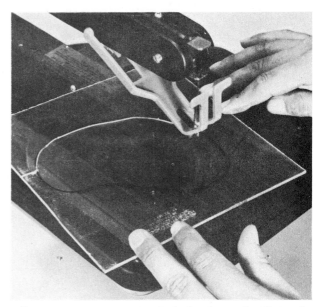

Illus. 503. Tape that is applied to both surfaces and that is cut under the same conditions as the unmasked pieces, which are shown in Illus. 501 and 502, cuts much cooler. See the results in Illus. 504.

Illus. 505. Sawing unmasked plastic on the Dremel saw.

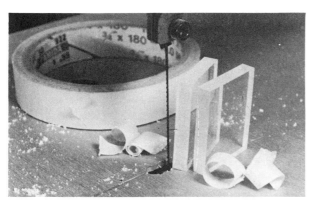

Illus. 504. Tape removed. Masked acrylic plastic cuts cooler than unmasked acrylic plastic. Note that the cut surface is cleaner than when sawn uncovered or unmasked.

cooler sawing will result if all layers are covered with masking tape. Use rubber cement to glue the masked pieces together.

The dust blower is another important help when sawing plastics. Adjust it so that it directs a stream of air to help cool the blade. One tip offered in the Dremel Power Tool Guide is: "Lubricate the line to be cut by rubbing it with the corner of a block of paraffin or a crayon." (See Illus. 505.) A slow and steady feed rate is best.

Softer plastics such as untempered polystyrene and polyethylenes will require slower speeds and coarser blades with more set. Sometimes very thin materials are best cut sandwiched between some inexpensive materials such as cheap plywood or corrugated cardboard. Remember, it's best to experiment to solve any problems associated with your own particular sawing job. The suggestions just discussed may or may not be useful in specific situations.

METAL

Sawing metal can become a very involved process. In some cases, sawing certain metals requires a varied range of cutting speeds and even, perhaps, the use of special cutting fluids to cut them effectively. On the other hand, some soft metals cut surprisingly well dry if the correct combination of blade, cutting speed, and feed rate is used. One-eighth-inch brass, for example, can be cut with a surprisingly fast feed rate. (See Illus. 506–508.) At a speed of 1,350 cutting strokes per minute, a No. 5 jewellers' blade with 36 teeth per inch will cut ⅛-inch-thick brass very well at a feed rate of 17 per seconds per lineal inch of cut. The result is an exceptionally smooth cut. (See Illus. 508.) Aluminum, thought of by many as a soft material, is best cut with a cutting fluid such as Tap Magic®. Aluminum is often a combination of various alloys, and the cutting qualities can range dramatically from very easy to very difficult. (See Illus. 509.) When using cutting fluids, remove or adjust the air hose so it points away from the cutting area.

Very hard metals such as steel will require

Illus. 506. One-eighth-inch-thick sheet brass cuts surprisingly easy. The sheet brass shown here was cut with a No. 5 jewellers' blade at 1,350 cutting strokes per minute. See Illus. 507.

Illus. 507. A remarkably smoothly cut surface on brass is produced by dry cutting with the correct blade and cutting speed.

Illus. 508. Smaller details obviously require finer blades. Here a No. 1 jewellers' blade makes an inside cut on ⅛-inch-thick brass.

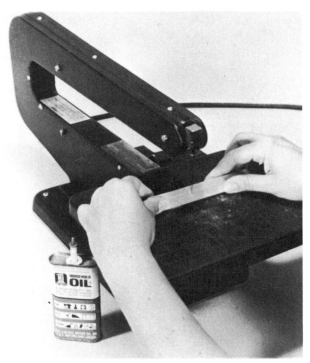

Illus. 509. Cutting light metal on the Dremel saw. The manufacturer recommends either lubricating the blade with light machine oil or rubbing it with a bar of paraffin.

Illus. 510. This detail was cut into ¼-inch-thick steel plate with a Hegner scroll saw.

proportionally slower feed rates and very sharp blades. A cutting fluid will keep the blade cooler and delay dulling. Thicker steel will require proportionally coarser tooth blades, slower speeds, and reduced feed pressures; this means you do not have to force the blade when it cuts. (See Illus. 510.) Very few scroll saws have good sawing capabilities for cutting steel over ¼ inch thick—the cutting speed becomes very slow.

Thin metals will likely "burr out" on the bottom edges unless supported on scrap plywood or similar material during cutting. Incidentally, chips from some cut metals can mess up the saw table's surface. When caught between the workpiece and the saw table, the metal sawdust chips can scratch and gouge the table surfaces. To protect your table from scratches and gouges from metal sawdust, attach an auxiliary table made from plywood or hardboard. Simply secure it with double-faced tape.

PAPER

Paper is easy to saw, providing it is stacked and held tightly together during sawing. (See Illus. 511.) Notepads with cutouts, as shown in Illus. 511, make some nice projects and personalized gifts. Stationery and greeting cards can be cut in the same way. The scroll saw craftsperson can make many projects when sawing paper.

The sheets have to be clamped tightly together. The cutout designs in Illus. 511 were simply sandwiched between two pieces of heavy corrugated cardboard, as shown in Illus. 512. Clamping pressure was provided by masking tape. Drill a hole, thread the blade, and saw as usual. The cut is surprisingly smooth, clean, and crisp. (See Illus. 513.)

If you plan to cut designs with a high degree of detail, use scrap plywood or hardboard for the flat pressure pads. Experiment-

Illus. 511. Paper cutouts are just one of many paper-cutting project possibilities.

Illus. 512. The paper is tightly sandwiched between corrugated cardboard and taped fast.

Illus. 513. The cut should be smooth and clean.

ing with various blades is also a good idea. The cutting capability of a blade can be checked quickly. Simply pinch the corner of an unneeded magazine together, tape it, and make a test cut.

MISCELLANEOUS MATERIALS

Cloth, felt, thin leathers, etc., can be cut in essentially the same way as paper when they are "pressed" tightly between some flat pressure boards.

Glass, ceramics, marble, clay products, and other extremely hard and brittle material can be cut on some saws. However, special cutting blades—like Remington's tungsten-carbide rod saw—have to be used. Remington's blades have particles of tungsten-carbide bonded to a steel rod. They have to be cut to length to fit into the scroll saw, which can be done easily with side-cutting pliers. Blades of this type are not recommended for cutting soft materials or metals, because loading will occur on the blade. They will fit only a few of the scroll saws available today.

Because these blades have no teeth, the cut is made on both the upstroke and down-stroke. However, the cutting isn't always fast. In fact, cut most of the very hard materials at a slow speed, and maintain an even-feed pressure.

The results of an experiment in sawing single-strength glass using an Excalibur variable-speed saw with the 12-inch Remington "grit-edge" carbide rod saw cut to length were good, but the cutting rate was extremely slow. With tape covering the cutting line to reduce chipping, and the speed dialed to 300 cutting strokes per minute, the rate of cut was about one lineal inch per four minutes of cutting time. That's certainly not spectacular when compared to sawing $13/16$-inch red oak. With a No. 7 blade, at 1,800 strokes per minute, oak this thick can be cut at approximately a rate of 5 seconds per inch.

Experiment before cutting any one particular kind of material that has not been discussed here. However, you should be able to make some fairly close comparisons to one of the several materials and the cutting suggestions that have been discussed.

CURRENT BOOKS BY PATRICK SPIELMAN

Alphabets and Designs for Wood Signs. 50 alphabet patterns, plans for many decorative designs, the latest on hand carving, routing, cutouts, and sandblasting. Pricing data. Photo gallery (4 pages in color) of wood signs by professionals from across the U.S. Over 200 illustrations. 128 pages.

Carving Large Birds. Spielman and renowned carver Bill Dehos show how to carve an array of large birds. All the tools and basic techniques used are discussed in depth, and hundreds of photos, illustrations, and patterns are provided for carving graceful swans, majestic eagles, comical-looking penguins, and scores of other birds. 16 pages in full color. 192 pages.

Gluing and Clamping. A thorough, up-to-date examination of one of the most critical steps in woodworking. Spielman explores the features of every type of glue—from traditional animal-hide glues to the newest epoxies—the clamps and tools needed, the bonding properties of different wood species, safety tips, and all techniques from edge-to-edge and end-to-end gluing to applying plastic laminates. Also included is a glossary of terms. Over 500 illustrations. 256 pages.

Making Country-Rustic Furniture. Hundreds of photos, patterns, and detailed scaled drawings reveal construction methods, woodworking techniques, and Spielman's professional secrets for making indoor and outdoor furniture in the distinctly attractive Country-Rustic style. Covered are all aspects of furniture making from choosing the best wood for the job to texturing smooth boards. Among the dozens of projects are mailboxes, cabinets, shelves, coffee tables, weather vanes, doors, panelling, plant stands and many more durable and economical pieces. 400 illustrations. 4 pages in full color. 164 pages.

Making Wood Decoys. A clear step-by-step approach to the basics of decoy carving. This book is abundantly illustrated with closeup photos for designing, selecting, and obtaining woods; tools; feather detailing; painting; and finishing of decorative and working decoys. Six different professional decoy artists featured. Photo gallery (4 pages in full color) along with numerous detailed plans for various popular decoys. 160 pages.

Making Wood Signs. Designing, selecting woods, tools, and every process through finishing is clearly covered. Hand-carved, power-carved, routed, and sandblasted processes in small to huge signs are presented. Foolproof guides for professional letters and ornaments. Hundreds of photos (4 pages in full color). Lists sources for supplies and special tooling. 144 pages.

Realistic Decoys. Spielman and master carver Keith Bridenhagen reveal their successful techniques for carving, feather-texturing, painting, and finishing wood decoys. Details that you can't find elsewhere—anatomy, attitudes, markings, and the easy step-by-step approach to perfect delicate procedures—make this book invaluable. Includes listings for contests, shows, and sources of tools and supplies. 274 closeup photos, 28 in color. 224 pages.

Router Handbook. With nearly 600 illustrations of every conceivable bit, attachment, jig, and fixture, plus every possible operation, this definitive guide has revolutionized router applications. It begins with safety and maintenance tips, then forges ahead into all aspects of dovetailing, freehanding, advanced duplication, and more. Details for over 50 projects are included. 224 pages.

Scroll Saw Pattern Book. This companion book to *Scroll Saw Handbook* contains over 450 workable patterns for making wall plaques, refrigerator magnets, candle holders, pegboards, jewelry, ornaments, shelves, brackets, picture frames, signboards, and many more projects. Beginners and experienced scroll saw users alike will find something here to intrigue and challenge them. 256 pages.

Working Green Wood with PEG. Covers every process for making beautiful, inexpensive projects from green wood without cracking, splitting, or warping. Hundreds of clear photos and drawings show every step from obtaining the raw wood through shaping, treating, and finishing your PEG-treated projects. 175 unusual project ideas. Lists supply sources. 160 pages.

ABOUT THE AUTHOR

Patrick Spielman's love of wood began when, as a child, he transformed fruit crates into toys. Now this prolific and innovative woodworker is respected worldwide as a teacher and author.

His most famous contribution to the woodworking field has been his perfection of a method to season green wood with polyethylene glycol 1000 (PEG). He went on to invent, manufacture, and distribute the PEG-Thermovat chemical seasoning system.

During his many years as shop instructor in Wisconsin, Spielman published manuals, teaching guides, and more than 14 popular books, including *Modern Wood Technology*, a college text. He also wrote six educational series on wood technology, tool use, processing techniques, design, and wood-product planning.

Author of the best-selling *Router Handbook* (over 200,000 copies sold), Spielman has served as editorial consultant to a professional magazine, and his prod-ucts, techniques, and many books have been featured in numerous periodicals.

This pioneer of new ideas and inventor of countless jigs, fixtures, and designs used throughout the world is a unique combination of expert woodworker and brilliant teacher—all of which endear him to his many readers and to his publisher.

At Spielmans Wood Works in the woods of northern Door County, Wisconsin, he and his family create and sell some of the most durable and popular furniture products and designs available.

Should you wish to write Pat, please forward your letters to Sterling Publishing Company.

CHARLES NURNBERG
STERLING PUBLISHING COMPANY

METRIC SYSTEM

UNIT	ABBREVIATION	APPROXIMATE U.S. EQUIVALENT		
Length				
		Number of Metres		
myriametre	mym	10,000	6.2 miles	
kilometre	km	1000	0.62 mile	
hectometre	hm	100	109.36 yards	
dekametre	dam	10	32.81 feet	
metre	m	1	39.37 inches	
decimetre	dm	0.1	3.94 inches	
centimetre	cm	0.01	0.39 inch	
millimetre	mm	0.001	0.04 inch	
Area				
		Number of Square Metres		
square kilometre	sq km *or* km²	1,000,000	0.3861 square miles	
hectare	ha	10,000	2.47 acres	
are	a	100	119.60 square yards	
centare	ca	1	10.76 square feet	
square centimetre	sq cm *or* cm²	0.0001	0.155 square inch	
Volume				
		Number of Cubic Metres		
dekastere	das	10	13.10 cubic yards	
stere	s	1	1.31 cubic yards	
decistere	ds	0.10	3.53 cubic feet	
cubic centimetre	cu cm *or* cm³ *also* cc	0.000001	0.061 cubic inch	
Capacity				
		Number of Litres	*Cubic*	*Dry*	*Liquid*
kilolitre	kl	1000	1.31 cubic yards		
hectolitre	hl	100	3.53 cubic feet	2.84 bushels	
dekalitre	dal	10	0.35 cubic foot	1.14 pecks	2.64 gallons
litre	l	1	61.02 cubic inches	0.908 quart	1.057 quarts
decilitre	dl	0.10	6.1 cubic inches	0.18 pint	0.21 pint
centilitre	cl	0.01	0.6 cubic inch		0.338 fluidounce
millilitre	ml	0.001	0.06 cubic inch		0.27 fluidram
Mass and Weight				
		Number of Grams		
metric ton	MT *or* t	1,000,000	1.1 tons	
quintal	q	100,000	220.46 pounds	
kilogram	kg	1,000	2.2046 pounds	
hectogram	hg	100	3.527 ounces	
dekagram	dag	10	0.353 ounce	
gram	g *or* gm	1	0.035 ounce	
decigram	dg	0.10	1.543 grains	
centigram	cg	0.01	0.154 grain	
milligram	mg	0.001	0.015 grain	

INDEX

Accessories, 51–54
AMT saws, 134–137
Asahi Koki saw, 68–70
Bevel sawing, 215–222
Blade(s), 12, 13, 20, 49, 50
  bending, 35–36
  breakage, 40
  changing, 38–39
  feeding pressure and, 49
  fret saw, 45, 46, 47
  jewelers', 46, 50
  metal-piercing, 46, 50
  pin-type, 42, 43, 150, 151
  plain-end, 42–43, 45, 150, 151
  plucking, 93
  reverse tooth, 55, 56
  sabre saw, 42, 43
  selection, 48–50
  speed of, 31–32
  spiral, 42, 44, 46–47, 49
  stock thickness, 49
  storage, 53, 54
  teeth size, 45
  twist-trick, 53
  types, 42–47
  using more than one, 51–52
  width, 49, 64
C-arm saws, 35, 138–144
Chamfers, 219–222
Compound sawing, 210–213
Constant-tension saws. See also specific saws, 28, 30, 33–34, 197
Cope joints, 202–204
Cope-dowel joint, 204–205
Corner lap joints, 201
Cornering, 165–168
Cutouts, 214–215
Cutting, 51–53, 163–172
Delta saws, 24
  24-inch, 58–59, 62–65
  C-arm, 138–144
  hobby, 73, 76–78
  sabre setup, 61
Dovetail joints, 206–209
Dowel pins
  spiral, 202

Dremel saws, 72–76
Eagle saw, 111–115
Excalibur saws, 101–110
Features, saw, 35–41
Feed rates, 54–55
Foley-Belsaw saw, 67, 68
Hawk scroll saws, 116–125
Hegner saws, 86–100
History of saw, 20–30
Hobbymax, 88, 93
Inlays, 223
  bevel-cut, 11
  combined, 236–237
  "sculpture," 231–233
  solid wood, 224–227
  woodturning, 227–229
Inside openings, 188–195
Jet saws, 61, 66, 134–137
Jigsaw puzzles, 181, 183
Joints, sawing of, 201–209
Kit saws, 79–84
Layout line, 165
Light-duty scroll saws, 72–78
Marquetry, 10, 12, 28, 80
  basics, 238–246
  bevel sawing, 244–246
  saw tables, 81–83
Metal, 249–251
Metrics, 255
Mitre joints, 205–206
Motors, 38, 98, 106, 131, 147
"Moto-Shop," 72, 73
Multimax-2, 88, 91, 92, 94, 96, 100
Multimax-3, 86, 87, 96
New Rogers scroll saw, 24–25
Nonwood materials, 247–253
Oliver saws, 58, 60
Operation, 31–34
Pantograph, 176
Paper, 251–253
Parallel-arm saws, 35
Patterns
  commercial, 176–181
  copying and transferring, 173–176
  enlarging, 174
Pedal saw, 84–85

Plastics, 247–249
Polymax-3, 86–87, 90, 92, 94, 96–98
Powermatic saws, 58, 59, 65–66
Preparation, 161–162
Project ideas, 181–187
Purchase of saw, 35–41
Puzzles, 181, 183–185
RBI scroll saws, 111–127
Relief, 233–236
Reproduction saw, 84–85
Rigid-arm saws, 28, 30, 32–33, 58–61
Ripping, 152–153
Safety, 12, 156–160
Sanding, 51, 64
Saw tables, 36–37, 81–83, 104, 128, 161–162, 214
Sawing basics, 161–172
Shopsmith, 68, 70–71
Signs, 216–218
Silhouettes, 29, 229–231
Sitting vs. standing, 163
Slip joints, 202, 203
Small pieces, 196–198
Speed, saw, 54
Stack sawing, 169–172, 239–243
Starting points, 163–164
Stock
  thick, 158, 159
  thin, 196–197, 199–200
Straight-line cuts, 169–170
Strong saws, 131–133
Style, saw, 32–35
Templates, 181, 182
Throat capacity, 32, 37, 103
Turns, 165–168, 216
Vega saw, 67
Velocipede saw, 23, 84–85
Veneers, 199–200, 244–246
Walking Beam saw, 145–154
Woodmaster saw, 128–131
Woodturning, 227–229